THE EASTERN STARS

ANTHOLOGY

Choice Cuts:
A Savory Selection of Food Writing
from Around the World and Throughout History

FICTION

Boogaloo on 2nd Avenue: A Novel of Pastry, Guilt, and Music

The White Man in the Tree and Other Stories

FOR CHILDREN

The Cod's Tale

The Girl Who Swam to Euskadi

The Story of Salt

TRANSLATION

The Belly of Paris, by Émile Zola

THE EASTERN STARS

How Baseball Changed the Dominican Town
of San Pedro de Macorís

Mark Kurlansky

Riverhead Books

a member of
Penguin Group (USA) Inc.
New York
2010

RIVERHEAD BOOKS
Published by the Penguin Group
Penguin Group (USA) Inc., 375 Hudson Street, New York, New York 10014, USA •
Penguin Group (Canada), 90 Eglinton Avenue East, Suite 700, Toronto, Ontario M4P 2Y3,
Canada (a division of Pearson Penguin Canada Inc.) • Penguin Books Ltd, 80 Strand,
London WC2R 0RL, England • Penguin Ireland, 25 St Stephen's Green, Dublin 2, Ireland
(a division of Penguin Books Ltd) • Penguin Group (Australia), 250 Camberwell Road,
Camberwell, Victoria 3124, Australia (a division of Pearson Australia Group Pty Ltd) •
Penguin Books India Pvt Ltd, 11 Community Centre, Panchsheel Park,
New Delhi–110 017, India • Penguin Group (NZ), 67 Apollo Drive, Rosedale,
North Shore 0632, New Zealand (a division of Pearson New Zealand Ltd) •
Penguin Books (South Africa) (Pty) Ltd, 24 Sturdee Avenue, Rosebank,
Johannesburg 2196, South Africa

Penguin Books Ltd, Registered Offices: 80 Strand, London WC2R 0RL, England

Library of Congress Cataloging-in-Publication Data

Kurlansky, Mark.
The Eastern stars : how baseball changed the Dominican town of San Pedro de Macorís /
Mark Kurlansky.
p.   cm.
Includes bibliographical references and index.
ISBN 978-1-59448-750-7
1. Baseball—Dominican Republic—San Pedro de Macorís—History.
2. Baseball players—Dominican Republic—San Pedro de Macorís—History.   I. Title.
GV863.29.D65K87   2010   2009041036
796.35707293'82—dc22

Printed in the United States of America
1   3   5   7   9   10   8   6   4   2

Book design by Chris Welch

While the author has made every effort to provide accurate telephone numbers and Internet addresses
at the time of publication, neither the publisher nor the author assumes any responsibility for errors, or
for changes that occur after publication. Further, the publisher does not have any control over and does
not assume any responsibility for author or third-party websites or their content.

A MIS VIEJOS AMIGOS EL PUEBLO DOMINICANO, EN LA ESPERANZA

QUE UN DÍA ENCUENTRE LA JUSTICIA Y PROSPERIDAD

QUE USTED SE MERECE

AND FOR TALIA FEIGA, WHOSE GREAT HEART IS BIG AS A MOUNTAIN

(¡Tanto arrojo en la lucha irremediable
Y aún no hay quien lo sepa!
¡Tanto acero y fulgor de resistir
Y aún no hay quien lo vea!)

(So much daring in the unresolvable struggle
Even though there is no one who knows it!
So much steel and flashing in resistance
Even though there is no one who sees it!)

—Pedro Mir, "Si Alguien Quiere Saber Cuál Es Mi Patria"
"If Someone Wants to Know Which Country Is Mine"

CONTENTS

PROLOGUE   Gracias, Presidente   1

PART ONE • SUGAR

CHAPTER ONE   Like the Trace of a Kiss   15

CHAPTER TWO   The First Question   33

CHAPTER THREE   The Question of First   47

CHAPTER FOUR   Who's on First   55

CHAPTER FIVE   The First Opening   67

CHAPTER SIX   San Pedro Rising   81

CHAPTER SEVEN   Draft Dodging   93

PART TWO • DOLLARS

CHAPTER EIGHT   The Fourth Incarnation of San Pedro   115

CHAPTER NINE   The City of Baseball   139

CHAPTER TEN   Three Three-Brother Families   165

CHAPTER ELEVEN   The Curse of the Eastern Stars   185

CHAPTER TWELVE   San Pedro's Black Eye   193

CHAPTER THIRTEEN   Fickle Judgment
from the Peanut Gallery   211

APPENDIX ONE   The First Seventy-nine: Major League
Baseball Players from San Pedro de Macorís   223

APPENDIX TWO   A Dominican Chronology   253

Acknowledgments   257
Bibliography   259
Index   263

THE EASTERN STARS

Gracias, Presidente

This is a book about what is known in America as "making it." And like all such tales, it is also a story about not making it. In this Dominican town, San Pedro de Macorís, the difference between making it and not making it is usually baseball.

If you do not make it, there is sugarcane—but only for half the year. Sometime between Christmas and the Dominican national holiday on February 27, depending on how rainy the summer was, the *pendones*—white feathery shoots—appear above the rippling green cane fields of San Pedro de Macorís. In the English-speaking islands of the Caribbean, where many of the families of San Pedro's sugar workers originated, the field is said to be "in arrow" because the *pendones* point upward. It means that the sugarcane is ripe for cutting and the cane harvest, the *zafra*, can begin.

It is an exciting moment, because most people who work in sugar here have employment only during the four to six months of the *zafra*. In an election year, such as 2008, at the beginning of the harvest a sign goes up at the Porvenir sugar mill, which is controlled by the ruling party. It says, *"Gracias, Presidente, por una nueva zafra,"* Thank you, President, for a new cane harvest, as though he, Leonel Fernández, the New York–educated caudillo—running again as he had in 2004 and in 1996, which was the last time Dominicans believed he offered anything new, his face on posters everywhere with the smile of an encyclopedia salesman—had personally caused the sugarcane to grow.

Some of the San Pedro mills—Santa Fe, Angelina, Puerto Rico, and Las Pajas—no longer operate. Four working mills remain, though not at full capacity: Quisqueya, Consuelo, Cristóbal Colón, and Porvenir. When the *zafra* is on, red glows can be seen from San Pedro along the northern horizon where the mill fires burn all night, cooking down cane juice. Porvenir, which in Spanish means "future," was originally on the edge of the city like the others, but the town grew around it and now trucks full of grape-red sticks of cane must drive through the traffic-clogged center of town to deliver to the mill.

Street kids, the ones who survive by shining shoes or washing the windshields of the cars that stop at traffic lights, run behind the trucks and pull off canes to suck. Sometimes they hold a stick of cane in a batter's stance. On the street, San Pedro boys regularly coil into a batter's stance anyway. Having a stick in hand, some can't resist taking a practice swing with a small rock—a dangerous habit in the crowded parts of town. But if they were to make a mistake and hit a rich man's shiny large SUV, chances are the wealthy driver hiding behind the smoked glass would be a baseball player who not that many years before had himself been whacking around stones with a stalk of sugarcane.

The road out of town that leads to the other mills begins at the green, white, and ocher Estadio Tetelo Vargas, home of the Estrellas Orientales, the Eastern Stars. San Pedro's long-suffering and always promising baseball team, founded in 1910, is older than many of the major-league clubs in America. With a center-field wall at 385 feet, Tetelo Vargas is a major-league-size field, though with fewer seats, more like a Triple A stadium. Behind the outfield wall, the drooping fronds of tall palms can be seen,

and in the distance, sticking up behind right field, the smokestack of
Porvenir.

The road alongside the stadium goes straight north—a rutted pockmarked remnant of the once paved two-lane route that has hosted too
many trucks, which now dangerously zigzag around potholes. The road
leads through the rural zone that is still San Pedro to whole villages that
have grown up around the mills after which they were named: Angelina,
Consuelo, Santa Fe . . . Soon—still in San Pedro—the road seems like a
causeway over a vast vegetable sea with lapping silver and green waves of
sugarcane. Some already-cleared fields look as if they had gotten bad
haircuts. Leggy white birds called *galsas* graze there until sunset, when
they nest in the trees at the fields' edges.

At lunchtime the *galsas* were still in the fields and the cane cutters in
Consuelo were under the trees, resting in the shade from a broiling midday sun. Cutting cane is the worst job in the Dominican Republic, the
hardest work for the least pay. It has always been said that no Dominican
would ever do such work—never even want to be seen doing it. Desperate
people from other sugar-producing islands with dying sugar industries
were brought in to cut the cane. And so places like Consuelo have a
polyglot culture with West Indian English and Haitian Creole as commonly spoken as Spanish and often mixed in the same sentence.

But that was in the nineteenth and twentieth centuries, when the Dominican Republic was an underpopulated country with a booming sugar
industry. Today it is the reverse, and the job market is becoming desperate. In this field the resting cane cutters were born Dominican.

No one really cared how long a lunch break they took. They would
not stop for long, because they were paid by the ton, not the hour. But
they needed some rest, especially while the sun was high.

There were several varieties of cane grown here, and this field had
been planted with what is called *Angola pata de maco*. It is a hard red stalk
that takes a mighty whack from a machete, the stroke repeated hun-

dreds of times in the course of a day. But it is not the toughness of the cane that cutters care about: it is the density and water content. Some types of cane are considerably heavier than other types, and a cutter negotiated to get a field like this, with "good cane," because they were paid by weight.

They were paid 115 pesos for chopping a ton of cane and piling it into open railroad cars with rods along the sides to hold the stalks in. One hundred fifteen pesos was about $3.60 in 2009 dollars. In one day, two cutters working together could fill a car, which held four tons. A locomotive that passed by regularly would haul the car off to the mill. In the sugar industry the Dominican cane cutter, left to do everything himself without the use of machines, is considered one of the least-productive cane cutters in the world. This is not from a lack of work but rather from the intensity of the work. Efficiency of labor, a normal concept in the development of most industry, did not exist in Dominican sugar. Equations such as the number of man-hours to produce a ton of sugar were of little interest to the unregulated adventurers who came to the Dominican Republic to produce sugar. The cost of labor was so low, the quantity of sugar that could be produced so enormous, and the profits so staggering that no one was pondering better means of production. After the initial decades when the sugar men arrived and built their state-of-the-art mills, there was not even a great effort to upgrade equipment.

So, while everywhere else the fields are set on fire so that the leaves burn away before harvesting, in the Dominican Republic the single cutter must chop the tough green stalk close to the ground, then chop it into three equal parts and toss them into a railroad car. In Jamaica, where the cane is burned first and the cane cutter does not do the loading, the cutter averages seven tons a day. A good cutter in San Pedro could cut two tons a day.

Cutters worked from seven in the morning to five at night, but in the middle of the day, when the sun was highest, they needed shade, food, and rest. It would be easy to imagine that men who did such work would be big, solidly built, muscular workers, but that would require an ample protein diet, which they didn't have. Elio Martínez, one of the cutters, was not a large man. He was lean and of middling height and had a soft voice. He was fifty-seven years old and had been cutting cane since he was sixteen. His father, who had also been a cane cutter, and his mother were both Haitian.

For lunch he was drinking cane juice, which, though of little nutritional value, was sweet and refreshing, and the sugar gave a momentary energy boost and made an empty stomach feel full. Part of the trick was to find the ripest stalk, and he felt through the hundreds of reddish stumps sticking out from the two-ton pile in a full wagon ready to be hitched to the locomotive. When he found a juicy one, recognizable by touch and its dark maroon color, he grabbed on and yanked the five-foot stick out of the wagon. He held it horizontally with his left hand and with his right lifted a hard wood stick, which he smacked several times into the center of the cane. Then he turned the cane and struck a few more blows until the fibers in the middle appeared slightly mashed. Then he leaned his head back and, holding the cane with both hands, twisted it until green juice poured into his mouth as though from a faucet. He repeated the process with several carefully chosen canes.

About five miles away, in the center of San Pedro, was a two-story apartment building constructed in the style of a motel. It had a chain-link gate so that it could be locked to protect the apartments, the large late-model SUVs parked in front of the building, and the privacy of the well-known tenants.

A fit-looking man in a bass-fishing T-shirt was on the lawn by the building with a bottomless metal cage. "Watch this, this is funny," he said to another muscular man. One end of the cage was propped off the ground with a plastic water bottle with a blue nylon string tied to it. The man in the bass-fishing T-shirt sat fifteen feet away, holding the string. He had spread corn under the cage for bait. Some pigeons were approaching it.

His name was Manny Alexander, and he had grown up not far away in downtown San Pedro. His family was so poor, their small house so crowded, that he shared a bed with several brothers and sisters. Then, in February 1988, when he was sixteen years old, he signed a contract with the Baltimore Orioles as a shortstop. The Orioles organization paid him a signing bonus of $2,500, a small bonus today but a respectable one in 1988.

"The first thing I did was I bought a bed," Alexander recalled. "I wanted a small bed all to myself. Then I got a radio, some clothes, food." More toys followed. Although his major-league career was not illustrious and he was not a top-salaried player, in his eleven years in the majors he did earn more than $2 million, which, here in San Pedro, could go a very long way.

Had he been working, this would have been lunchtime. But Manny was on no particular schedule. He wanted to show his pigeon trap to his friend José Mercedes. Mercedes was born in El Seibo, northeast of San Pedro, but had been living here since the late 1980s. He was a pitcher who also signed with the Orioles. His major-league career began at the age of twenty-three in 1994 and lasted only nine years. But that was enough time to earn several million dollars. He was relaxing this day after having started the night before for the Santo Domingo team, Licey, which had defeated the home team, the Estrellas Orientales, further diminishing San Pedro's fast-vanishing lead in the final games of the season. Licey had a largely major-league pitching staff.

Manny squatted on the ground, string in hand, waiting to yank the bottle out and trap the pigeons as soon as they mustered the foolhardy courage to venture under the cage to eat the corn. The birds were inching toward the trap with jerky steps when suddenly a new bright copper-colored Ford van pulled up, blasting a merengue, which is the accepted way to play the national music. The pigeons, lacking a Dominican sensibility, left in a panic.

On the back of the vehicle in large figures was the number 47, the uniform number of the pitcher Joaquín Andújar. Andújar was an exceptional pitcher who had helped the St. Louis Cardinals win the World Series in 1982 with successful starts in two games. Curiously, many of the former ballplayers had smoked windows on their cars so that the driver could not be identified, as though to preserve their anonymity, but then they placed their numbers on the outside to make sure that everyone would know who they were. Many of the former major leaguers in San Pedro drove large, expensive cars. However, the real status was not the value of the cars but the cost of the gasoline they ate up. Most people in San Pedro could not have afforded to drive one of these cars if it were given to them.

The pigeons weren't the only ones startled by Andújar's midday arrival. It was well known in San Pedro that Andújar, who was out late every night, was seldom up and out of his apartment by midday. His days usually began in the afternoon.

Andújar, a trim six-foot man, not particularly big for a pitcher, and on this day meticulously dressed in a yellow sweater—unusual dress for midday in the Dominican Republic unless you spend your time in air-conditioning—came over and argued with Mercedes about his trap. Mercedes insisted that the string should be tied to the cage and not the bottle. They tried it his way and the pigeons returned, but they were now too cautious to chance going under the cage.

The three men joked about eating the pigeons they caught. But they weren't eating them, just keeping them in a large cage as pets. It was just for fun. Manny Alexander laughed. "That's why the Dominican Republic is so good: we're free here," he said.

Back in the Consuelo cane field, Dionicio Morales, known to cane cutters as Bienvenido, which means Welcome, strolled sleepily over to the wagon for his lunch. He was not as lean as Elio and the others resting under the trees. A slight paunch indicated a somewhat better position in life. The son of a Haitian father and Dominican mother, he was the exact same age as Elio but had six more years' experience. He had started in the cane fields when he was ten years old. "I've done every job," he said, but it sounded more like a complaint than a boast. "I cut, I planted, I cleaned fields."

Now Dionicio was a field supervisor, on this day in charge of the handful of weary cutters resting in this field. He earned 8,000 pesos a month, about $250, which worked out to about a dollar more a day than a cutter who averaged two tons. But he had the luxury of a stable salary, at least during the four-month *zafra*. In the mid–twentieth century his father crossed the island from Haiti to cut cane for three cents a ton. Dionicio remembers those even harder days when only a dirt trail led from Consuelo into town, and sugar people never left the fields. The sugar companies provided housing in the fields in little villages called *bateys*, a word that before the Spanish came to this country was the name of a ball game. Field workers and their families lived there and bought supplies and food from the company store, which gave them credit. These purchases ended up consuming most or all of their meager pay. If the cane workers wanted their children to go to school, the children had to walk for miles, but this was a considerable improvement over earlier times when there was simply no school. The major difference was that with the paved road, the baseball stadium in the center of San Pedro was only fifteen minutes away. The cutters still owned no transportation. But for the amount of money they earned cutting a few hundred pounds of cane—a few pesos—they could get a ride into the center of town on the back of a motor scooter. This was the leading form of transportation in San Pedro, known as a *motoconcho*.

Dionicio and Elio both lived, along with a few hundred other families of field workers, near this field in the Batey Experimental. The workers there did not live in barracks, as in some of the worst *bateys*, but in separate tin-roofed concrete houses with one to three small rooms. From time to time running water and electricity functioned. Families grew some of their own food in the *bateys*, especially *plántanos*, cassava root, which was known here as yucca, and pigeon peas—all Caribbean staples that were easy to grow. Some made extra money by buying oranges and selling them along the unpaved streets of the *batey*.

"It's not so bad if you earn good money," Dionicio said of the *batey* he called home. "If you don't earn much money, it's hard." Many of the people in Batey Experimental—especially between *zafras*, the period known as the "dead time"—didn't earn anything.

There were not a lot of choices for work in San Pedro de Macorís. Asked how he liked his work, Elio Martínez shook his head emphatically in the negative as though he had just tasted something bitter. Then he quickly added, "But I have to earn money."

Not everyone in San Pedro cut cane. Some worked in the sugar mills. Some were fishermen. Some sold oranges and some drove *motoconchos*. Some played baseball, which was increasingly what San Pedro was known for, now that the sugar industry was dying.

Sugar and baseball had exchanged places. A town where some baseball was played but was known in the world only by the sugar industry had become a town with some sugar that was known in the world chiefly by baseball organizations and fans. The sugar town of San Pedro had become San Pedro the baseball town. It was, of course, also a place where people wrote poetry, fell in love, raised children, built good and bad marriages, fished the sea, grew other crops, had shops and businesses—even played other sports, such as basketball and boxing. But it was San Pedro's fate to be known in the world for only one thing at a time. That a town of this size would achieve fame at all in a small, poor country seldom looked at by the rest of the world except when it was invaded is remarkable. A century ago, if San Pedro was mentioned abroad, if there was any response at all, it was likely, "Oh, yes, the sugar place." Today it is usually, "Oh, yes, that town where all the shortstops come from."

Back when San Pedro was that sugar town, baseball began in these sugar fields. In San Pedro the history of sugar—a story of poverty and hunger—and the history of baseball—a tale of millionaires—have always been tightly intertwined. It was sugar companies that brought in the game and cricket-playing Eastern Caribbean sugar workers who provided the players. In some cases sugar even supplied the baseball itself, a hardball fashioned from molasses. Later, when the game came to other parts of the country, different balls were used. In Haina, farther down the coast on the other side of Santo Domingo—where the Alous, one of the great baseball-playing families, grew up—there was no sugar but there were lemon groves, and so lemons became balls—not nearly as durable as sugar.

This is a story about making it; about the slight twists and turns that determine success and failure, and how each changes lives—about a world where the right or wrong nod from a coach on a farm team, so called for their obscure American locations, can make the difference between earning a few million dollars a year or going back home and earning a few hundred dollars a year. And that is a difference that determines the lives of more than a dozen family members too. Life is a precarious thing often decided by the strength of an arm, the fluidity of a swing, or the sureness of a gloved hand. Even in San Pedro, not everyone has the talent to be a baseball player. What it most always comes down to in life is how well we play the cards that are dealt us. Like poker, life is a game of skill that stems from luck. It does not come as a revelation to most of us that life is essentially unfair. That is why we so admire the ones who play it well.

Throughout the Caribbean, the poor live on dreams. Generation after generation goes by and the hard life gets no easier. But there is always hope. In Kingston, Jamaica, slum kids practice their singing and hope to be the next Bob Marley or Jimmy Cliff. In San Pedro de Macorís they practice their swing and dream of Sammy Sosa.

By 2008, seventy-nine men from San Pedro had already made it into the major leagues, where the average salary was $3 million. But Elio Martínez did not play baseball. He beat one more stalk of cane and twisted it above his mouth for a last drink. Soon lunch would be over. *Gracias, Presidente.*

PART ONE

SUGAR

La caña triturada, como una lluvia de oro,
en chorros continuados, baja, desciende y va
allí donde la espera la cuba, para hacerla
    miel, dulce miel, panal.

El sol que la atraviesa con rayo matutino,
de través, como un puro y muy terso cristal,
sugestiona, persuade, que se ha liquefacto
    la misma luz solar.

The ground-up cane, ring of gold,
continuously spurting, comes down, goes down and goes
where the bucket awaits it, to make of it
    Honey, sweet honey, honeycomb.

The sun shining straight through it with morning rays,
crosswise, like a pure, terse glasswork,
suggesting, persuading, that what has liquefied
    Is the very light of the sun.

—Gastón Fernando Deligne, "Del Trapiche"

CHAPTER ONE

Like the Trace of a Kiss

I t is easier to describe San Pedro de Macorís, and the unique history and cultural blend that formed it, than it is to explain the country in which it was formed. There is a strange ambivalence to the Dominican Republic. Pedro Mir, the Dominican poet laureate from San Pedro de Macorís, described his country as:

> *Simply*
> *transparent,*
> *Like the trace of a kiss on a spinster*
> *Or the daylight on rooftops.*

Of the nations called the large-island Caribbean, the ones that by size should dominate the region, the Dominican Republic is the one with the least impact and the least distinct culture. The others all have poetic names: Haiti, Cuba, Jamaica, Puerto Rico, and Trinidad. The Dominican Republic has a name that seems a temporary offering until a better idea comes along. Even Puerto Rico, which has the odd history of having never been an independent nation, seems to have a stronger sense of itself. The Dominican Republic, one of the first independent nations in the Caribbean, seems to struggle with its identity.

It is a country that has usually been out of step with history, left behind in the Spanish empire, left behind in the independent Caribbean; even on its own island, it is the country that isn't Haiti. Almost as poor as Haiti but not quite, neither as tragic nor as romantic, the Dominican Republic missed the first sugar boom in the eighteenth century and came late to the second one in the nineteenth century. As with baseball, its sugar industry ran behind those of Cuba and Puerto Rico, and the Dominicans had trouble positioning themselves.

Dominicans speak Spanish, but it is not a very Spanish place. It is neither as Latino nor as African as Cuba. Dominicans have developed distinctive and celebrated music forms, but they are not as influential nor as recognized as the many forms of Cuban music or Jamaican reggae or Trinidadian calypso. It does not have the strong tradition of visual arts and folk crafts for which Haiti is known, and in fact Dominican tourist shops are filled with Haitian paintings and crafts and bad knockoffs of them. They also sell tourists Cuban cigars because Dominican ones, some of which are very good, don't have the same cachet.

The Dominican Republic is nothing like its neighbor across the island, Haiti, which is a far more African place. But except for the Spanish language and baseball, it doesn't very much resemble Cuba or Puerto Rico, either. Despite a long and mostly painful relationship with the United States and the fact that money shipped home by Dominicans in the United States is a major prong of the struggling economy—the third poorest in the Americas—the Dominican Republic has not become very Americanized, either. Major League Baseball is acutely aware that the Dominican ballplayers sent to the U.S. are lost in a very strange and different land.

It is tempting to say that baseball defines it, but it got the game from Cubans, Puerto Ricans, and Americans. Dominicans have excelled in the game, and in the last few decades baseball has at last become something at which Dominicans dominate—at last, something they can be known for—and this is a source of pride. From 1956—when Ozzie Virgil, from the northern Dominican town of Monte Cristi, became an infielder for the New York Giants—through 2008, 471 Dominicans played in at least one major-league game. One in six of them have come from the relatively small town of San Pedro de Macorís.

But even this celebrated accomplishment may be slightly tarnished by the fact that Cubans dominate Caribbean play and always have. It is U.S. law, which forced Cuban ballplayers to defect if they wanted to play in the U.S., that gave Dominicans their opening in baseball. In February 1962, when the United States imposed an embargo on Cuba, only six Dominicans had ever played in the major leagues.

Despite all its murky ambiguity, the Dominican Republic really is a distinct country with its own society and culture and way of doing things unlike anyplace else. This has made Dominicans love their homeland and yearn for it when they are away. It is just not very easy to articulate what it is. In the past twenty years there has been a marked growth in tourism, but it has been a style of tourism that spirits away visitors to walled-off resorts, safely away from the Dominican reality. The impression these visitors are left with is so false that the country may be even less known than it was when almost no one came.

There are Dominican characteristics. Not surprisingly, given the violent history of the Dominican Republic, there is violence in everyday Dominican life. There is domestic violence, but also the recent decline in the economy has been accompanied by a rise in street crime, especially by young men. The mayor of San Pedro, Ramón Antonio Echavaría, said street crime was the biggest problem facing his town. But also national human rights groups complained that in 2008 alone almost 500 people, most of them under the age of thirty-five, were shot and killed on the street by police, who admit to only 343 of the killings.

Despite all this, Dominicans have a sweetness to their demeanor. They smile and embrace one another far more easily than most people. Americans, trying to instill American ideas of sportsmanship, tell ballplayers in Dominican youth programs to come out and shake their opponents' hands after a game. They come out to the field and for a brief moment begin the unnatural hand-shaking ritual but quickly begin hugging each other. That is what Dominicans do.

Dominican men are infamous for sexism. Yet women are common—though far from dominant—in the professions, especially as doctors. The image of the strong Dominican woman is celebrated—notably the three Mirabal sisters, upper-class women who resisted the Trujillo dictatorship and were murdered on their way home from visiting their husbands in prison. In fact, the founding legend of Dominican resistance was a Taino woman named Anacaona. After her husband was killed by the Spanish, Anacaona became leader of all the Tainos and was captured by the Spanish while trying to negotiate peace. The Spanish governor, Nicolás de Ovando, had her hanged.

Mothers are revered, and it is not unusual for a man to decide to use his mother's last name rather than the traditional father's name. In Spanish names, there are two last names, the father's and then the mother's. Although the father's name is in the middle rather than the end, by tradition it is the one that is used. But Dominicans often choose their mothers' names. An example is the slugger Ricardo Jacobo Carty. Jacobo was his father's name and Carty his mother's, and by Spanish tradition he would have been called either the full name or Ricardo Jacobo, but instead he always called himself Rico Carty, after his mother. There are many other San Pedro examples.

Dominicans are very attached and loyal to their families. This, of course, is not uniquely Dominican, but what is striking is how much they focus on immediate family and often how little interest is shown in the broader community. The sense of nation is even weaker still.

Like many Caribbeans, Dominicans love to dance, often excel at it, and find fellow countrymen who can't dance to be odd. It seems that a love of dance has always been a Dominican trait. The eighteenth-century Spanish colonial rulers were disturbed by the ubiquity of Dominican dancing, and in 1818 the governor finally issued an edict prohibiting dancing on public streets at night without a permit. Many Dominican dances of the period, as in other Caribbean islands, were rooted in the European dances of the day, such as the minuet.

Then, in the nineteenth century, the merengue appeared. To Dominicans, this music form is one of the few things that are distinctly and uniquely Dominican. But musicologists point out that a number of islands, such as Cuba and Puerto Rico, had merengues and may possibly have had them significantly earlier. Worse, from the Dominican point of view, one of the earliest merengues originated in Haiti, and the music appears to have first turned up on the Dominican side in the late eighteenth and early nineteenth centuries, when Haitians started coming over during the very violent Haitian revolution. Dominicans can live with the idea that *their game*, baseball, came from America and Cuba but not that *their music* came from Haiti. The Dominican Republic was invaded and occupied several times by the black nation with whom it shares its island, and anti-Haitianism, often expressed in racial terms, is a central Dominican obsession. In fact, it is popularly believed, though probably not true, that merengue was created to celebrate the end of Haitian occupation in 1844.

The music was named after meringue, the sweet and fluffy confection that is nothing more than egg whites, air, and sugar. Both the word and confection are French, suggesting a Haitian connection.

Merengue was always dance music. Throughout its many changes, it has remained in swiftly bouncing 2/4 time, heavy on the downbeat. It was originally played on numerous variations of guitar made of a gourd with ridges that is scraped, called a *güiro*—the modern metal version is called a *güira*—and a drum that was beaten on one end and played with sticks on the other. Dominicans have tried to attach symbolic importance to this drum because it has a male and a female side. The pounded side has a billy-goat skin and the stick side is covered with the skin of a she-goat.

Dominicans commonly say that the *güiro* is an authentic Dominican instrument invented by the pre-Columbian Taino Indians. Anthropologists have refuted this. In fact, there is some troubling evidence that it may really have come from Puerto Rico.

About the time the accordion was added to the merengue band, the music was denounced by prominent citizens, including former president Ulises Francisco Espaillat. Espaillat claimed that merengue was dangerous and called it "fatal" because it attacked the nervous system and caused imagination to spin out of control.

He may have had a point. Like sex, it is a physical excitement that presents an alternative to rational thought. In the years since Espaillat, the instrumentation has gotten both more elaborate and louder with the inclusion of a brass section. The beat remains frenetic and engaging, an exhilarating and somewhat numbing expression of energy for energy's sake. With large speakers and powerful boom boxes, merengue has ensured that Dominican towns are not quiet at night; and now, with the advent of iPods and tiny earphones, it can be blasted into the ear canal and directly patched into the brain. Things you cannot do while listening to merengue: reflect, stand still, be sad.

Since the 1960s a newer music, *bachata,* has emerged from poor rural areas. This is the Dominican equivalent of country music: sad ballads of unrequited love. While it is also claimed as a distinctly Dominican form, it clearly has its roots in the Cuban bolero.

The ambiguous and confused Dominican identity, like all national identities, is rooted in history. The Dominican Republic, in a region known for harsh histories, has a particularly difficult, somewhat strange story of a land and a people struggling for centuries to find a path to nationhood. In five hundred years it was invaded twice by the Spanish, three times by the Haitians, twice by the French, and twice by the Americans—if you don't count sugar companies or Major League Baseball. Dominicans have also on their own initiative at different times asked to be annexed to Spain, Britain, Colombia, France, and the United States.

The one Dominican moment with an undisputed claim to world history was in 1492 when Columbus landed there, named the island Española to leave no doubt about ownership, and established the first European colony in the Americas. It became a base for the Spanish conquest of America, and most of the butchers who conquered for Spain—including Cortés, Pizarro, Ponce de León, and Balboa—passed through there.

Gold was the Spanish obsession of the time, and when they found some they enslaved the locals to mine it. Only twenty-five years later, most of the gold and most of the locals were gone. The Spanish had worked to death or infected with fatal diseases all but 11,000 of the estimated population of 400,000, earning Santo Domingo an important place in the history of genocide.

Understandably, Dominicans do not feel comfortable with their founding history. There is no Columbus Day holiday in the Dominican Republic, because they knew him too well. Yet there is a certain pride, especially in the capital city, in the firstness that Columbus gave them—that Santo Domingo is the oldest European city in the Americas and its university the oldest in the Americas.

But with both the gold and the population gone, Santo Domingo became a backwater, never again to play a major role on the world stage. Sugar, which for a thousand years had been a Mediterranean product, could be produced more cheaply in the Caribbean tropics. The Dominicans were one of the first sugar producers in the Americas. The original colonists tried it, harvesting the first Dominican sugar crop in 1506. But despite high sugar prices in Europe, Dominicans failed to become major sugar producers. Sugar requires a great deal of labor, and the Spanish, having killed most of the locals, were left with an underpopulated island. Like other islands, they began importing African slaves, but starting in 1522 the slaves began rebelling. Soon there were more runaway slaves than Spaniards in the colony.

Away from the capital, in the far western regions of the second-largest

Caribbean island, local sugar was being sold illegally to enemies of Spain, such as France and Holland. The Spanish solution was to burn and destroy all the coastal agriculture on the western side of the island, where the smuggling had taken place, and forcibly vacate the area. As a result, it was taken over by the French, who turned it into the most profitable colony in the world, while the eastern Spanish half remained impoverished and neglected.

In the late eighteenth and early nineteenth centuries—when the French side exploded in what would be the Americas' first successful African slave rebellion and in what became the world's first postcolonial black nation— the Santo Domingo side continued to drift.

In 1795, during the Haitian revolution, the French took the Spanish side away from Spain. The Dominicans rebelled and threw the French and the Haitians out but, instead of declaring independence, asked the Spanish back. From 1809 to 1821 the Spanish ruled again, but they ruled harshly and were indifferent to developing the colony. Tired of Spanish rule, the Dominicans rebelled again—as did most of the Spanish colonies at the time—and in a rare moment of triumph the Dominicans drove the Spanish out and declared their independence. This should have been the moment of national glory, the founding moment in the nation. But immediately a sense of panic seemed to grip Dominicans about being alone in the world. They entered into negotiations with Simón Bolívar, the great South American liberator from Venezuela who dreamed of one large independent Latin American nation called Gran Colombia.

Instead the Haitian army invaded in 1822 and, with little resistance, took over and immediately abolished slavery. The Dominicans never even had their own abolitionist movement. Haitian rule was not only antislavery, it was antiwhite—even antimulatto—and the Haitians, wishing to make the eastern side of the island blacker, encouraged black immigration from the United States and got five thousand blacks, mostly from New York and Philadelphia—many of them freed slaves—to move to underpopulated areas. After twenty years of occupation, the Dominicans were left a little bit Spanish, a little bit French, not quite black or white—the only mulatto country, obsessed with race and deeply insecure.

Dominican history teaches of the Dominican military victory that drove the Haitians out in 1844. But one of the Dominican leaders, Buenaventura Báez, was educated in France and seems to have suffered from that age-old affliction Francophilia. When he returned from France, he collaborated with the Haitian occupiers while opening a dialogue with the French government on having France take over the Dominican Republic, known at the time as Haiti Español. There is some evidence that the French had a hand in negotiating the Haitian retreat. Even as Haiti Español was being christened the independent nation named the Dominican Republic, negotiations were under way for the French takeover.

Dominican historian Frank Moya Pons wrote about a "defeatist attitude" that set in, with a conservative upper class preoccupied with the fear that the Haitians would return and take their property. In the first years as an independent nation, Dominicans discussed possible takeovers by not only the French but the Spanish, the Americans, and the British. This was threatening to the Haitians—particularly their leader from 1847 to 1859, Faustin-Élie Soulouque—who feared above all else an attempt by outsiders to reestablish slavery in Haiti. Soulouque, a black brought to power as a puppet of the upper-class mulattos, had a surprising cunning and quickly consolidated power and crowned himself Emperor Faustin I. A militant black nationalist, his fear of foreigners—especially Americans, who by then ran the leading slaving nation—led to three attempts to retake the Dominican Republic. This in turn led the Dominicans to a desperate desire to be taken over and rescued by a foreign power.

None of the four powers under consideration was particularly interested in acquiring the Dominican Republic. Columbus, it seems, was the first and last to have considered it a prize. The French were interested only in Haiti and had gotten the Haitians to agree to a huge indemnity in exchange for recognition of the nation. The only French interest in the Dominican side was to stop the Haitians from spending all their money trying to take over the Dominican Republic instead of paying them. The British and the Spanish were concerned only about American designs on the real prize, Cuba, and feared that the U.S. saw the Dominican Republic as a stepping-stone. Far from worrying about preserving their nation while all these militarized world powers were looking them over, many Dominicans, not all of them white, were claiming Spanish citizenship. Spanish law promised citizenship to any descendant of a Spanish colonist. As Spanish citizens, they were exempt from Dominican military service.

But at the end of the international debate, in 1860 the Spanish came back. Dominicans did not like Spanish rule this time any more than they had the other times, and they fought a war of independence against the Spanish, which they won in 1865. They were independent at last, and from 1865 to 1879 had twenty different governments.

In despair and defeatism, Dominicans tried to become part of the United States. U.S. president Ulysses S. Grant was interested but the American people had no interest in the Dominican Republic, and so most politicians were not particularly receptive; the project was rejected by the Senate in 1871. In fact, Massachusetts senator Charles Sumner, an old-time abolitionist, was remembered in the U.S. as a hero for opposing the measure and sparing the U.S. the annexation. Once Dominicans came to know the U.S. better, Sumner came to be remembered with equal admiration by Dominicans.

An independent Dominican Republic, without economic resources, went deeper into debt and was increasingly controlled by foreign financial institutions. In everything the Dominicans tried to do, they were divided between two bitterly opposed groups: the reds and the blues, the Partido Rojo and the Partido Azul.

It was the fate of the Dominican Republic to fill odd footnotes in history and never center stage. World War I was the pretext for a U.S. invasion of the Dominican Republic. As World War II approached, when the world turned its back on German Jewish refugees, the Dominican dictator Trujillo took them in—welcoming them not out of a sense of humanity but to *blanquear*, whiten, the racial makeup of Dominicans, just as the Haitians had welcomed American blacks to darken it.

When World War I was breaking out, the Americans discovered that Dominican waters were in danger of a German takeover, so they took over instead. In truth, the invasion was part of a policy that went back to 1898 of securing the Caribbean for building the Panama Canal. The U.S. during this period found excuses to invade six Caribbean nations, including both Haiti and the Dominican Republic. The Americans suspected that the Dominicans, given their history and their deep debt to European banks, would one day throw in with the Europeans, right in their own backyard, at the gateway to Panama.

In remarkable similarity to the invasion of Iraq not quite ninety years later, the U.S. invaded in 1916 with few clear goals or explanations and was surprised to find that locals resented the American presence. Dominicans formed into small bands that sporadically attacked U.S. troops, who called them bandits. The U.S. created a Dominican national police force to control the rebels but struggled to get Dominicans to effectively take charge of this force.

The U.S. military established an officer training school in Haina. Among the graduates in the first class was a drifter and petty criminal named Rafael Leónidas Trujillo Molina. Although there had been some problems with this young enlisted man trying to extort money from the locals, the charges had been dropped and he was approved for officer training. Graduating a second lieutenant, Trujillo befriended high-ranking American officers and rose so rapidly that in 1924, when the Americans left, claiming they had stabilized the country and built an effective police force, Trujillo was a major. Soon after, he became a lieutenant colonel. The Americans had said they wanted to achieve stability, and indeed they had. Within six years of the American withdrawal, his opposition exhausted by its eight-year war with the U.S. Marines, Trujillo had gained complete control of the country. He kept it for thirty-one years, one of the longest-running dictatorships in history, until he was assassinated in 1961 with the complicity of the CIA.

Trujillo ruled by personal whim—"megalomania" was the word used by Jesús de Galíndez, a Basque refugee of the Spanish Civil War, in his doctoral dissertation on Trujillo at Columbia University, for which the general had Galíndez kidnapped from New York and brought to Santo Domingo. His body was never found, and the variety of gruesome stories that circulated about his end were testimony to the dark Dominican imagination. Of course, Trujillo himself had a Dominican imagination—none darker—and one of these grim stories was probably true. Galíndez, like many in the decades of Trujillo government, came to a very bad end. In his dissertation, which chronicles meticulously both the eccentricity and brutality of the regime, Galíndez reported that in 1935 Trujillo's henchmen had assassinated a political opponent in exile in New York; that they had murdered another Dominican in 1952 on Madison Avenue; and that in 1950, in Havana, they had murdered Mauricio Báez, a union organizer from San Pedro de Macorís. None of this turned the U.S. government against General Trujillo.

The Jewish refugee incident is only one of many examples of Trujillo's obsession with "whitening the race." He whitened merengue by insisting on the version from the white Cibao region. Another attempt to whiten the race was made in 1937. While everyone was consumed with the epic baseball showdown between Ciudad Trujillo and San Pedro, Trujillo launched Operación Perejil, more ominously nicknamed the *corte*, the cutting down.

Most Haitian-born people cannot say *perejil*, the Spanish word for parsley. Haitians speaking their mother tongue, Creole, tend to pronounce *r* as *w*, which is an African influence. And, like many English-speaking people, they struggle with the Spanish *j*, the *jota*, which, coming from Arabic, has a raspy *h* sound. Trujillo sent soldiers to the border region armed with sprigs of parsley. When encountering anyone who seemed suspiciously dark or had African features, a soldier would take out the sprig and ask the person to identify it. If he said something sounding like "pewidgil," he was either sent across the border or killed. It is not known exactly how many were executed. *The New York Times* initially estimated between 2,700 and 3,000, but the killing continued. Galíndez guessed that there were more than 20,000 dead, and some estimates have been as high as 30,000 murdered. Those on sugar *bateys* were not touched, and it is supposed but not certain that Trujillo's message was that Haitians could come to the Dominican Republic but had to keep to their *bateys*. Afterward the merengue composer Julio Eladio Pérez came out with the song "Trujillo en la Frontera," "Trujillo at the Border," in which the Dominicans of the border thank the caudillo for bringing peace and progress to the region.

Trujillo also tried to whiten himself. He was rumored to have some Haitian blood and was a little dark—nothing that couldn't be fixed with the right amount of Pan-Cake makeup. According to journalist Bernard Diedcrich, who covered Trujillo in the 1950s, the general's foundation would start to streak in the tropical heat and he would shoo away press photographers.

Trujillo's story says much about the relationship of the United States and the Dominican Republic. Trujillo rose to prominence because of the U.S. military occupation. His murderous rule was tolerated by Presidents Hoover, Roosevelt, Truman, and Eisenhower—even in 1956, when his agents kidnapped Galíndez in New York. Although Trujillo was torturing and murdering Dominicans by the hundreds, what was important to Roosevelt was that Trujillo sided with the Allies; to Eisenhower, it was that Trujillo was a staunch anticommunist. But in June 1960, before Kennedy was elected, Trujillo tried to assassinate Rómulo Betancourt, the president of Venezuela. Then, shortly after Kennedy was elected in November, Trujillo killed the three Mirabal sisters. Once in office, Kennedy decided that the U.S. did not want him anymore, and soon Trujillo was dead.

In British novelist Graham Greene's *Our Man in Havana,* police captain Segura, an infamous torturer, explains the idea of a torturable class: that a dictator could murder and torture as many people as he liked as long as he did not touch the kind of ruling-class people to whom other world leaders could relate. Trujillo had crossed that line. No longer just a killer of nameless brown people, he had become a rogue menace in the world. To deal with him, the CIA linked up with a Dominican underground that the U.S. had not helped for thirty years, and that was the end of the general.

Trujillo ran the most successful kleptocracy in Caribbean history—not an insignificant achievement, considering the contenders. For a kleptocracy, success is marked by the amount stolen and the number of years in a position to keep stealing. Trujillo, although he ran only a small, poor country, became one of the richest men in the world and lasted longer than even the Duvaliers in neighboring Haiti—father and son combined. Of course, in reality the longest kleptocracy in Caribbean history was the centuries in which Europe sucked every ounce of wealth it could find out of its Caribbean colonies. Corporate America tried its best—after all, sugar could be grown in Florida and Louisiana, yet it was this history of kleptocracy that made the Caribbean seem appealing for business—but never lived up to the kleptocratic success of Europe. Then the Europeans and the Americans wondered at the tendency toward kleptocracy in these islands as though this were a peculiarly Caribbean affliction, perhaps caused by climate.

The key to Trujillo's success was ruthless brutality and relentless egotism that sought to control and redefine everything in Dominican life. He owned most of the industry—including the sugar mills but also rice, beef, salt, and shoes—and controlled the baseball teams, and even dominated merengue with hits such as "Glory to the Benefactor," "Trujillo Is Great and Immortal," and the 1946 smash "We Want Reelection." He danced the merengue to gain popularity with the peasant class, but he also whitened the music to appeal to the upper classes by imposing forms that came from Spanish poetry.

Dominican children placed bottle caps on their chests to resemble the leader with his self-awarded medals and custom-designed uniforms. It has long been believed that Dominican feelings of insecurity and ambivalence demanded a certain type of paternalistic strongman for leader: what is called in Spanish a *caudillo*—the type of leader that expected to be thanked for the sugar harvest. It is also widely recognized that this tendency, caudilloism, is one of the great problems of the Dominican Republic. When Trujillo came to power, one of the first officially sanctioned merengues said:

> *We have hope in our caudillo;*
> *Everything will change with great speed,*
> *Because now Trujillo is president.*

After Trujillo was killed, for the next thirty years Dominican politics replaced the reds and the blues with Joaquín Balaguer and Juan Bosch. These two eternal brotherly enemies—Balaguer, the right-wing caudillo who had served as Trujillo's president, and Bosch, the leftist idealist, friend of Fidel Castro—had so much in common that they appeared to be mirror images of the same person. Balaguer was born in 1906 in the northern Cibao region, a member of an elite group in the country's wealthy region with the whitest population. Bosch was born in the same region and social class three years later. Bosch had a Puerto Rican mother, and Balaguer a Puerto Rican father. They were both white in a country where only about fifteen percent of the population is white. They both had literary aspirations, although Bosch's tough and realistic short stories garnered more respect than Balaguer's flowery, nineteenth-century-style poetry. More highly regarded was Balaguer's writing on literature, which always reserved ample space for praising the work of his *frère-ennemi*, Juan Bosch.

One worked for Trujillo, the other opposed him and went into exile. They both lived and played central roles in the nation's political life into their nineties, both seemingly refusing to either retire or die. The two old enemies could even join together to keep a third party out.

Balaguer was an aesthete who never married and lived in the servant quarters of the house of his six sisters. He wore dark suits and a fedora, and his only extravagances were a specially made limousine known as the Balaguermobile and a huge, dark, elaborately carved desk that he inherited from Trujillo, his extravagant predecessor. It was rumored that Balaguer had fathered illegitimate children throughout the country, but this speculation may have come from the difficulty Dominicans had in accepting men of power who were not oversexed. The sexual exploits of most of them, especially Trujillo and his son Ramfis, were legendary. When Trujillo's assassins caught up with him on the road, it was said the dictator was on his way to a tryst.

But just their haberdashery showed the difference between the caudillos: Trujillo looked like a feathery cross between Napoleon and Lord Nelson as seen in a Gilbert and Sullivan operetta, while Balaguer resembled actor Karl Malden doing a credit card commercial.

Balaguer, with or without sex, lived to be the oldest head of state in the world—was he preserved by celibacy, another worrying rumor mill asked—hanging on after he was legally blind and his hearing had faded. Interviewed at his huge desk, which made the small man look even smaller, this writer asked him why the electrical system was constantly failing. While he was denying this obvious truth, the electricity went off in the palace, but Balaguer continued with his denial, too blind to know what had happened.

Bosch was also a colorful octogenarian. He liked to take journalists to the slums and show his outrage at the wretched housing by pulling shacks apart while the poor family helplessly watched what little they had being torn up. Successive U.S. governments liked Balaguer, who had formed his right-wing party while in exile in New York. The Kennedy administration initially supported Bosch despite the claim of opponents that he was a communist. But once in power, as a result of one of the rare untainted democratic elections in Dominican history, Bosch made the mistake of seeking economic independence from the U.S. by awarding public contracts to Europeans. Washington began to fear Bosch, and after he was removed in a military coup in 1963, the U.S. invaded to prevent him from coming back to power. They put in his place Balaguer. In most Balaguer elections, fraud was suspected and violence was employed: in 1966, Balaguer had 350 Bosch supporters killed in order to ease his return to power. The U.S. accepted this as long as it was keeping Bosch from office. Once Bosch was no longer the opponent, the U.S. started criticizing the nearly nonagenarian president's proclivity for fraud.

In 1992, for the four-hundredth anniversary of Christopher Columbus's arrival, Balaguer ignored how badly the explorer is regarded in the Dominican Republic and spent $200 million to build a monument to him that could project light in the shape of a cross into the sky that would be visible for ten miles—that is, if they can ever get enough electrical power to light it up.

Having seen the U.S. completely manipulate the destiny of their country for generations, Dominicans understandably make the mistake of thinking that their country is a major priority of U.S. policy. But, in fact, the mistake of the nineteenth-century annexationists—who, once their proposal came to a Senate vote, discovered that no one in Washington was really interested in their country—is continually repeated. After President Lyndon Johnson sent troops to occupy the Dominican Republic, he sent down his top national security adviser, McGeorge Bundy, to report on the situation. But it turned out that the main reason for the assignment was not Johnson's concern about the Caribbean nation he had just invaded but to force Bundy to cancel a planned debate with leading scholars on Vietnam policy. It was Vietnam, not the Dominican Republic, that was preoccupying Washington. It is always something else.

CHAPTER TWO

The First Question

The first question most people ask when they learn how many Major League Baseball players have been produced by this one small town of San Pedro de Macorís is "What's in the water?" There seem to be numerous things in the water, some from the Mexican cement factory along the Higuamo River. But there is probably nothing in the water that would help with baseball. San Pedro baseball was not born from the water but from the history of the town.

Dominicans tend to be more attached to their regions than to their country, a fact that has proved important in the organization of baseball. One of the reasons it is so difficult to define Dominican culture is that although it is a small country—it is large only by Caribbean standards—the Dominican Republic has distinct regions with different histories, different economies, different traditions, even different racial makeups. This was true to some degree even before Europeans arrived. The previous people, the Tainos, had divided the island into five regions, each with its own ruler, or cacique. San Pedro, along the southern coast, forty miles east of the capital, is in the eastern part of the island, which is why its baseball players are called the Eastern Stars. It was part of the Taino region of Higüey, ruled when the Spanish arrived by a cacique named Cayacoa. Once the Spanish took over, the history and culture of the regions diverged even more dramatically. Baseball came out of the unique history of San Pedro de Macorís and the southeastern region.

The Tainos of Hispañola were from a group known as Arawaks who came from South America but spread northward into the Greater Antilles. Two of their best-known inventions were hammocks, which they called *hamacas*, and a musical instrument known as maracas. Two things that they had in common with the current inhabitants: they ate the root of the cassava plant, known today in Spanish by the word *yuca*, said to be of Taino origin, and they played a ball game for which they constructed fields throughout their communities. The Taino word for both their ball game and their ballpark is the Dominican word for a cane-worker village, a *batey*. While Tainos are clearly the reason that today's Dominicans eat so much yucca, the fact that the current residents are also a ballpark-building people is a coincidence, an accident of history, like the fact that the Tainos, too, had extreme reverence for their mothers.

The Tainos were a seafaring people, which is why these South Americans spread so far north in the Caribbean. Another reason is that they were driven there by a more aggressive South American group, the Caribs, who were also expanding into the Caribbean. When Columbus came to the Caribbean, he sailed into an ongoing war between the Tainos and the Caribs. When he first encountered the Caribs, on Guadeloupe, he claimed that they were breeding Tainos for food and that their body parts were hung to cure like sides of beef. He said he was so revolted by this that he attacked and killed every Carib he could find, but since that was what he generally did, it has to be wondered if this was a fabricated excuse. However, the Caribs and the Tainos were clearly at war, and the Tainos seemed to be losing. Gonzalo Fernández de Oviedo, an early Spanish historian of Santo Domingo, wrote that the cacique Cayacoa was one of the more ferocious resisters of the encroaching Caribs.

The Tainos built excellent dugout canoes, and in fact invented the word *canoe*, or *canoa*. They caught fish in nets, with hook and line, with spears or with traps, which are the same techniques used in San Pedro today.

In Taino Higüey, a people settled at the mouth of the Higuamo, where the river is wide and brackish and full of fish. No doubt drawn there by the fishing, this people called themselves Macorixes. Not only did the Macorixes have abundant river fish to net, oysters to pluck from the mangrove roots of the brackish water, and crabs to chase out of the holes they dug in the earth of the marshlands, but they could go to sea and try to land giant fish such as marlin, which were sometimes longer than the Macorix canoes. In short, it was a good spot for fishing and, set as it was a little upriver from the sea, was safe from all but the most furious of storms, known in Taino as a *huracán*.

Soon after the Spanish arrived, they began the conquest of Higüey and, when the Tainos resisted, unleashed a war of extermination. By 1504, with the territory more firmly under control, Juan Ponce de León was appointed governor of Higüey.

At the mouth of the Higuamo, people continued to fish, primarily from the eastern bank; but as time went on, a village also grew on the western bank. The area went by various names. The original settlement was and is still called Punta de Pescadores, Fishermen's Point. But just as pragmatic and illustrative was another name, Mosquito or Mosquitisol, named for the other creatures besides fish for which the marshy area was known.

Soon after independence in 1844—some say in 1846, others insist not until 1858—the town started to be called San Pedro de Macorís, after both Saint Peter, the patron saint of fishermen, and the Macorixes, the original Taino fishermen. The people were for the moment free of the Spanish, and Taino names were starting to come into fashion: throughout Dominican history, Taino names have become in vogue whenever anti-Spanish sentiment or Dominican nationalism is popular.

San Pedro de Macorís, with its sheltered riverfront and its short sea voyage to the capital, became a commercial port for local products, especially fish and plantains. In fact, there was a period in the late 1860s and 1870s when the town was referred to as Macorís de Plántanos. Other crops, such as corn and beans, were also shipped from the port. But Macorís de Plántanos was about to undergo a dramatic change.

The booming Cuban sugar industry started to spread to San Pedro, which had the flat, humid tropical land suited for growing cane, was close to the capital, and had its own seaport. The return of Spanish government in 1861 brought in Spanish and Italian entrepreneurs looking for opportunities and interested in sugar.

Then, on October 10, 1868, in Cuba, a wealthy Cuban landowner from Yara named Carlos Manuel de Céspedes made a speech from his farm, forever after known in Cuban history as the *grito de Yara*, in which he renounced both Spanish rule and slavery. He set his own slaves free. Thirty-seven other planters around Yara also freed their slaves and formed an army. So began a failed war of independence known as the Ten Years' War. Since this was largely an agricultural war—in fact, historians often attribute the movement's failure to its inability to attract support from Havana—wealthy Cuban landowners fled. Many of them were sugar producers who went to the Dominican Republic.

The Dominican Republic, which did not have slavery, was not competitive with Cuba and Puerto Rico until the 1870s, when the practice began to be abolished in Spanish colonies. In 1876 a Cuban, Juan Antonio Amechazurra, began exploring the possibilities of sugar production in San Pedro, and on January 9, 1879, just north of town, he opened the first *ingenio*, a steam-powered sugar mill named Ingenio Angelina. The *ingenio*—the word means "ingenuity"—was a modern wonder—state-of-the-art technology for its day in the Dominican Republic—and became the name of both the machine and the entire sugar mill. Until then, cane had been fed to a grinder powered by oxen or other livestock, a machine known in Spanish as a *trapiche*.

In both the U.S. and Europe, sugar was losing its luxury status and becoming a basic food for the working class, an important market in the Industrial Revolution. In November 1880 the government facilitated a San Pedro sugar industry by granting permission for San Pedro de Macorís to become an international port. The following year another Cuban, Santiago W. Mellor, founded Ingenio Porvenir on the edge of town. In 1882, Puerto Ricans started a mill and two different Dominican companies founded Ingenio Cristóbal Colón and Ingenio Consuelo, which was sold to a Cuban in 1883. By 1884, five years after the first San Pedro mill had opened, six modern steam-powered sugar mills were operating in San Pedro and shipping their sugar abroad from the port in town. Another, Quisqueya, opened in 1892 and an eighth, Las Pajas, in 1918.

In a town of a few thousand people, millions of dollars were spent on infrastructure: the port facility, the mills, *bateys* for the workers, train lines to carry the cane from the field to the mills . . .

Throughout the nineteenth century, starting with the Haitian revolution and continuing through the abolition of slavery in the French, British, and Danish colonies of the Caribbean, there was a move in Europe away from labor-intensive sugarcane processing, replacing it with sugar beet production. By the end of the century, more sugar from sugar beets—which grew well in Europe—was being produced than cane sugar.

Meanwhile, the Spanish colonies of Cuba and Puerto Rico were maintaining a slave economy and, almost free of competition, still developing sugarcane production, which continued to increase even after the Spanish ended slavery in the last two decades of the nineteenth century. After the turn of the century, the cane sugar industry overtook the beet sugar industry. Subsequently the European sugar industry was destroyed by World War I, leaving Caribbean sugar as the only alternative. During the war, U.S. investment in the Spanish Caribbean, much of it in sugar, reached heights never seen before or since. By the end of the conflict, Cuba, Puerto Rico, and the Dominican Republic produced almost a third of all the sugar sold in the world market. Between 1913 and 1926, Dominican sugar production quadrupled. Most of that growth was under U.S. military occupation.

In those years, sugar replaced coffee as the leading export of the Dominican Republic, a shift that had already occurred in Cuba and Puerto Rico. With this expansion, Europe, including Spain, ceased to be the primary consumer of sugar from the Spanish Caribbean, replaced by the sweet tooths of America. This switch in markets was a harbinger for the future of the Caribbean. Between the end of the American Civil War and 1890, American sugar consumption tripled. American sugar companies in mid-century were buying sugarcane and processing it in American cities. In 1870, sugar refining was the leading industry of New York City.

Gradually it became apparent that refining the sugar where it was grown and shipping it, a far less bulky product than cane, was more cost-effective. While foreign capital brought new technology to the mills— better grinders, railroads, and electricity—the fields remained equipped with little but the muscle of the worker and the machete. Few Dominicans were available for this labor.

While slavery continued in Puerto Rico until 1873 and in Cuba until 1886, the Dominican Republic had not had slavery since it was stopped by the Haitian occupiers in 1822. There were few Dominicans with agricultural skills looking for work, because over several generations they had settled into family farming. The Dominican Republic was a nation of small-scale farmers, and an underpopulated one at that. Estimates of the total population of the country in 1875 are as low as 150,000 people.

But land was available, and the Dominican government charged little in export duties. By the late nineteenth century, San Pedro de Macorís became the sugar center of the Dominican Republic. Two-thirds of Dominican land planted in cane was in San Pedro. After the World War, sugar companies aggressively searched for more land. In 1923 a subsidiary of an American firm, South Porto Rico Sugar Company, burned to the ground two small villages near San Pedro—El Caimonal and Higueral—so that it could expand fields in neighboring La Romana. The company offered no compensation to the 150 families they had made homeless. To the Americans, both the sugar companies and the military, clearing peasants off land around San Pedro created not only land for planting but landless peasants in search of agricultural work. As long as peasants had land to cultivate, they were not interested in underpaid wage labor in the sugar fields: at the turn of the century, mill owners had been arguing that the Dominican Republic was unsuited for the sugar industry because the combination of underpopulation and abundant fertile land made it easy for peasants to operate small farms, so they were not interested in working for the mills.

The fact that sugar companies, especially the American ones, took possession of far more land than they planted—more than half the land owned by sugar companies was never used—is evidence that they wanted the farmers more than the farms. But this never really worked. The various schemes by which the sugar companies and the Marines tricked or forced peasants off their land during U.S. occupation did not mobilize them to work for the sugar companies but instead incited them to organize an armed guerrilla movement against the occupation that was active in the east from 1917 to 1922.

The sugar producers' next idea was to bring in temporary workers from the Canary Islands and Puerto Rico. But then they realized that sugar workers from the British Caribbean were available. After slavery was abolished in the British Caribbean in 1838, the sugar industry on those islands went into decline and their mills did not take advantage of the improved technology of the Industrial Revolution. English-speaking black workers began to migrate seasonally for sugar harvests in Cuba, the banana harvest in Central America, dock construction in Bermuda, and, later, construction work on the Panama Canal. Just as the Dominican sugar industry was developing in the 1870s, steamships were replacing sail-powered transportation in the Caribbean, and workers were becoming more mobile.

At the same time, the sugar companies in San Pedro were beginning to appreciate the advantages of recruiting a more desperate foreign workforce, especially after a strike by Dominican workers in 1884 forced the companies to back off from a wage reduction. Starting in 1893, the sugar companies in San Pedro started recruiting workers from Saint Thomas, Saint John, Saint Kitts, Nevis, Anguilla, Antigua, and Saint Martin. On some islands, such as Anguilla, almost the entire male workforce would leave for the Dominican Republic at harvesttime. Every year about 4,500 workers would arrive at San Pedro just as the *zafra*, the cane harvest, was about to start. One result was that wages in sugar fields steadily declined. The migrants in San Pedro would work for twenty-five cents a day, half of the salary of a Dominican agricultural worker. The migrants had no negotiating power. Dominicans could threaten to go back to the land, but the immigrants had to accept wages and conditions or face deportation. Furthermore, once the companies discovered this source of labor, they had an endless supply of replacements for disgruntled workers.

In San Pedro they called the migrant workers *cocolos*. There is great debate on the origin and meaning of the word and whether or not it is pejorative. Regardless of its original tone and meaning, today in San Pedro, descendants of Eastern Caribbean sugar workers proudly call themselves *cocolos*. Some have speculated that the word is of Bantu origin. The usual explanation is that it was a mispronunciation by the Spanish-speaking people of San Pedro of the name of the British Virgin Island of Tortola, from where some *cocolos* came. But some nineteenth-century writers referred to Haitians as *cocolos*, and a late-nineteenth-century poem by José Joaquín Pérez of Santo Domingo referred to a Taino boy as a *cocolo*.

The big issue that Dominicans had with the *cocolos* was not their language or nationality but their skin color, which in most cases was black. It has made San Pedro, even today, one of the blackest areas of the Dominican Republic. Because this is a mulatto country, there has always been a sense that it could change, gradually becoming blacker or whiter: just as the Haitian occupiers had wanted to blacken it, Dominicans who developed a historic resentment and fear of Haitians wanted to whiten it.

And here were the *cocolos* coming to San Pedro and blackening the population. Dominicans in other parts of the country were growing concerned not only about the blackening of San Pedro but about foreign labor working for foreign-owned sugar companies: the eastern provinces were separating from the Dominican Republic. With great resentment, Dominican merchants complained that the *cocolos* took their money home with them rather than spending it in San Pedro. After some fifteen years of importing *cocolos*, newspapers started running articles about this "undesirable" immigration. In 1912, the legislature in Santo Domingo passed a law imposing restrictions on bringing in people who were not white. But in San Pedro both the sugar companies and the general population that was benefiting from the sugar boom ignored this legislation. Given the quantities of money they were generating, no one wanted to fight with the sugar companies.

The Dominicans wanted them to stay through the *zafra*. As early as the 1890s, sugar companies were advancing the *cocolos* their salaries in the form of credit at overpriced company stores. This kept them on the *bateys*, since they no longer had any money to spend elsewhere. Of course, such practices made sugar work even more unattractive to Dominicans and ensured that the sugar companies would have to import labor.

While by contract the sugar companies agreed to pay for foreign workers' voyages home, a 1919 law made it illegal for them to receive their return fares until the harvest was done. At Angelina the company would not even return a worker who had been incapacitated by injury. Also in 1919 a law was decreed barring immigration to the Dominican Republic by anyone who was not Caucasian. Nonwhites who entered the country were required to register and get a permit within their first four months in the country.

Yet Eastern Caribbean *cocolos* kept coming until the late 1920s, when they were almost entirely replaced by Haitian workers, sometimes also referred to as *cocolos*. Because of the 1912 anti-immigration law, statistics started to be kept. Between 1912 and 1920, according to official records, 39,000 of these Eastern Caribbean people came to San Pedro.

During World War I, with U.S. troops occupying both Haiti and the Dominican Republic, Haitians started replacing the Eastern Caribbeans as migrant workers. A total of 22,121 Haitians came for the *zafra* in 1921, and forty-three percent of them went to the mills of San Pedro. But by then thousands of Eastern Caribbean workers had come, many with women, and settled in San Pedro in mill communities such as Consuelo. By 1914, one in four legal immigrants was female.

All of these many thousands of foreign workers were to have an enormous impact on small, underpopulated San Pedro. Less and less Spanish was spoken in San Pedro. The Haitians spoke Creole, their own Africanized French, and the Eastern Caribbean people spoke English, except for the occasional French speaker from Saint Martin.

American mill owners liked English-speaking workers and gave them easier, better-paying jobs in the mills. They were upwardly mobile and were able to bring in relatives from their native islands and find them positions too. Some left the mill and got jobs in town at the bustling port on the Higuamo River. Almost all sugar loading at the ports was done by *cocolos* and the railroads that operated at the sugar mills were almost entirely operated by *cocolos*.

During the American occupation, Americans were less interested in race than money, and with Europe and its beet production destroyed, fortunes were being made on Caribbean sugar. At its peak in 1922, Cuba, Puerto Rico, and the Dominican Republic produced thirty-eight percent of the world's cane sugar and twenty-seven percent of total world sugar. Cuban sugar alone sold that year for $1 billion.

Even though in the Dominican Republic a higher percentage of sugar production was American owned than in Cuba and Puerto Rico, the Dominican producers did not receive the same preferential treatment as the other two islands. Puerto Rican sugar could enter the U.S. tariff-free, and Cuban sugar had a twenty-percent reduction in sugar tariff. This made it difficult for Dominican sugar to be competitive in the U.S., but fortunately Europe in ruins created a huge market for Dominican sugar mills. Historians termed the sugar boom in the Spanish Caribbean during the early decades of the twentieth century the "Dance of the Millions"—millions of dollars generated in the sugar fields.

The Dominican Republic now had an export-based economy, and the center of that export economy—the center of the Dominican economy from the late nineteenth century into the 1930s—was the sugar industry and the *ingenios* of San Pedro de Macorís: Consuelo, Las Pajas, Quisqueya, Angelina, Santa Fe, Cristóbal Colón, and Porvenir.

From the eastern bank of the Higuamo River, an affluent town of elegance and culture was emerging. In 1888, the leading poet of the nineteenth-century Dominican Republic, thirty-year-old Gastón Fernando Deligne, a native of Santo Domingo, abandoned the capital for San Pedro de Macorís, where he wrote much of his important work until his death in 1913. Joaquín Balaguer, the right-wing caudillo, literary scholar, and poet, rated him one of the best poets and wrote that he had the ability "to put together in the same composition, at times the same stanza, the most prosaic of realistic details along with the loftiest thoughts and most evolved forms."

Other literary figures followed, and San Pedro for a time was known for its poets. The year Deligne died, Pedro Mir, the leading Dominican poet of the twentieth century, was born in San Pedro. Typical of the increasingly cosmopolitan nature of San Pedro, Mir's father was a Cuban sugar mill engineer who had come to San Pedro to work for Cristóbal Colón and there met and married Pedro's mother, who was from Puerto Rico. Mir was working in the Cristóbal Colón mill, when the leftist Juan Bosch, a major literary figure in the 1930s, took an interest in his poetry. The reverse of Deligne, Mir started in San Pedro but ended up building his reputation in Santo Domingo—except during the period from 1947 to 1961, when he fled the Trujillo regime and lived in Cuba. In 1984 the Dominican legislature named him poet laureate. Typical of the bizarre contradiction that was Balaguer, the literary critic praised Mir for using his poetry to stand up to the "despotism and social injustice" that Balaguer the politician participated in.

Ludín Lugo Martínez, born in San Pedro, was a leading Dominican woman poet and novelist. René del Risco Bermúdez, born in San Pedro in 1937, was a poet and short story writer who suffered prison and exile in the Trujillo years and then, in 1974—just when his reputation was growing— died in an automobile accident at the age of thirty-seven. And there have been numerous others. If San Pedro had not been so successful at baseball, it would have been famous for its poets.

During the sugar-boom years, there was considerable intellectual life in San Pedro. Among the young people involved in the poetry scene was Evangelina Rodríguez Perozo, born in 1879, who went off to Paris to study medicine and returned to be the first native-born doctor in Dominican history. There was considerable interest in the advancement of women in San Pedro. In 1886, Deligne began championing the idea that women were entitled to the same education as men. In 1922, the first feminist political organization in Dominican history, the Dominican Feminist Association for the Rights of Woman, was established in San Pedro by Petronila Angélica Gómez, a journalist and teacher. Its magazine, *Fémina*, was the first in the Dominican Republic to be edited by women. It published for seventeen years.

Built on sugar money, a handsome town emerged with ornate homes and stores in architectural styles from Belle Époque to Art Deco. A central park with tropical gardening was created, and a new white cathedral, finished in 1913, defined the skyline as it gleamed in the sun. A stately two-story balconied yellow and white City Hall, pretty as a cake, was built next to the cathedral. When Macorisanos walked around the elegant center of town—even if they were poor sugar workers—they dressed up in white linen.

After the 1916 invasion, Rear Admiral Harry Shepard Knapp, who headed the military government that now ruled the Dominican Republic, began touring his fiefdom. He did not arrive in San Pedro until January 25, 1918, by which time he had already seen most of the country. He was stunned by San Pedro, a town of elegance and culture and economic development far beyond anywhere else he had been. Indeed, the very first automobile ever seen in the Dominican Republic was a Ford brought over by the owner of the Santa Fe sugar mill in 1912. San Pedro also had the first asphalt-paved street in the country. It had the country's first automatic telephone line, which connected with the capital. It also was the first city in the country to use concrete construction and built the first three-story building.

In 1922, when the first census in San Pedro was conducted, 38,609 people lived there, of whom more than a third, 10,145, were foreigners. These were not just cane workers; they included the Americans, Italians, Cubans, and other foreigners who ran the sugar industry. And there were immigrants from Lebanon who in the first decades of the twentieth century were settling in the Dominican Republic, Haiti, Jamaica, and other parts of the Caribbean.

After Trujillo took power in 1930, Pan Am began offering flights by seaplane from Santo Domingo. The planes would land in the Higuamo River and let passengers out at the port, which was a short stroll to the cathedral, the town hall, the shops, and the park in this little pearl of a city. But by then San Pedro's fortunes were beginning to change.

By 1931 the value of goods shipped from the port of San Pedro was less than half of what it had been in 1926. The sugar boom was cooling off, and the Dominican Republic was the producer with the least access to foreign markets. But sugar production continued, increasing faster than demand on all three islands, and the Cuban government—and soon after, the U.S. government—began imposing restrictions on production aimed at preserving the price. Since the early 1930s, with the exception of a few brief bubbles, the value of sugar on the world market has steadily declined.

Neither was Trujillo good for San Pedro. While the city had its share of Trujillo supporters, it had come to the general's attention that he had a considerable number of opponents in the sugar city to the east. In any event, he did not want any competitors with Santo Domingo, the capital, which he regarded as "his" city. In fact, he changed the capital's name to Ciudad Trujillo: Trujillo City. He had come to power on August 16, 1930. A few weeks later, on September 3, Hurricane San Zenón destroyed Santo Domingo. Trujillo saw this as his opportunity to rebuild the city in his image. San Pedro was forgotten as sugar faded and the dictator who completely controlled the economy diverted all resources to the city that now bore his name.

But San Pedro de Macorís had one thing left. During the half-century sugar boom, among all the firsts of the small eastern town on the Higuamo, there was this: in 1886, Dominican baseball began to be played in the sugar mills of San Pedro.

The Spanish-American War is generally credited for launching America's great imperialist adventure in the Spanish Caribbean, because the U.S. in effect replaced Spain as the colonial power in Cuba and Puerto Rico. But American businessmen had long been interested in the two islands, and sugar producers began operating in Cuba back in the time when baseball was just getting started in the U.S., in the 1830s and 1840s. And these same Cubans came to San Pedro. It is ironic that when the sugar producers built housing for workers and named them *bateys* after the Taino ball fields, they did not know that these *bateys* would be one of the greatest wellsprings of ballplaying talent ever known.

CHAPTER THREE

The Question of First

Baseball is a game that loves facts but spawns myths. It is often stated that the first baseball game was organized in 1839 in Coopers-town, New York, by Abner Doubleday, who invented the baseball diamond and codified the rules. This was the conclusion of a commission established in 1908 to once and for all determine the sport's ambiguous origin. It was led by sporting-goods entrepreneur Al Spalding. Abner Doubleday, a Civil War general, in 1839 was a cadet at West Point, which was a long journey to Cooperstown, a town that has no record of Doubleday's having ever been there. There is no record that Doubleday himself ever said anything about his connection with baseball, and most historians—including those at the National Baseball Hall of Fame in Cooperstown, where it is a founding myth—discount the story. What is known is that baseball came out of English sports, possibly including cricket, which goes back to at least the sixteenth century, with roots centuries earlier. Round-ers, another English game, was almost certainly a precursor of baseball in America. There were many eighteenth-century variations on both the game and its name. There was town-ball, round-ball, and a game called base, and it is still being argued which of these or which combination was the origin of baseball.

The only fact in the Abner Doubleday story that seems to be true is the date: 1839. Somewhere around then these games had evolved into something recognizable as baseball. It was originally a sport for city people, and in 1845 a Manhattan book dealer, Alexander Cartwright, wrote a rule book for his local club, the Knickerbockers, who would later change their name to the Yankees. Cartwright's rules became the rules of baseball, and he traveled around the country establishing baseball clubs in various cities. By 1857 there were sixteen clubs in New York City alone. The Civil War helped spread the sport throughout the United States. But it was sugar—that is, American sugar executives—who brought it to the Caribbean during the Dance of the Millions.

The American presence in Cuba predates baseball and even sugar interests. When America was a British colony, there was a considerable British presence in Cuba. In 1762 the British even took over Havana for several months. While the Dominican Republic seemed a distant, unknown place to Americans, Cuba was regarded as nearby and familiar. In 1817, when the Spanish declared Cuban ports open to international trade, American business stepped in. Cubans became familiar with Americans and American culture. American companies won contracts for development, especially in Havana, where both the gas street lighting and the granite cobblestone pavement were American. There were American consulates throughout the island.

And so by the 1860s, when baseball was becoming established as the American national pastime, the Cubans were learning about it and started playing it. The Spanish may have inadvertently tied the independence movement to baseball in a self-fulfilling prophecy when in 1868, at the start of the Ten Years' War, they banned the game, suspecting that it was somehow a pro-independence conspiracy. There was no clear tie, at least until the ban, but affluent young men were becoming *independentistas,* and they were also taking up baseball, which the Spanish saw as an incursion by Americans and also an excuse for the rebels to arm themselves with wooden clubs.

The failed 1868–1878 war cemented Cubans to the American sport not only because the Spanish had made the accusation but because pro-independence Cubans, including José Martí, fled to the United States, where baseball was becoming a craze. The Cubans learned the game and even organized Cuban and Cuba-versus-U.S. games. Martí himself was seen at a Key West game in which the Cubans beat the Americans. Martí, always aware that after the Spanish were defeated the Americans would be the next problem, reportedly claimed the victory was a good omen for the cause of independence.

Cuban baseball, like American baseball, has a mythical first game. In Matanzas in 1866 according to one story, the crew of an American ship decided to teach the game to the Cuban dockworkers who were loading sugar. In another version an American ship tied up for repairs and taught the men fixing their ship. In some of the versions the Americans were trying to sell the Cubans baseball equipment. But there is also another story that says the first game was not even in Matanzas but in Havana, from where two affluent young Habaneros named Ernesto and Nemesio Guillot had been sent off to Spring Hill College, a prep school in Mobile, Alabama. They came home in 1864 with bats, balls, and Cartwright's rule book and trained a team in the affluent Vedado section of Havana, making this neighborhood, according to some baseball historians such as Peter Bjarkman, the true birthplace of Cuban baseball—not the always cited Matanzas of two years later. The Guillot story, unlike the Matanzas versions, is unromantic enough to be true.

According to official history, the first organized game between Cuban club players was on a ball field in Matanzas that still exists called Palmar del Junco on December 27, 1874. Unlike Abner Doubleday's game in Cooperstown, it is well documented that this game between a Matanzas team and the Habana Base Ball Club did take place. But it is not clear that it was the first organized game between clubs. Historian Roberto

González Echevarría suggests that it may simply have been the first game to have been written about in the press. Historians like the story of Cuban baseball beginning in Matanzas because it was a port where American ships docked, and Cubans, like Dominicans, have always been drawn to the idea of baseball being a contest in which the locals stood up to the Americans.

But the 1874 game at Palmar del Junco was between Cubans. Havana won by the astonishing score of 51 to 9. Hitting skills developed earlier than fielding skills, and early games often had such scores. Emilio Sabourín, one of the revered martyrs of Cuban independence, played left field for Havana that day and hit eight home runs. Sabourín was one of the early promoters of not only Cuban baseball but also Cuban independence. He founded and managed one of the three Havana clubs that played fourteen series between 1878 and 1892. His club won nine of them. But the worst fears of the Spanish were confirmed when it was discovered that the money Sabourín had raised by organizing baseball games was sent to the independence movement. In 1895 he was arrested and baseball was once again banned. Sabourín was shipped to an infamous military prison in Ceuta, on the Moroccan side of the Strait of Gibraltar. The left fielder, sometimes called the "father of Cuban baseball," died there two years later.

In the 1890s, Spain was fading from the three islands and America was taking hold, and so soccer, the once popular Spanish sport, fell out of favor and was replaced by the American sport, baseball.

As in Cuba and the United States, it is not clear where baseball began in the Dominican Republic. Certainly, in the late 1870s baseball-loving Cuban *independentistas* and American baseball enthusiasts met to develop a sugar industry in San Pedro de Macorís. In San Pedro it is said that the first Dominican game was played there in 1886. But many historians and people in Santo Domingo refute this. Sugar makers were not the only Cubans to come to the Dominican Republic, and San Pedro was not their only destination. At the same time that sugar makers were building San Pedro, Ignacio Aloma and his brother Ubaldo came to Santo Domingo. They were ironworkers who built balconies and grillwork. In 1891 they formed two baseball clubs with Cuban and American players and even a few Dominicans. The two teams were known to Dominican fans by their colors, the Rojos and the Azules. Another Cuban started two teams in La Vega, in the north near the Cibao, and they were also known as the Reds and the Blues. In Cuba there were also red and blue teams, but the labels were particularly meaningful in the Dominican Republic, where politics for many decades had revolved around the Red and Blue parties.

In the 1880s, when the big new *ingenios* were being put into operation in San Pedro, experienced baseball players were not easily found. The normal way to establish a baseball club in both the U.S. and in Cuba was to find athletic young men and teach them the game. And it occurred to the Americans, the Cubans, and the Puerto Ricans that in their mills they had the potential for ball clubs. They began teaching the game to sugar workers. Each mill could have its own club and they could play each other. Soon they would have an eight-club league just in the San Pedro sugar industry.

In Santo Domingo, baseball was a game for the wealthy elite. As in Havana, upper-class Dominicans sent their sons to schools in the U.S. and they came back playing baseball. This was very different from the sugar-mill sport of San Pedro.

A few years after the games began in 1886, the *ingenios* started importing Eastern Caribbean *cocolos*. The *cocolos* kept not only their own language—English with a West Indian lilt—but their own culture. They drank dark, strong, smooth rum that was steeped in the small fruit of the tropical plant guavaberry, known to science as *Myrciaria floribunda*. They made soup with the broad-leaved callaloo and served meat or fish with little hard-boiled flour dumplings or a cornmeal mush called *fungi*. They danced to their own music with their own drums, and on their holidays dressed up with costumes and masks to perform ritual dances of David and Goliath or Wild Indians.

They also had their own sports, and the most popular of these was cricket. Historians argue about the role of cricket in developing baseball in the United States, but there can be no argument about the important role of cricket in developing baseball in San Pedro. The sugar companies simply had to give the *cocolos* round bats and a new set of rules. They already knew the concepts of hitting, catching, baserunning, pitching, making outs, and scoring runs.

Cricket and then baseball were diversions in very hard lives. In a land once called Mosquito, malaria was rampant. So was leprosy, the disease that killed the poet Gastón Deligne. With the bad water supply of the *bateys*, dysentery was a frequent problem. The diet of most of the workers did not include sufficient nutrition for the twelve-hour shifts during the *zafra*. Serious injuries from the machinery in the mills or machetes in the field were frequent. If an injury such as loss of a limb meant that the laborer was no longer eligible for work, he received no compensation.

Coming from a different world and with a limited but better education, *cocolos* knew about things that Dominicans had never heard of, such as labor struggles and black people organizing. Marcus Garvey, born in Jamaica in 1887 and a forerunner of the Black Power movement, was organizing black people all over the English-speaking world, and he did not forget about the *cocolos* of San Pedro de Macorís. In 1919, Garvey's Universal Negro Improvement Association sent an organizer. Within months they had their own building in San Pedro, and within a year San Pedro was the center of an important Dominican chapter of the Garvey movement with more than a thousand members. Garvey promoted the idea of black people reuniting in Africa, and many of the *cocolos* talked about how they would soon be leaving the sugar mills and going to the continent of their ancestors. During the 1921 *zafra, cocolos* went on a strike that was quickly crushed.

The *cocolos* were a well-organized society, and one of the keys to that organization was a network of cricket clubs. They made their own white uniforms. But the mills were more interested in baseball. They sometimes even paid cricket players for baseball. No one paid for cricket. By the 1920s baseball had largely replaced cricket, and many of the fields where they had played it became baseball diamonds.

During the *zafra*, sugar workers only worked and slept, but the other six months of the year, the dead season, they had time for baseball. This free time corresponded more with the American summer baseball schedule than the winter schedule that became traditional in the rest of the Dominican Republic and the other Caribbean islands. The mills would each sponsor a team with uniforms and equipment and they would play *regionales* against the other mill teams. Some mills, especially Consuelo, would have so many gifted players that the team couldn't use them all and would send a few to other mills. Several, such as Alfredo "Chico" Contón, went to play in Cuba or Puerto Rico or even the Dominican Winter League, once it started. But none of these tremendously talented players was going to the major leagues because the leagues did not hire black players.

The sugar-mill players of San Pedro were even separate from La Vega and Santo Domingo players as well as Cubans and Puerto Ricans, because all those other Caribbeans played in the winter during the *zafra*. But the San Pedro teams had the advantage of constant U.S. contact, since the sugar companies were always bringing in new Americans. In the years since the game had been introduced to the Caribbean, both the rules and the equipment had been rapidly changing. In 1873 it was ruled that catching a fly ball in a hat, a common practice until then, would award the hitter a single and the ball could not be put back into play. In the 1880s the number of balls for a walk gradually was reduced from nine to four, and the number of strikes to an out was changed from four to three. In the 1890s the distance between the pitching mound and home plate was increased from fifty feet to sixty feet. In the first decade of the twentieth century, the first two foul balls started being counted as strikes, greatly reducing the number of pitches in an at-bat. Every decade the game was considerably different, and Dominican players needed contact with the U.S. in order to keep playing current American baseball.

Communities at the mills, especially the *cocolos*, were knit extremely tightly, and within their world these games were closely followed and considered important. They were, after all, the closest thing these people had to a leisure activity. Baseball took on great meaning for the players and the fans, and the quality of their Cuban and American instruction from the cadre of the sugar companies was thought to be excellent. During the early decades when baseball was spreading in the Dominican Republic, the baseball played in the mills in San Pedro is remembered as the best Dominican baseball of the time. There is no way to verify this, and baseball has a way of fostering uncertain myths, but this was the beginning of the legend of San Pedro baseball. To baseball fans who ask, "Why San Pedro de Macorís?" the answer is not the water but the sugar.

CHAPTER FOUR

Who's on First

W hile San Pedro was hosting regular hard-fought contests between the mills, Santo Domingo was developing their own
league. For fifteen years there were two teams, red and blue:
Ozama Club, named after the river on whose western bank the city was
first built; and Nuevo Club. There were other teams, but these were the
two with uniforms and an official schedule. They got their baseball knowledge from Dominicans who had spent time in the U.S.

Lulu Pérez, who led Nuevo Club, learned the new curveball from the
Americans and taught it to his ace pitcher. A curveball is a difficult pitch
to master. It is accomplished by pressing the middle finger against the
seam of the baseball and snapping the wrist as the ball is released. This
sends the ball spinning so that it seemingly goes straight but at the last
moment veers off course. A good curveball appears to be going right at
the batter and, just as he ducks or prepares to step back, drops into the
strike zone and a strike is called. What makes it even more difficult is that
a good curveball drops from head level to the strike zone or from the strike
zone to below the knees, just before reaching the plate. Very few batters
can hit a good curveball. But it is a dangerous pitch to throw. If it doesn't

have enough motion, it will either be a ball or fly predictably through the strike zone—a very easy pitch to hit because it is not a fast pitch.

In the first decade of the twentieth century, there were still only a few good curveballs, which of course meant that batters had little experience against the pitch that was invented in the 1870s by Candy Cummings. Even today it is rare to find a good curveball from a young Dominican pitcher who has not played in the U.S. In fact, good curveballs are fairly rare in general. But in the early years of the twentieth century, Lulu Pérez taught Nuevo Club ace Enrique Hernández how to throw one, and he did it so well that no one in Santo Domingo could hit it. Because Hernández claimed to have some Taino blood, fans started calling him Indio Bravo. At a time of undeveloped outfield defense, it was pitching that kept the score from going into double digits. When Indio Bravo pitched, Nuevo Club was undefeatable.

In 1906 a group of young Santo Domingo players met in a house in the old part of Santo Domingo, the Colonial Zone, once ruled by Columbus and today favored by tourists. Their subject was how to beat Indio Bravo. They built a baseball club designed to take on the Nuevo Club and they called it Club Licey, after another river, this one in the Cibao. At first uniformed in gray, they soon switched to white with blue stripes and ever after they were nicknamed the Azules. Licey fans still celebrate the November anniversary, but more than the founding of the Licey team it was the beginning of the modern Dominican Winter Baseball League that has become the centerpiece of Dominican baseball.

Originally it was a Santo Domingo competition in which the other baseball regions, the north and San Pedro, were not involved. But Licey began traveling outside the capital to find other competition. To play in the north, the entire team would have to travel long hours on dirt roads and even organize mule trains through mountain trails. On the other hand, San Pedro de Macorís had its long-standing commercial advantage: it was only a short ship's crossing from Santo Domingo. In 1911, Macorisanos put together a team with local Americans, Cubans, Dominicans, and *cocolos* to face Licey. In the first encounter in 1911, pitching dominated with twenty-one strikeouts. But the baserunning kept it lively with twenty-two stolen bases. To the shock and disappointment of Macorisanos, Licey won.

But back in the capital, Licey was unable to match Nuevo Club, which won the first championship in 1912. Indio Bravo was impossible to get a hit off of, even after an unbalanced Licey fan tried to slow him down by stabbing him in his throwing arm.

The U.S. invasion and occupation of the Dominican Republic, like most military occupations, was deeply unpopular. In San Pedro an angry Dominican opened fire on U.S. Marine officers and killed one as the troops were arriving at the port. After the U.S. invasion the interest in baseball increased, not because of a love of things American, but from a strong desire to beat the Americans at their own game. And the Americans provided knowledgeable and equipped opponents. The Americans, who showed little respect for things Dominican, were impressed with the baseball players. One Dominican pitcher, Felito Guerra, was so respected, he was offered a contract to pitch in the U.S. He would have been the first Dominican major leaguer but instead became a national hero when he refused to go, to protest the occupation.

Cuba, Puerto Rico, and Panama had all been occupied by the U.S., and because of that exposure all three became better baseball-playing countries. Now the Dominican Republic followed the same pattern. After the Dominican invasion, the U.S. occupied Nicaragua and their game greatly improved also. It seemed that baseball was the one thing a small Latin American nation could gain from a U.S. invasion.

Licey built up their team with Puerto Ricans, Cubans, and Americans. Their star pitcher was a Cuban called El Diamante Negro. But Nuevo Club was still holding its own because they had Indio Bravo, who was still accomplishing Homeric feats. After the U.S. occupation, Nuevo Club took on the U.S. Navy cruiser *Washington* and Indio Bravo struck out twenty-one Navy batters. But he got into a dispute with his ball club and went over to Licey, making them undefeatable. The demoralized Nuevo Club disintegrated.

The Licey Tigers had become the dominant club. By 1921 northern baseball had shifted from La Vega to the capital of the Cibao, Santiago de los Cabelleros. It took the Licey team five days to get there and two days to rest. They then won all eight games against Santiago.

But this same year a new Santo Domingo team, Escogido, was formed for the purpose of taking on Licey. They made their color red because Licey was blue. Because Licey had stripes on their uniform they called themselves Los Tigres, the Tigers, so Escogido became the Lions. In 1928, Santiago named its team Sandino after Augusto César Sandino. The year before, three years after leaving the Dominican Republic, the U.S. invaded and occupied Nicaragua and Sandino became a folk hero throughout Latin America for his armed resistence to U.S. occupation. But once Trujillo— a product of U.S. military anti-insurgency efforts—came to power, the name Sandino was no longer allowed and, conforming to the Santo Domingo teams, the Santiago team became the Águilas, the Eagles, and then the Águilas Cibaeñas, the Cibao Eagles. Only San Pedro de Macorís did not have an animal. True to their tradition as the city of poets, they called their team Las Estrellas del Oriente, the Stars of the East. But they needed an animal, too, to give fans an image to use in the spectacle that erupts in Dominican stadiums. And so they declared their mascot to be an elephant so that fans could trumpet like elephants when the Estrellas scored a home run. Noise is important in Dominican culture.

These four teams—the Tigres del Licey, the Leones del Escogido, the Águilas Cibaeñas, and the Estrellas Orientales—from these three towns became the core of Dominican professional baseball. They played long seasons against one another, with grueling final contests for the Dominican championship.

The games in Santo Domingo, Santiago, and San Pedro drew huge crowds and were avidly covered by sportswriters, who always used pseudonyms to protect themselves from the ire of fans. For a few years it was an amateur passion, what is known by Dominicans as baseball's romantic era. But the clubs could make so much money at these packed stadiums that inevitably the romance was soon overtaken by commerce, and baseball became a professional sport. Players sought the highest salary in a circuit that included not only the four Dominican teams but the teams of Cuba and Puerto Rico and a few other Latin American countries as well as the Negro League in the United States. And players from these foreign teams, especially the Negro League, the Cuban League, and the Puerto Rican League, also came to the Dominican Republic to play.

The most famous player of the Dominican League was Juan Esteban Vargas, known as Tetelo Vargas. Born in Santo Domingo in 1906, he was a phenomenally fast runner nicknamed "the Dominican Deer." He broke a world record rounding a baseball diamond in 13:25 seconds. There is an unconfirmed rumor that he once beat Olympic track star Jesse Owens in a sprint. Vargas played all three outfield positions, shortstop, and second base, and was a great hitter with a strong throwing arm. He played for Escogido, for the Negro League in New York, for Puerto Rico, for Mexico, for Venezuela, for Cuba, for Colombia, for Canada, and finally, past the age of retirement, for the Estrellas in San Pedro. This was the world of Dominican ballplayers. Vargas was never allowed in the major leagues because he was black, but in Puerto Rico in the 1940s he played in a tournament against the Yankees during their spring training and batted .500, getting seven hits in fourteen at-bats. In 1953, playing for the Estrellas at the age of forty-seven, he was the Dominican League batting champion with an average of .353.

With professional careers like Tetelo Vargas's the cane workers of San Pedro had even more motivation to play their sugar-mill games hard and well and maybe someday leave the mill for Estrellas or the other teams or even the Negro League.

Trujillo was not a baseball fan, but that did not mean he wasn't interested in controlling it. His son Ramfis and other family members and many of his generals liked the game. Besides, his concept of governance was to own everything, so that the profits went to himself and the rest he could distribute as he pleased to those who said, "*Gracias, Presidente.*"

When sugar prices started to rise in the late 1940s, he took over mills to get the profits. By the mid-1950s he controlled two-thirds of the sugar production in the country, mainly for his personal profit. Among his assets were the San Pedro mills of Porvenir, Quisqueya, Santa Fe, and Consuelo.

But even before taking over sugar, when he first came to power and sugar did not look profitable, Trujillo took over baseball. It was at this time that some of the best players came to the Dominican Republic. Top players of the Negro League came to the Dominican capital—in fact, some of the best players in the world, including Josh Gibson, who came with a Venezuelan team in 1933. Gibson, one of the best catchers and hitters of all time, was called the black Babe Ruth, and some said he was a better hitter than Ruth. He had the best lifetime batting average in the history of the Negro League, possibly as high as .384. Batting averages show how difficult it is to get a hit in professional baseball. A batter who got a hit every time he went to bat would have a 1.000 batting average. In reality, any professional who can get a hit once out of every three times at bat—an average of .333—is considered an excellent hitter. Anyone who hits over .300 is considered formidable. Gibson had a .467 batting average for 1933, a hit almost every other time at bat.

The Santo Domingo teams, bankrolled by the dictator, started bringing in foreign talent such as Cuban pitcher Luis Tiant, Sr., the left-handed father of the right-handed pitcher of the same name. Fewer and fewer positions were left for Dominicans unless they were remarkable players such as Tetelo Vargas. Dominican teams recruited whoever they could get to win.

Until then, the San Pedro team had not won a championship. Unlike the Santo Domingo teams, who usually won, San Pedro did not draw foreign stars. They were not even drawing a great deal on the tremendous talent at their sugar mills, because they played during the *zafra*. The home team was mostly made up of upper-class gentlemen players, some of them doctors—something else San Pedro was known for—and they generally lost. San Pedro wanted to compete too. Instead of playing on the local team, a group of prominent Macorisanos, centered around a judge originally from Santo Domingo, Federico Nina Santana, decided to organize, with the judge financing it. He spent money buying top players and was willing to lose money to see San Pedro win. This is when the team was given its name, Estrellas del Oriente, and later Estrellas Orientales, Eastern Stars. Before, it had been El Macorís. The Eastern Stars were mostly from Cuba. They took on the Cubans and Puerto Ricans of Licey and Escogido and beat them both, winning the 1936 championship.

By 1936, Licey and Escogido were used to bringing the championship to the capital, with an occasional strong showing from Santiago. Losing to San Pedro came as a shock. And the Estrellas in San Pedro kept buying even more talent, giving them every hope of winning the championship again in 1937. Although Trujillo did not care about baseball, he did not like seeing the city that now bore his name lose. The general had no feelings for Licey or Escogido, both of whom lost their stadiums in Hurricane San Zenón. But Trujillo felt that Trujillo City should have a baseball team, and that team had better win.

Trujillo's brother José was a baseball fanatic—an emotionally unstable one who once lost his temper in a game and hit an American player. José and his sister had been the money behind Licey. Dr. José E. Aybar, a dentist, who had run Licey since 1929, had an endless source of money from the Trujillos to conduct a bidding war with Escogido over Cuba's greatest talent. Now the dictator decided that there would be only one team in his city, that they would buy the greatest players on the market, and that they would beat San Pedro de Macorís for the championship. Dr. Aybar was put in charge of the Dragones de Ciudad Trujillo.

Aybar then went to New Orleans, reportedly with suitcases full of money, and bought the best talent of the Negro League, including Josh Gibson and Satchel Paige, the high-kicking right-handed pitcher who threw breaking balls that were so unique, he gave them his own names, such as the bat dodger, the jump ball, and the two-hump blooper. Some baseball writers claim he was the greatest pitcher of all time. Aybar also got "Cool Papa" Bell, a small, wiry center fielder said by some—Tetelo Vargas fans may disagree—to be the fastest runner in the history of baseball. According to legend, he once scored from first base on a sacrifice bunt, a dribble off the plate designed to move the runner to second. But Dr. Aybar had Trujillo's money behind him. Reportedly, Paige was handed $30,000 in cash, an enormous amount of money at the height of the Depression, to divide as he saw fit between himself and eight other players. Top players in the Negro League, which was supposed to be high-paying baseball, were earning less than a thousand dollars for an eight-week contract.

Word was spreading in the Negro League that the Dominican League paid better than their clubs. Nina also went shopping for players in the U.S. and brought four back to San Pedro. They arrived at the port by seaplane. Waiting for them was General Federico Fiallo, Trujillo's military commander and a former pitcher for Licey in its 1906 opening season. Fiallo took the four players to Ciudad Trujillo to play for Trujillo's team, and Nina had to return to the U.S. to find more recruits.

Throughout the thirty-six-game season, all three teams went on a spending spree to bring in more and more stars. The 1937 season is remembered as the best baseball ever seen in the Dominican Republic, some of the best in baseball history—an epic battle played out with some of the all-time greatest players. Determined to beat San Pedro, Ciudad Trujillo, with its Americans and Cubans and one Puerto Rican, ended up with only one Dominican player on its roster. For the American players it was a novel experience. When Ciudad Trujillo lost, the military would angrily fire weapons in the air. The police would arrest Negro League players and keep them in jail the night before a game to prevent them from going out on the town. Paige later wrote, "I started wishing I was home when all those soldiers started following us around everywhere we went and even stood out in front of our rooms at night." During one game against San Pedro, the manager told them menacingly, "Take my advice and win." By the seventh inning they were behind by one run. "You could see Trujillo lining up his army," Paige said later. "They began to look like a firing squad." Ciudad Trujillo scored two runs that inning to take a one-run lead and then Paige pitched two scoreless innings.

As sometimes happens today in the major leagues, Ciudad Trujillo spent the most money and they won. The capital erupted with loud merengue and dancing in the streets. More than elation over the victory, the players felt relief, because no one could be sure what the murderous and mentally unstable Trujillos might do if they lost. Paige said, "I hustled back to our hotel and the next morning we blowed out of there in a hurry."

But it all cost too much money. The plan was to switch to winter baseball so they could raid U.S. teams in the off-season without upsetting American managers. Trujillo did not like to upset the Americans. But San Pedro had no money to bring back the American and Cuban stars, and without the threat from San Pedro, Trujillo wasn't going to pay for a big-roster Ciudad Trujillo team. No one had any money left, and for more than ten years the league didn't play professional ball at all. The best Dominican players went abroad. It was amateur ball that kept Dominican baseball alive. And it was widely recognized that the best amateur baseball in the country was in the cane fields of San Pedro de Macorís. Even Santo Domingo's leading baseball historian, Cuqui Córdova, acknowledged that in the 1940s most of the best Dominican players were poor sugar workers playing mill games in San Pedro.

After the *zafra* was over, some of the cane cutters had work weeding and hoeing the fields. But when Trujillo bought up the refineries, he eliminated this type of work and used chemicals to kill weeds. Then times were even harder in the San Pedro fields. But they could grow their food in gardens and they could keep themselves together by playing baseball.

In 1951 the Dominican League was reorganized as professional baseball again. Tetelo Vargas, now in his mid-forties, settled in San Pedro to play for the Estrellas; with his bat, it was a contending team. But that first year Licey beat Escogido for the title. The next year Águilas beat Licey and then in 1953 Licey beat Águilas, establishing a competition between those two teams that has dominated the league. The following year Estrellas won, beating Licey. By then baseball was integrated and there was no more Negro League. Dominican teams started hiring major-league players to play winter baseball. The Estrellas got Roger Maris, but they were not very impressed with him. Although Maris was a famously serious and hardworking player in the major leagues, Macorisanos complained that he did not play hard the way they did in San Pedro. That summer he went back to the Yankees and beat Babe Ruth's sixty-home-run season record.

Between 1951 and 2008, in the fifty-four championships—with time off for coups and invasions—thirty-nine have been won by either Licey or Águilas, with Águilas having one more championship than its competitor and the Eastern Stars winning only twice, in 1954 and 1968. They became a heartbreaking club, much like the twentieth-century Red Sox, with a history of collapsing just before victory. Twelve times they made it into the final series but lost.

In 1959, the Estrellas Orientales got a new home, a stadium on the edge of town by the rural road that led to the sugar fields. It was named for Ramfis Trujillo, the dictator's murderous, baseball-loving son. There was originally some question of the paternity of Ramfis, whose real name was Rafael Leónidas Trujillo Martínez. Ramfis's mother, María Martínez, had had him while she was married to a Cuban who insisted that he was not the father of the baby. María left him and became Trujillo's third wife. From an early age a family resemblance became apparent, as young

Ramfis—Trujillo gave him the nickname from a character in the Verdi opera *Aïda*—delighted in obliterating farm animals with a large-caliber pistol. Trujillo had proudly named Ramfis a colonel at the age of four. A lover of baseball and polo, he was also given to inflicting particularly barbaric forms of torture on people he believed to be his enemies.

It was a double insult for San Pedro to have its stadium named after this killer, both because of his brutality and because Ramfis had always been an outspoken fan of Escogido. After his father was assassinated, San Pedro changed the name of the stadium to Estadio Tetelo Vargas. But the masters of the republic continued to stake their claim to San Pedro's baseball stadium. At the entrance is a plaque to Joaquín Balaguer for renovations in 1993, and next to it one to President Leonel Fernández for renovations in 1999. One of the trappings of president was to get your name on the Tetelo Vargas Stadium.

CHAPTER FIVE

The First Opening

I t was not the home team but Major League Baseball in the U.S. that made the world realize that this little sugar town produced great ballplayers. Three things happened in the mid–twentieth century that opened the major leagues to San Pedro de Macorís.

The first thing that happened was an end to the so-called color line in Major League Baseball, the segregation that had created the Negro League. Originally baseball was integrated, but a movement grew to exclude African-Americans. It was led by Cap Anson in the 1880s. Anson was one of the greatest players of his day, with a twenty-seven-year career—mostly for the Chicago White Stockings, who later became the Cubs—during which he became the first player with three thousand hits. He was so influential in baseball that his racism infected the entire game. On numerous occasions Anson refused to play because there were black players either on his team or the opposing one. Famously, in 1883 he objected to playing with the catcher Moses Fleetwood Walker, a well-educated son of a doctor and considered the first African-American major leaguer. Other players followed Anson. There was never a stated rule barring black players, but increasingly in the late nineteenth century they were not allowed to play. Some called it a "gentlemen's agreement." After the 1898 season, blacks were not even allowed in the minor leagues. Being the instigator of this injustice did not stop the National Hall of Fame from inducting Anson in 1939, one of the first nineteenth-century Hall of Famers.

Occasionally lighter-skinned players passed by claiming to be Latin or Indian, but they would be discovered and forced out. In 1916, Jimmy Claxton played two games for the Oakland Oaks as an American Indian. When it was revealed that he had some African blood, he was fired. The somewhat darker skin of such players as Alex Carrasquel from Venezuela, Hiram Bithorn from Puerto Rico, and several Cubans did not pass without comments from press and fans, but they did manage to play in major-league games, though never for long or illustrious careers. Some signed forms certifying the Spanishness of their background. In the 1920s, two Cubans, outfielder Jacinto "Jack" Calvo and pitcher José Acosta, pulled off the feat of playing for both major-league teams and Negro League teams.

For two decades there was no permanent organization for African-American professional baseball until 1920, when Rube Foster, a black former pitcher—not to be confused with the white Red Sox pitcher of the same name—founded the Negro National League. The Negro League was a separate major-league-quality baseball system. In addition to their U.S. season they played in Cuba, the Dominican Republic, Puerto Rico, Panama, and Venezuela. African-American players became part of the Latino world.

In 1920, Judge Kenesaw Mountain Landis was appointed the first commissioner of baseball. Theodore Roosevelt had appointed him judge to the Northern District of Illinois, where he distinguished himself by his trials against unionists, leftists, opponents of World War I, and black people. Many of his rulings were overturned on appeal. He was the judge who managed to get the first black heavyweight champion, Jack Johnson, banned from the sport; backed by bigoted white players and club owners, he managed to maintain segregation in baseball.

But race relations were changing in the 1940s. The military was becoming integrated, there was a nascent civil rights movement, and there was a wealth of talent in the Negro League—some of the best players in baseball, waiting for the team with the courage to tap them. Landis died in 1944, and the new commissioner, Happy Chandler, a Kentucky politician nicknamed for his comportment, was willing to allow integration. In 1945, Branch Rickey, the Brooklyn Dodgers' general manager, held tryouts for black players. He said he was thinking of forming a black Brooklyn team. That same year he signed Jackie Robinson, an all-around athlete and talented infielder, sending him to the minor leagues with the stated intention of bringing him up to the Dodgers.

Rumors had been floating around for some time about giving Negro League players tryouts in the majors. It was widely thought that Satchel Paige would be given one of the first tryouts. Paige had grumbled about the idea of a tryout, but he was bitter for years that he did not get to be first. However, he probably would not have agreed to starting in the minor leagues because he was considered one of the best pitchers of his day.

There is some evidence that Rickey was considering a Cuban for the first black. A Latino might have seemed more acceptable to fans because, oddly, Americans were more willing to accept blacks if they were foreign. He was looking at Silvio García, a famous Cuban infielder who was also famous for his alcoholism and for his menacing statements about what he might do to white people who dared to bother him.

Robinson, though talented, was a rookie and not the best the Negro League had to offer. But he was good and he had something else Rickey was looking for. When he signed Robinson, Rickey told him that he wanted him to accept abuse stoically. That was something Paige or García would never have done. Paige was famous for his tantrums and antics on the mound. Robinson withstood verbal abuse and death threats with a calm façade few other players could have mustered—not because of a stoic or passive nature but because of a strong and disciplined character.

Robinson fascinated the press and the public. In 1947 he became the first Rookie of the Year, making it a coveted award forever after. Eleven weeks after Robinson signed with Brooklyn, Bill Veeck of the Cleveland Indians signed a Negro League outfielder named Larry Doby. Several years earlier Veeck had tried to buy the Philadelphia Phillies and sign numerous top black players, but after he told Landis of his intention, the club was suddenly sold to another bidder. Doby, who endured all that Robinson did, has been largely ignored by history because he was the second and not the first. This was why Satchel Paige had so wanted to be first. Doby was the first black player to hit a home run in a World Series, in 1948, which helped Cleveland win that Series. Satchel Paige was also signed, and helped the Indians win. Robinson was instrumental in helping Brooklyn win a World Series, but not until his final season, 1956, long after he became a legend.

The third black player was Hank Thompson, signed by the St. Louis Browns twelve days after Doby. The fourth, Willard Brown, played his first game for the Browns two days after Thompson. Thompson then went to the Giants in 1951, joining Monte Irvin and Willie Mays in the first all-black outfield.

Major-league teams were acquiring tremendous talent from the Negro League and winning pennants and World Series with them. But there was still enormous resistance from owners, players, and fans. The minor-league Class AA Southern Association refused to hire black players and was eventually the target of a civil rights movement boycott. The organization finally died in 1961 but maintained segregation to the last. Tom Yawkey, owner of the Boston Red Sox—today a favorite team of many Dominican fans—refused to hire black players. He turned down both Jackie Robinson, who tried out in Fenway Park, and Willie Mays. By the 1960s, while integrated teams were prospering, the Red Sox stubbornly remained at the bottom with their all-white team.

With only fifteen percent of the population white, mostly from a privileged class, the Dominican Republic rarely produces white baseball players. But by the 1950s, Dominican players had a chance at the major leagues. If they could get there, they would find themselves in a strange country, very different from theirs, and face a very different kind of racism.

Dominicans are not strangers to racism. The Dominican—in fact pan-Caribbean—obsession with the calibrating of racial differences is profoundly racist.

But the Dominican ballplayer is confronted with something entirely different in the U.S. It is because Dominicans are so familiar with the notion of racism that they find the American variety so baffling. Dominicans did not worry about issues of segregation and integration. In the Dominican racist logic, it made no sense to have separate baseball teams or lunch counters because racial traits are not transmitted over lunch counters or on baseball diamonds.

Most Dominican parents are so mixed that the children could come out most any shade. There are rural superstitions about pregnant mothers consuming white foods to ensure light-colored babies. As citizens of a mulatto country, Dominicans' skin color could easily get darker or lighter, depending on whom they mixed with. According to the theory, if they got whiter, they would be a happier, more prosperous country, because white people enjoy happy and prosperous countries. On the other hand, were the population to get darker, the Dominican Republic would eventually become a black country. If that happened, it would simply be absorbed into Haiti, a barbarous and impoverished land. Since the first Haitian invasion the main concern has always been the threat of a Haitian takeover.

Historically, the answer in the Dominican Republic was to keep adding white people to the mix and to get rid of the black people. The problem is that this keeps raising a difficult question: Who's going to cut the cane?

The Dominican Republic needed black people, so white people were needed to offset them. Sugar was the only industry exempt from Trujillo's decree—designed to prevent the importation of neighboring blacks—that any company's workforce had to be seventy percent Dominican.

Concern about whitening the race was continued after Trujillo's death by his former puppet president, Balaguer, who in 1983 wrote a book titled *La Isla al Revés*, The Island in Reverse, that claimed the Haitians were still trying to invade though no longer using the military. He called it a "peaceful invasion," an *invasión pacífica*, a favorite term of Trujillo's. The new invasion, he wrote, was "biological" and he warned of the "fecundity" of black people, saying that they "multiply with a rapidity that is almost comparable to that of vegetable species." To further illustrate his point, he included five pages of color photographs of families from his native region to show what fine Caucasian faces they had.

When José Francisco Peña Gómez—a popular politician with black skin and African features—ran for president in 1996, Balaguer insisted he had a secret plan to reunify the country with Haiti. Peña Gómez was a Dominican born of Dominican-born parents with one Haitian grandparent, and yet he was frequently said to be Haitian.

Even as recently as 1997, President Leonel Fernández, who said he would be different, discovered that the Dominican Republic was threatened by a Haitian "mafia"; some 35,000 Haitians and Dominicans of Haitian ancestry were subsequently deported.

But unlike the Americans, Dominicans do not see their society as divided between white people and black people, with anyone with any touch of African blood considered black. Dominicans are mostly mulattos, and in Dominican society mulattos are not considered black. In fact, *mulatto* is too vague a term for all of the variants—*morenos, indios, chabins,* people with African hair, commonly known as "bad hair," and green eyes, people with "good hair" but bad noses—all recognized classifications that in America were considered black. Dominicans had not expected to be treated as though they were *haitianos.*

It was predictable that the first black Latin players would be Cuban. White Cubans had always been in the major leagues. Thirty-two Cubans had played in the majors before 1948, starting in 1871 with the first Latino major leaguer, Esteban Bellán, known in the majors as Steve Bellán, who was one of the founding forces in Cuban baseball. Cubans such as pitcher Dolf Luque, nicknamed "the Pride of Havana," were mainstays of the majors during the white-only years. There was no gentlemen's agreement on white-skinned Latinos.

In 1951, Minnie Miñoso from Havana, the speedy outfielder nicknamed "the Black Comet," moved from the Negro League to the Cleveland Indians and then to the Chicago White Sox. Miñoso was the first black Latino player in the major leagues. The door was slowly opening for San Pedro.

In 1952, Sandy Amorós moved from the Cuban League to the majors—a good story, since he was black but didn't speak a word of English, and so reporters never talked to him. A spectacular player in Cuba, he was a shy man who seemed lost in the English-speaking world of the 1950s major leagues. When he played for the Brooklyn Dodgers he had no home but lived on the yacht of Roy Campanella, the Dodgers' black catcher who had learned Spanish playing in the Mexican League. The unseen Amorós had his one moment of fame, a spectacular catch of Yogi Berra's hit by the low left-field wall of Yankee Stadium that turned into a double play, saving the 1955 World Series for the Dodgers.

In the 1950s, when there were few Spanish-speaking players and few black players in the majors, it was not going to be an easy move for Dominicans. The first Dominican to play major-league ball was Osvaldo Virgil. Virgil left his small village near the Haitian border a Dominican named Osvaldo Virgil and ended up in the major leagues a black man named Ozzie Virgil.

Dominicans were not being recruited in those days, and Ozzie probably would never have been found by Major League Baseball had his father not so vociferously opposed the Trujillo regime that the family had to flee to Puerto Rico. From there, like many Puerto Ricans of the time, the Virgils moved to the Bronx, where Ozzie played sandlot ball in his neighborhood—which happened to be near the Polo Grounds, home of the New York Giants. Later he played for the Marines. Virgil could do almost everything in baseball: he was a utility player—someone who filled in where needed—and in his nine years in the major leagues, he played every position except pitcher and center field.

The Giants at the time had hired Alejandro Pompez as a scout. Alex Pompez, born in Key West, Florida, of Cuban parents, had owned two Negro League franchises: the New York Cubans and the Cuban Stars. He was known for bringing Latinos into the Negro League, including Minnie Miñoso and pitcher Martín Dihigo, regarded in Cuba as one of their all-time greatest players.

Pompez was out scouting in the Bronx. He was always looking for Latino players and had even expressed a desire to find some Dominicans when he stumbled on a very talented one right in the neighborhood. Virgil played his rookie year for the Giants in 1956 and later said that he was so nervous during his first major-league at-bat that he could not stop his legs from shaking. He batted four times and failed to get a single hit; he even made an error at third base. This was the official debut of Dominican Major League Baseball.

There was not a great public reaction to the first Dominican—at least not to his nationality. Everyone was too preoccupied with his skin color—especially in 1958, when Virgil was traded to the Detroit Tigers. The *Detroit Free Press* reported the trade with the headline "Tigers Call Up First Negro," and on the day of his first game another page-one headline announced, "Tigers' First Negro to Play 3rd Tonight." The *Detroit News* front-page story ran with the headline "Tigers' Decision to Play Negro

Hailed by Race." Suddenly a man too light to be considered black in his native land was a symbol of racial integration in America. His historic significance as the first Dominican player was almost completely forgotten, despite the fact that at the time the major leagues had forty-six black players and no Dominicans but him. At that point the Tigers were the only major-league club other than the Red Sox that had not integrated, and so his race was the single most important fact about him. A June 9, 1958, editorial in the *Free Press* began "The Tigers now includes a Negro" and misspelled his name. The same paper thirty-nine years later ran a profile that revealed, "Ozzie Virgil doesn't think of himself in terms of black and white."

But even though Virgil was willing to accept his role in Detroit as a black icon, American blacks did not see him as one of their own. "They thought of me more as a Dominican Republic player instead of a Negro," he once complained to the *Detroit Free Press*.

The same year that Virgil started, the next Dominican, Felipe Alou, came to the U.S. to play minor-league baseball. His name was actually Felipe Rojas Alou. He went by the surname of Rojas Alou, with the traditional use of the father's name first, but the scout who recruited him did not understand the Spanish custom with names and assumed that Alou, his mother's name, was his last name and Rojas was simply a middle name. All the Rojas boys—Felipe, his brothers Matty and Jesús, and Felipe's son, Moisés, all major leaguers—changed their name rather than contradict the Americans. In 1992, Felipe Alou became manager of the Montreal Expos, the first Latino manager in Major League Baseball.

But it was Ozzie Virgil who had led the way. Juan Marichal, one of the first five Dominican major leaguers and the only Dominican in the Hall of Fame as of 2009, has said that in the Dominican Republic he never thought about playing in the major leagues until Ozzie Virgil started playing for the Giants.

In 2006, when ten percent of major-league players were Dominican, a reporter from *The Miami Herald* asked José Reyes, the young Dominican shortstop for the Mets, about Ozzie Virgil, the first Dominican to play in the majors. Reyes did not know who Virgil was.

Dominicans only very slowly started being signed with Major League Baseball. After Virgil in 1956 came Felipe Alou in 1958, then his brother Matty in 1960. Julián Javier, a sure-handed infielder and swift baserunner, debuted with the St. Louis Cardinals in 1960. Also in 1960, Diomedes Olivo started pitching for the Pittsburgh Pirates at the age of fourteen. In 1961 his brother Chi-Chi started pitching for the Braves. Rudy Hernández, a pitcher who spent most of his career in the minors, was called up and pitched twenty-one games for the Washington Senators, also in 1960. The first Dominicans—Virgil, the Alous, the Olivos, Marichal—were all from small towns. The only exception was Hernández, who was from Santiago. Four out of the first seven were pitchers. None of the seven were from San Pedro. The first were found in places where the first Dominican scouts knew to look, such as the Pan American Games and the military teams built up by the Trujillo regime. Virgil was found because he was in New York, Felipe Alou because as a pre-medical student at the University of Santo Domingo he played for a college team that happened to be coached by Horacio Martínez, who had recently signed on to scout for the New York Giants.

Of the first seven, the one who established the most enduring image of a Dominican ballplayer in both positive and negative ways—an image that would impact on both players and fans—was Juan Antonio Marichal Sánchez, from the small northern village of Laguna Verde near the Haitian border.

Marichal was an intimidating pitcher with what in the 1960s was already an old-fashioned delivery: an elaborate windup that sent one leg straight in the air and made it impossible for the batter to get any inkling of what type of pitch he was about to release. He had mastered a wide variety of different pitches, which added to the batter's confusion.

He came from a tough world. He was a discovery of Ramfis Trujillo, who grabbed the young Marichal to play for the team he was developing in the Dominican air force. The dictator's son watched Marichal pitch one game and drafted him into the air force on the spot. Although working for a homicidal maniac can be frightening, the Trujillos favored the military and paid their recruits well.

Marichal became a major-league pitcher in 1960 for the San Francisco Giants and was stellar from his first game. His career earned run average was 2.89, one of the lowest in the history of the game. The earned run average, or ERA, measures the average number of earned runs—runs that are the pitcher's fault—scored in a game. In an age when ball clubs have huge pitching staffs and a starting pitcher seldom stays in the game for more than seven innings, it is astonishing to recall the night of January 2, 1963, in San Francisco's Candlestick Park, when Marichal pitched sixteen innings against Milwaukee Braves pitcher Warren Spahn until finally Willie Mays hit a home run off of Spahn.

Marichal seemed to have the attention of the entire Dominican Republic each time he pitched. According to legend, the first Americans to realize there had been a coup d'état in Santo Domingo in 1965 were the Western Union operators at Candlestick Park in San Francisco. It was their job to wire each play to the Dominican Republic when Marichal was pitching. Something cataclysmic must have happened to block scores. In fact, the government-controlled communications had been seized by conspirators.

Marichal would have seemed more spectacular if he had not pitched in an age of spectacular pitchers. Don Drysdale, Sandy Koufax, and Bob Gibson all pitched at the time. During Marichal's career, the top annual pitching prize, the Cy Young Award, was won once by Drysdale, twice by Gibson, and three times by Koufax but never by Marichal. Was it because

Marichal was Dominican? Some make that accusation, but had he beaten Koufax or Gibson, some might have said it was because Koufax was Jewish or because Gibson was black.

Hitters feared Marichal because of his unusual variety of pitches and his ability to conceal the ball until the last moment. Art Shamsky, a top hitter for the Cincinnati Reds at the time, called Marichal "the toughest pitcher I ever faced." Shamsky was what is called a contact hitter: he would always try to get his bat on the ball, even if it led to an out. He prided himself on rarely striking out. He could make contact with Koufax, but Marichal would strike him out. "Hitting is all about seeing the ball out of the pitcher's hand," Shamsky said. "With that high kick you couldn't see the ball until it was there."

In a game that loves statistics, Marichal had spectacular numbers—sometimes even better than Koufax's. The press, the people who choose the Cy Young Award, stereotyped them both. Koufax, the Jew, was an "intellectual" pitcher, whereas Marichal, the Dominican, was a "hot-blooded Latin" pitcher. Giants manager Al Dark, who had three Latins on his roster, mused publicly on whether Latins could truly understand the game of baseball. He said that Latins lacked "mental alertness."

The press called Marichal "the Dominican Dandy," a slightly denigrating label implying that he did not know what to do with his money and so indulged in clownish foppishness. Nothing better illustrates the impact of Marichal than the fact that, years after he stopped playing, the press would still occasionally refer to some Dominican player as a dandy.

Since baseball players earn their living playing their childhood game, they have much less pressure than most people to act like adults in the workplace. There is no shortage of incidents of American ballplayers having temper tantrums and outbursts of violence. But when a Spanish-speaking player does it, he is being a hot-blooded Latin. Marichal did not originate the stereotype of the hot-blooded Latin ballplayer. The original hot-blooded Latin was Adolfo Luque, a Cuban who was one of the all-time great pitchers, enshrined in American literature because Hemingway mentions him in *The Old Man and the Sea*. Luque never hesitated to threaten other players, umpires, or fans. Once, when heckled by an out-fielder named Bill Cunningham, who was shouting at the pitcher from the bench, Luque put down his ball and glove, marched over to Cunning-ham, and threw a mighty roundhouse punch—which Cunningham side-stepped. Luque's fist landed squarely on the jaw of outfielder Casey Stengel. A brawl ensued and Luque was ejected from the game, but he returned in a rage, swinging his bat clublike at players and umpires. Lat-ins are like that, a lot of people in baseball concluded.

All the worst fears about Marichal were confirmed on August 22, 1965. The Giants were playing against their main rival, the Los Angeles Dodg-ers, with Marichal pitching against Koufax. At bat, Marichal got into an argument with Dodgers catcher Johnny Roseboro, who, Marichal claimed, deliberately threw the ball too close to Marichal's head. In some versions the throw nicked Marichal's ear. Words escalated and finally Marichal hit the catcher with a bat. Roseboro needed fourteen stitches.

Marichal gave baseball an enduring and unfair image of Dominicans as rough and violent people—a backward people. It was the baseball version of a long-standing Dominican stereotype. In the tough Latino neighborhoods of New York where Dominicans move in on the Puerto Ricans, the Puerto Ricans often insist that Dominicans don't wear socks—that is, that they are primitive.

But Marichal was an inspiration to Dominican players. He was one of the greats. A player becomes eligible for the Hall of Fame five years after retirement, which in Marichal's case was 1981. He failed to get positive votes from seventy-five percent of the members of the Baseball Writers of America, which is the requirement for induction. He was turned down the following year as well. Some thought it was because of the Roseboro incident. Others, especially in the Dominican Republic, thought it was because he was Dominican. The following year Roseboro himself, who had become a good friend of Marichal's, urged his election to the Hall of Fame, and that year he was accepted—the first and, more than 460

Dominican major-league players later, the only Dominican to be so honored.

As recently as 2008, Marichal found controversy. He and Dominican pitcher Pedro Martínez were filmed in the Dominican Republic attending a cockfight. And there was the old accusation once again: barbarous and primitive Dominicans are cruel to animals. Martínez tried to argue that cockfighting was simply "part of the Dominican culture."

In the 1960s, young ballplayers in the *bateys* and barrios of San Pedro de Macorís followed Marichal's career and gleaned two contradictory lessons: First, it was very difficult for a Dominican to get along in the United States; second, those who braved it had a chance at a great deal of fame, money, and glory. But it was never going to be easy.

In the southern towns that many young baseball players are sent to, the strange American breed of racism persisted for years, long after baseball and even the South were integrated. Rogelio Candalario, a player from San Pedro, signed with the Houston Astros. He was a promising left-handed pitcher until he broke his arm in 1986. The Astros sent him to their Double A team in Columbus, South Carolina. "People would just stare at me," Candalario recalled. "I'd say, 'What's wrong?' 'Nothing,' they would say."

CHAPTER SIX

San Pedro Rising

I n 1962, something happened that had an enormous impact on baseball, sugar, and tourism. On February 7, in response to the expropriation of American assets in Cuba by the new revolutionary government of Fidel Castro, the U.S. declared a trade embargo. First of all, this meant that the U.S. would now buy its sugar elsewhere, while the Cubans responded by opening trade with the Soviet Union. Until then, a Caribbean vacation had largely meant Cuba; there was little tourism in the rest of the region. Now Americans were suddenly looking for other places for Caribbean winter holidays. But also it meant that Cuban baseball players could no longer play in the United States. To be eligible for work in the United States, a Cuban had to defect permanently, leaving behind friends and family, which few Cuban baseball players wanted to do. Major League Baseball would have to look elsewhere for Latino talent.

The first ballplayers from San Pedro de Macorís entered the major leagues in 1962, the year of the Cuban embargo. Not surprisingly, these players came from the sugar mills. Amado Samuel, a shortstop from Santa Fe, was the first Macorisano in the majors. He signed with the Milwaukee Braves in 1958 and played his first major-league game at the beginning of the 1962 season. He lasted only three seasons in the majors, his last one for the Mets. The second Macorisano to make the majors, Manny Jiménez, was also from Santa Fe. He missed being the first Macorisano by one day, beginning the 1962 season with the Kansas City Athletics. He had a seven-year career as a left fielder and, unlike Samuel, was a respectable batter with a kick to his swing that back in the sugar fields of Santa Fe had earned him the nickname *"El Mulo."* In his best years he batted over .300.

Pedro González, from the Angelina sugar mill, was the third player from San Pedro to play major-league ball. His father was Puerto Rican and his mother was a French *cocolo* from Saint Martin. As a small child he lived in downtown San Pedro, in a neighborhood on the shore of the Caribbean Sea that is called Miramar. When his parents separated, González's mother took him back to the sugar mill at Angelina, where he became a *cocolo* and a baseball player. He laughs now about the equipment he and his friends played with. Occasionally they had real baseballs, because in the Dominican League whoever catches the last out of the game, by tradition, keeps the ball and generally gives it to the street kids of his choice.

The rest of the time balls were made out of socks, also a San Pedro tradition. Socks are stuffed tightly into an outer sock, which is then sewn closed and dipped in water before playing to give it a little density. Socks, too, were hard to come by. When Julio Franco, the durable major-league shortstop, was growing up in Consuelo, he used to steal socks from his big brother, Vicente. This is another way of looking at the Puerto Rican assertion that Dominicans don't wear socks.

For a time *batillas* were used. Bottled water came in large jugs with a big cap that could be used as a ball. But in recent years manufacturers have switched to lightweight plastic and the cap does not have enough weight for throwing.

Bats were another problem. The real bats were broken and glued, taped, or even nailed back together, but often a stick of tough tropical wood or even light sugarcane served instead. Sometimes a milk carton could be shaped into a glove—a fairly good glove if you knew how to shape it, especially if you were not catching anything harder than a wad of socks. If anyone had a real glove, he left it in the position on the field so that the other team could use it too. Dominican children were resourceful: girls skipped rope with palm fronds.

The best way to get bats and balls was to play on a team, and there were teams all over San Pedro. There were the sugar mills, and González did not limit himself to Angelina. One year he played on a team run by the Haitian vice consul, who was based in San Pedro to look after the many Haitians who cut cane there. Also on that team were Manny Jiménez and his brother Elvio, a shortstop, who would be a teammate of González's again in 1964 with the New York Yankees. But Elvio's major-league career lasted only one game.

In 1957, Ramfis Trujillo drafted not only Juan Marichal but several San Pedro players from the mills, including González and both Jiménez brothers. In San Pedro it was becoming clear that the Dominican military was a pathway to the major leagues. The army, navy, air force, and police all had teams that competed against one another, and still do. This was top-quality Dominican baseball, and players who did well on these teams got noticed. San Pedro youths in the sugar mills even today will point out that the military teams are a good opportunity because "that is how Juan Marichal got discovered."

González, a large and affable man, signed with the Yankee organization in 1958, the year Marichal began his major-league career. He arrived in America speaking no English. There were few Spanish speakers to help him. "I ate ham and eggs for breakfast and the rest of the time chicken and french fries," González recalled. "It was all I knew how to order."

When he started in the majors in 1963, Dominicans were still not completely accepted. After distinguishing himself as a hitter in the minors, González started playing for the Yankees in 1963. He was the first Dominican to play for the Yankees. He was a novelty, nicknamed "Speedy

González" after a vaguely racist Looney Tune stereotype: a Mexican mouse with a gold tooth and a big sombrero who spoke in an exaggerated singsong nasal accent—the Latino as a cartoon character. Or he may have been named not so much for the cartoon as for the 1962 hit single by singer Pat Boone that seems to be about this same cartoon mouse, but is really about nothing at all.

Because of injuries, González never lived up to his batting potential, but he was a smooth and artful infielder who made only thirty-one errors in his five years of Major League Baseball. In 1964 he covered five positions and made only three errors in sixty-six games.

As with Virgil, González's skin color was a bigger issue than his ethnicity. "I remember when the Yankees came to play the Baltimore Orioles in 1963," he said without a trace of bitterness in his voice. "The whole team stayed in the Sheraton in Baltimore, but they wouldn't serve me in the restaurant. I used to have to go to the black part of town to find a place to eat. But I always said I didn't come to integrate, I came to play baseball."

At bat, González was often hit by pitches. He believed it was intentional: "Pitchers used to bean black players. The managers would say 'get the black guy.'" Surprisingly, González insisted that Charles Dressen, a legendary Hall of Fame manager for Brooklyn who was managing Detroit at the time, "always told them hit the black guy." A hit batter moves to first base, but he will have been intimidated—which is known in baseball as "having his power taken away." Racists believed that blacks could be easily intimidated, and so pitchers often threw at them. Longtime club owner Bill Veeck openly criticized the practice.

But González tried not to make trouble, concentrating instead on building his career. "I learned a lot because I was in love with baseball and I worked my tail off," he recalled. One time, tired of the stinging blow of fastballs, he lost his temper. Toward the end of the 1965 season, while batting for the Cleveland Indians against Detroit Tigers pitcher Larry Sherry, two pitches in a row barely missed him. It is not certain that Sherry was trying to hit González—often a pitcher will throw inside very close to the batter to force him to move back off the plate—but González was furious. Bat still in hand, he ran up to the pitcher and swung at him, hitting Sherry's arm before being restrained. González was fined $500 and suspended for the rest of the season, which was not many games. He did not injure Sherry the way Marichal had injured Roseboro, and it was not a notable game—González was not a famous player like Marichal—but for those who noticed, it was another hot Latin Dominican running amok, even though baseball had a long tradition of cool northerners doing similar things.

González did not make a huge amount of money. Most baseball players didn't in the 1960s. One of his best years, 1966, the Cleveland Indians paid him $15,000 for the year. He probably made more money in baseball after he retired. He could do this because as a former major leaguer, he was somebody. In 1964 he had even played in a World Series. He went on to manage Tampico in the Mexican League and then the Estrellas back in his hometown. His Estrellas were filled with future major leaguers from San Pedro, including Julio Franco, Alfredo Griffin, and Rafael Ramírez.

Later González became a well-liked fixture around San Pedro as a scout for the Atlanta Braves. "I just look around and keep kids off the street," he said. "They might turn out to be good players too." A successful man who sent his children to the local medical school, he was proof for young Macorisanos that you can build a life if you make it to the majors.

San Pedro slipped into the major leagues almost unnoticed until its first star, Ricardo Adolfo Jacobo Carty, known as Rico Carty. The first hint of his *cocolo* roots was the pronunciation of his nickname, "Beeg Mon"—an accurate description, as Carty was a muscular six feet, three inches tall. He was from Consuelo, where there is a Carty Street, running from the church to the fenced-off sugar mill, named after his mother, Oliva Carty, who was a midwife. By the twenty-first century there were more than one hundred Cartys in Consuelo, a subdivision with about 45,000 people. They were originally French-speaking sugar workers from Saint Martin but with roots in other islands as well. When Rico spoke his fluent English, it was hard to discern if his accent was French, Spanish, or West Indian. Probably it was all three.

Carty has said in interviews that when he was growing up in Consuelo there were two choices: cut cane for the mill or work in the mill. Carty's father worked in Ingenio Consuelo for sixty years. He loved boxing and cricket. Rico was born in 1939, and when he was a child the older men in Consuelo played cricket. The boys tried it too, but the lure of baseball, encouraged by the mills, was irresistible. The Carty family lived in mill housing behind the *ingenio*, simple wooden houses in a little Caribbean barrio called Guachupita.

Rico was one of twelve sons and four daughters. The fields that surrounded them were for growing cane. Baseball was played in the unpaved streets. Owing to his ability to hit deep into center field, Carty was known as an "up-the-middle" hitter, which he attributed to the fact that under Consuelo rules you had to keep the ball in the street: if it went into the houses it was an out. He attributed his ability to hit breaking balls to the fact that wadded socks or rags are not balanced, so the pitches had a lot of unpredictable movement.

Carty's mother understood the value of education and hoped her son would study to become a doctor. But Rico did not like to study—he wanted to play baseball—so she banned him from the baseball fields, hoping that would force him to concentrate on schoolwork. Instead he would sneak off and play games in the street with teams from competing Consuelo barrios.

Since Rico was clearly not a student his parents got him a job cutting wood for the mill. He hated it, but working for the *ingenio* gave him the opportunity to play on their baseball team. At that time Dominicans could not break into Major League Baseball; the sport that could lift them out of poverty was boxing. Rico's father, who loved the sport, gave him books on it and trained him. Rico was undefeated in seventeen fights, twelve by knockouts. Then he lost his eighteenth. He always claimed it was because he had eaten too many beans before the fight. He gave up boxing and in 1959 went back to baseball for Ingenio Consuelo, where he was much talked about as the boy who could hit the ball four hundred feet straight up the middle on any kind of pitch. But his father was disappointed: although he lived to be ninety, he never went to see his son play baseball. In 1959, Rico and some five hundred other young Dominicans tried out for the Pan American baseball team. The Dominicans had won the 1955 Pan American Games and were a team to watch in the 1959 games, which were in Chicago at Comiskey Park.

The major leagues sent scouts to look at the reigning Dominican team. The team did not do well but Carty did, hitting home runs over center field the way he had learned on the streets and making a spectacular throw to home plate off the right-field fence. Everyone wanted to sign this Dominican kid with the perfect swing, the powerful throwing arm, the tall, lean, and muscular body, and the strikingly sculpted face.

Many of the new Dominican players—unlike the Cubans, who played a season in Mexico, a season in Venezuela—were leaving the Dominican Republic for the first time. The Dominican Republic is not a very big place, and a few dozen miles to Santo Domingo or up to Santiago was as far as Carty had ever been until he played in Chicago at age nineteen. Being a *cocolo*, Carty always thought he spoke English. But now he discovered that he did not understand Americans and they could not understand him. Scouts went to talk to him, but he could not understand them. Every time someone offered him a contract, he signed. Before long he had signed with six major-league organizations, and by some accounts eight or nine. At the very least he had signed with the Cardinals, the Braves, the Yankees, the Giants, the Cubs, and the Dodgers. In his confusion he had also signed with Estrellas, Licey, Escogido, and Águilas.

George Trautman, who headed Minor League Baseball, interceded. He pointed out to the various angry clubs that there was no legal issue, since Carty had neglected to take any money. But he told Carty that he had to choose a team. Carty picked the Milwaukee Braves, because he liked the team. Only later did he understand that the $2,000 signing bonus they offered was small money and he could have gotten far more from the St. Louis Cardinals.

Back in the Dominican Republic, it was more complicated to sort out his contracts. Realizing what he had done, he said that he wanted to play for his hometown Estrellas Orientales. Trujillo was furious and Carty was taken to court—a Trujillo court. But in the end, a good ballplayer could be forgiven in a Trujillo court, and he was allowed to play for Estrellas.

The Braves sent Carty to play minor-league baseball in Waycross, Georgia, where he thought Jim Crow laws did not apply to him because he was a Latino. Like Pedro González, he ate a lot of chicken because he could say that. Later he learned how to order hamburgers.

In the United States, it was difficult to find familiar foods. In his autobiography, Felipe Alou wrote of being revolted by the coldness of the milk. In rural Dominican Republic, milk generally arrived unpasteurized and was boiled for safety and served warm. But chicken was the one familiar food they could find.

This story about only knowing how to order chicken is repeated over and over again by the early San Pedro major leaguers. Why was that the word they knew? Not all of them even knew that. San Pedro players tell stories of Dominican rookies favoring fast-food restaurants that offered photographs so they could simply point to the chicken picture or even walk in, flap their arms, and make chicken noises to indicate their orders. Poor Dominicans live on a diet of rice, beans, tropical fruits, root vegetables, and occasionally a chicken.

On the wide main curving street that runs by the Tetelo Vargas Stadium, there are many small restaurant-bars where fans can watch American baseball games on large-screen TVs. They serve mostly chicken. Chicken may have been, as González suggested, the word they set out to learn. Chicken is popular and good in San Pedro. As in much of the Caribbean, most of it is free-range, because sending chickens foraging is the most cost-effective approach in the tropics.

Not all Dominican players chose chicken. "Ham and eggs" was another phrase the Dominican players quickly learned to say. When José Mercedes got to the Orioles, he learned the phrase "same thing" and simply waited for someone else to order and then said, "Same thing."

Carty was not as isolated as González had been, because there were some Dominicans in the Braves organization, even other Macorisanos— even one whose father had played cricket with Carty's father. But only Rico made it to the majors.

Carty was liked and certainly respected by the other players, but he was always somewhat of an odd man out, a colorful character. They were puzzled by his habit of carrying his wallet in his uniform into the game because he was not confident that his money would be safe in the locker room.

He found American racism hard to understand. He could see that, as a Latino, he had a slightly better standing than American black players. So he always presented himself as a Latino. But American black players were resentful of this. Carty did not understand much about black America at the height of the civil rights movement. He called himself "Big Boy," and the black players resented it because they did not want to see a black man call himself "boy." He changed it to "Man": "Beeg Mon." But he never really understood the issue.

It was after the Braves moved to Atlanta that Carty got a taste of what it was like to be a black man in America. In September 1971, after Carty had established himself as a baseball star, he was driving in Atlanta with his brother-in-law, Carlos Ramírez, at about midnight. Ramírez was visiting from the Dominican Republic and spoke no English. Racial tension had been heightened in Atlanta by the killing of two white policemen in a black neighborhood. According to Carty, who described the incident in a 1975 interview with the Cleveland *Plain Dealer*, another car pulled up with two white men. The two called out to a black man in the street, "Hey, nigger."

Ramírez asked Carty in Spanish what was happening. When Carty told him, his brother-in-law asked, "Do they do that here?"

"Yes," Carty replied. "Sometimes between the blacks and whites."

"Why?" Ramírez asked.

"I don't know," said Carty. "I just play ball and go home." And the two laughed. Then the two in the other car started shouting "Nigger!" at the Dominicans. Still not understanding the ways of American racism, Carty shouted back in English, "You may be more nigger than me, because you are American and I'm not."

Carty was not his usual athletic self, because he was just recovering from a severe leg injury. Spotting a uniformed white policeman, he got out of his car and limped up to him and asked for his help, saying he had an injury and didn't want any trouble from the two men in the car. But the two he was complaining about were plainclothes policemen. The police took out their guns and one of them said, "These are the cop-killing niggers." He hit Ramírez over the head with his handgun, and then they began beating Carty with a blackjack, kicking him on the ground, then handcuffed and arrested him before finally one of the policemen recognized him.

The policemen were suspended; one already had a record of brutalizing black people, and the police chief and mayor apologized profusely. The attorney for the three suspended policemen said that it was a minor incident that had been blown up because it involved a famous baseball player. But in truth, Carty had been saved by his standing in baseball. The Atlanta press expressed concern that the finger injuries and black eye might somehow keep Carty from finishing the season.

Carty was what is known as a natural hitter, or, as they say in San Pedro, *nació para batear*, he was "born to bat." His swing had both power and grace, and he had that mysterious ability to see pitches and put his bat where they were going. For seven years he maintained the highest lifetime batting average of any current player. At the time, few players were hitting well—a period known in baseball history as "the second dead-ball era." The first dead-ball era, a time when hitters inexplicably were all slumping, was the first two decades of the twentieth century. The second dead-ball era, from 1963 to 1972, corresponded almost exactly with

Carty's career. The phenomenon is only partly explained by the fact that it was an era of great pitchers. Carty was, along with Roberto Clemente, Hank Aaron, Carl Yastrzemski, and only a few others, one of the rare great hitters of his time. The reverse of Marichal, who was underappreciated because of the wealth of great pitchers, Carty enjoyed great renown because so few others were hitting so well.

Had he stayed healthy, Carty might have been one of the all-time greatest hitters in baseball. In 1963 he had a brilliant rookie year, but the following year he had back problems. In 1967 he missed weeks of play from a shoulder injury caused by a bad slide into second base. In 1968 he seemed to run completely out of luck: that year he missed the entire season, spending 163 days in the hospital with tuberculosis. He missed fifty-eight games in 1969 with three shoulder separations. Often his injuries were sustained in the winter, playing for the Dominican League, which he insisted on doing every winter.

In 1970 he had a phenomenal batting average of .366, which was the best in the major leagues since 1957, when Ted Williams hit .388 for the Red Sox. Then, triumphant, Carty went home to San Pedro to play for the Estrellas, but he was traded to Escogido. While playing for Escogido, he broke his leg in three places and shattered his knee colliding with Matty Alou in the outfield. The Braves did not have their batting champion for the entire 1971 season. After the knee healed and a hip-to-calf brace was removed, he went back to Escogido and, in a game against Licey, Cincinnati Reds pitcher Pedro Borbón hit Carty on the left side of his face and broke his jaw.

Carty never did make tremendous amounts of money in Major League Baseball. A restaurant he started in Atlanta, Rico Carty's Open Pit Barbecue, burned down when flames leaped out of the open pit after the restaurant had been operating only fifteen days.

He did wear rings that spelled out his name and uniform number in diamonds. When he was in Atlanta, he earned a reputation as a shopper after buying twenty-five pairs of shoes at one time. He also once bought six suits and another time twenty-four shirts. When a reporter asked him about this, he said, "I go into a store and I can't help myself. I see all the beautiful things and I have to have them."

In Carty's best-paying year of his fifteen seasons in the majors—1977, at the end of his career—he received $120,000. Most years he earned half of that or less. But back in San Pedro he did not need a lot of money. He bought a large, comfortable house in downtown San Pedro for $45,000—a one-story ranch house large enough for his wife, four daughters, and son. In the 1960s, when his mother picked the spot, it was an undeveloped neighborhood on the edge of downtown, and Carty had to pay to get electricity brought in. He was a popular figure in San Pedro, the local boy from Consuelo who became a star. Most of the next generation of players, including Carty's own nephew, Julio Santana, cite Rico Carty as their inspiration. In 1994, with neither political nor administrative experience, he was elected mayor of the town. This may not have been a measure of his popularity, since he was handpicked by Joaquín Balaguer, and Balaguer did not permit his candidates to be defeated. Carty explained, "Joaquín Balaguer is a good friend of mine, so when he asked me to run I could not tell him no." He pledged as mayor to keep the youth of San Pedro supplied with bats and balls from the major leagues.

But then something else happened to open the door of Major League Baseball even wider for the boys of San Pedro and produced perhaps the most important generation San Pedro has ever sent out.

CHAPTER SEVEN

Draft Dodging

B y the 1970s, boys had been playing baseball in San Pedro for nearly a century without dreaming that it could change their lives. But after the first few major leaguers—especially once Rico Carty became a star—baseball turned into something much more serious than a sport: it could be the salvation of an entire family. What had changed was not so much San Pedro but Major League Baseball.

Until 1976, once a player signed a contract with a franchise, he was theirs until they did not want him anymore and traded him or released him. When a contract expired, the franchise always had the option to renew it. The rule, known as the "reserve clause," came into effect in 1879. An owner could even cut a player's salary by twenty percent. In 1969, after distinguishing himself as a hitter and outfielder for the St. Louis Cardinals for twelve years, Curt Flood was traded to the Philadelphia Phillies. The Cardinals had traded three players for three Phillies. But Flood refused to go, saying he didn't like the Phillies, their stadium, or their fans. The Phillies were infamous for racism. The manager, Ben Chapman, had led his team in shouting racist insults at Jackie Robinson. Flood sued baseball and got former Supreme Court justice Arthur Goldberg to argue his case, which went to the Supreme Court. Among Goldberg's arguments was the claim that the current system unfairly repressed wages. The Court ruled against Flood.

But many people felt that Flood, who had been active in the civil rights movement, was fighting a just cause. He had written to the baseball commissioner, Bowie Kuhn, in 1969: "I do not feel that I am a piece of property to be bought and sold irrespective of my wishes." Since he was black, the comparison to slavery was evident, and his struggle was seen as one for civil rights at a time when there were many such struggles in America. It was not seen as being about money. Had he let himself be traded, his $100,000 salary would have been one of the top paychecks in baseball. The celebrated sportswriter Red Smith, writing in *The New York Times*, satirized: "'You mean,' baseball demands incredulously, 'at these prices, they want human rights too?'"

Yes, they did.

In 1975 two pitchers, Andy Messersmith and Dave McNally, refused to sign their contracts, and after they had played a season without contracts it was ruled that they then had the right to be free agents.

A player who becomes a free agent by fulfilling his contract puts himself on the market and can go to the team he chooses, often the highest bidder. If a player has been doing well, this can produce highly competitive bidding. This has made agents important because, with millions of dollars at stake, there is often considerable negotiating. Before free agents, players negotiated contracts with management on their own.

Regardless of the high principles that had guided Flood, one of the results was that baseball became a game of millionaires. Salaries like Flood's $100,000 became laughable. Before there were free agents, in the Rico Carty years, the average salary in the major leagues was $52,300. Carty's salaries, which seem meager today, were above average. But by 1980 the average had leaped to $146,500. A decade later it was more than $800,000. By 2008 the average was $3 million a year. Signing bonuses, an extra one-time bonus on signing the first contract, also went up; the once token handouts for the most promising players are now in the millions.

At this same time, with jets replacing trains for traveling teams, Major League Baseball began a process of expanding from sixteen teams in the Northeast and Midwest to the current thirty around the country, and this, too, created a hunger for fresh young talent. The most important source of new young players was the draft, in which every franchise got to pick from a pool of undeveloped talent. The lower the standing of a club in the previous season, the higher the pick in the draft so that the last-place teams got the first picks.

But the draft was a highly regulated operation, and teams were limited in the number of draft picks they could take. This placed the player in a good negotiating position. A very promising prospect could refuse the offer. Then he had to wait a year, but a year later he would probably be worth more money to whoever got him. In the meantime the franchise had wasted a pick, because they were limited to the players they drafted whether those players signed on or not. So it might be in the club's interest to sweeten the deal—fatten the bonus—in order to get the prospect signed, which was why bonuses had been going up.

However, players who were not born in the United States were not subject to the draft. They were declared "amateur free agents," and there was no limit on hiring free agents, and you did not have to be a last-place team to be first to grab a top prospect. Foreigners became an unlimited source of new talent. This internationalized baseball, opening it up to Venezuelans, Colombians, Panamanians, Nicaraguans, Koreans, Taiwanese, and Japanese. Today, more than a quarter of major-league players are foreign born, and the percentage will probably rise, since the minor leagues are about half foreign born. Moving beyond the limitations of the draft was the original reason, but then a wealth of talent was discovered and they were cheaper to sign than American drafted players of comparable promise.

The first country to profit from this search for nondrafting talent was the Dominican Republic. This was partly because, by the mid-1970s, base-ball was accustomed to the idea of Latin players. There had been Cuban and Puerto Rican players, but Cubans were no longer available and Puerto Ricans were U.S. citizens and therefore subject to the draft. With a tradition of baseball and the second-worst economy in the Americas—Nicaragua has recently fallen lower and bumped the Dominican Repub-lic up to third—Dominicans were ready to be saved by baseball. When Major League Baseball went looking for foreign players, the first place they looked was the Dominican Republic.

San Pedro and other parts of the Dominican Republic became the feed-ing grounds of major-league scouts. A scout had to identify a young teen-ager, develop his ability, and get him signed—a process that sometimes took years—without another scout grabbing the prospect. And so these scouts were cruising the ball fields, often running into and trying to out-maneuver one another. Some, like Pedro González, were ex-players, but many of the more successful ones were not. Epifanio Guerrero, commonly known as Epy, from Santo Domingo, never made it as a player. His brother Mario, a shortstop, never got out of the minors, and neither of Epy's two sons got beyond AAA ball. But Epy was the most famous Dominican scout, signing 133 young Dominicans, thirty-seven of whom—including George Bell and Tony Fernández—made it to major-league rosters.

At the start, Guerrero was scouting for the Toronto Blue Jays and his archcompetitor Rafael Avila was scouting for the Los Angeles Dodgers. From Los Angeles, the Dodgers—the same management that had opened the sport to black players in Brooklyn—pioneered Latino recruitment. Avila was a Cuban, a veteran of the ill-fated 1961 anti-Castro Bay of Pigs invasion. In 1970, when Avila moved to the Dominican Republic, there had still been only twenty-four Dominican players who had risen to the major leagues. But at a time when baseball was not very international, for twenty-four players to have turned up on major-league rosters in fourteen years from one small foreign country was a phenomenon.

At first the scouts tried to raid the military teams, where Marichal had been found. But this had the complication of getting the player released from the military. Then they looked at the Dominican League. Avila started working with Licey. But eventually they discovered an untapped wealth of very talented teenagers who lacked proper training, in the sugar fields of San Pedro. The scouts needed to find places to train the young players and feed them—they were all undersized and undernourished— without attracting too much attention. Avila built two rooms in Elvio Jiménez's backyard and housed and fed fifteen players there, the forerunner of what came to be known as a baseball academy.

The competition for San Pedro ballplayers was lively. In 1976 a Cuban scout for the Cleveland Indians, Reggio Otero, picked up a fifteen-year-old *cocolo* from Consuelo named Alfredo Griffin, who had honed his skills playing every Sunday for the sugar mill where his stepfather worked. Epy Guerrero never forgot that Griffin had gotten away from him, and after three years of slowly rising in the Indians organization, he was able to get Griffin away to Toronto, where he started his career winning the Rookie of the Year Award.

Alfredo Griffin, Pepe Frías, Julio Franco, Rafael Ramírez, and Tony Fernández were all shortstops from San Pedro who went to the majors in the ten years between Frías in 1973 and Fernández in 1983, and all became stars. Griffin, Frías, and Franco were from Consuelo. Soon San Pedro de Macorís, the city of *plántanos*, sugar, and poets, became known as the city of shortstops. To date, only thirteen of the seventy-nine Macorisanos who have played in the major leagues have been shortstops, compared with twenty-seven pitchers, mostly in recent years. But when this town was first getting noticed by the fans of professional baseball, it seemed that it was turning out more excellent shortstops than anything else, and even today when the name San Pedro de Macorís is mentioned, often the response is "That town with all the shortstops."

A shortstop is one of the most important players on a team—certainly the star of the infield. He roams between second and third base, between infield and outfield. Because most hitters are right-handed, they tend to hit toward the left, and so the shortstop is in more plays than anyone else. If it were a left-handed world, the shortstop would have been placed between first and second. It is a role that requires great athleticism because he is involved in tight critical plays, including double and triple plays. Often by the time a ground ball has gone the distance to reach the shortstop, there is little time to beat the runner on a long throw to first base. A shortstop's moves often appear spectacular, and good shortstops usually become fan favorites.

Since the youth of San Pedro dreamed of being stars, they dreamed of being shortstops. But also, since they had hard lives and poor nutrition, Macorisanos tended to be small, with powerful throwing arms, which is the classic shortstop—or at least it was until large men such as Cal Ripken, Jr., and Alex Rodriguez started playing the position.

Griffin's family came from Nevis. His father, Alberto Reed, was a musician and a dockworker in Santo Domingo. They lived in Villa Francisca, a poor crumbling and crowded one-story neighborhood in the old part of the capital near the Ozama River. Reed performed at a nearby nightclub called Borojol. He played in a musical tradition that reached its height in Cuba in the 1940s and 1950s with singers who earned international reputations such as Tito Rodríguez and Beny Moré. The music was called *son*, an Afro-Cuban hybrid. Eventually *son* would mutate into salsa, but before that happened, in the 1940s, Arsenio Rodríguez introduced big conga drums to *son*; by the time Alberto Reed was playing, conga drumming was an important part of the band. This made a huge impression on young Alfredo, who developed a permanent love for conga drums.

When Alfredo was only eight years old, the rough, fetid streets of the capital, in which boys from rival barrios fought one another for dominance, got even rougher. A U.S. invasion followed a coup d'état, and a civil war meant street battles with high-caliber automatic weapons.

Alfredo's unmarried mother, Mary, a Macorisana, wanted to leave the dangerous town, where young Alfredo liked to run loose and watch both the violence and food distribution by American soldiers. She took her three sons and left Reed and moved back with her family in her native Consuelo. She later became involved with the sugar worker whom Alfredo still refers to as his stepfather. Although Alfredo always used his mother's name, clearly Reed was an important influence. People in Consuelo who recall growing up with Alfredo say that their earliest memories are not of him laboring in the mills, because he didn't work there, or playing on the Consuelo ball team on Sundays, for which he was paid, but of Alfredo playing the conga in a band and entertaining at *cocolo* parties and fiestas. Other things they remember are that he earned money shining shoes and that he was a tough street fighter.

Griffin credits the mill with making Consuelo a place that produces baseball players. "They all come from here," he said, "because we played ball for the mills every Sunday." Certainly Consuelo, a small subdivision that has produced eleven major leaguers as of 2009, is per capita the most productive neighborhood in modern baseball history. Griffin first learned baseball playing street ball in Santo Domingo, but he is not certain he would have ended up a baseball player if he had stayed in his tough city neighborhood. None of the boys he grew up with there played pro ball, and some of them ended up in jail.

Were it not for baseball, Alfredo Griffin might have become a very different person, but Alfredo had an uncle, Clemente Hart, who was a cricket player turned baseball player and played for the Estrellas. Hart steered Alfredo toward Consuelo baseball. Soon Ingenio Consuelo was paying him to play on their team. Managed by a former major leaguer, Pedro González, this was not the usual company team: it had Alfredo Griffin, Nelson Norman, Rafael Ramírez, Rafael Santana, and Julio Franco—all future major leaguers. This was a team that scouts watched.

In fact, Consuelo played in a league consisting of six mill-sponsored teams, the Circuito de los Ingenios, which played a thirty-game season in the dead season and which scouts closely monitored. The mills supplied uniforms with the name of the *ingenio* across the chest. Well known for the quality of their baseball, the league games were the primary entertainment in the sugarcane communities.

Teams also developed in the various barrios of central San Pedro, which formed a league. The top San Pedro team would play the top *ingenio* team at Tetelo Vargas Stadium for the September season finale. The *ingenio* players and their families would cram into buses and go to the stadium, where the playoff took place in front of a screaming crowd of about nine thousand fans. In October the *zafra* would begin, the workers would take off their uniforms and return to the mills or the fields, and professional baseball—the Estrellas—would take back the stadium.

San Pedro's amateur leagues and their playoffs gave scouts many games in which to look for prospects. Young ballplayers initially tried out for love of the game, but they quickly became aware that they were being considered for the majors.

Cleveland Indians scout Reggie Otero, a Cuban, spotted fifteen-year-old Griffin playing second base. This was one Otero would not let Epy Guerrero grab for the Toronto Blue Jays, so Otero quickly developed Griffin as a shortstop, signed him in 1973, and sent him off to the Cleveland farm system by the age of sixteen.

Despite his *cocolo* background, Griffin spoke little English and lived a lonely existence in America, away from family and friends for the first time. For three years in the minors he got occasional starts with the Indians. In his first major-league at-bat, in 1976, he got a hit. The following winter he went back to San Pedro, to the Estrellas, where he developed skills as a switch-hitter. The ability to bat either left- or right-handed is a great advantage, because pitchers usually do better against batters who bat on the side from which they throw. A switch-hitter can bat on the opposite side no matter who is pitching, so Griffin returned from San Pedro a more valuable hitter.

After three years in which he played only occasionally, Griffin was traded to the Toronto Blue Jays for Victor Cruz. According to legend, Epy Guerrero stole him. But the truth is that the Blue Jays simply made a great trade. Cruz had been an excellent relief pitcher for Toronto, and Toronto fans could not understand why the Blue Jays would give up a top pitcher for an unknown who was not greatly appreciated in Cleveland.

But Griffin was noticed immediately in his new home. When the press saw him working out in 1980, he became the talk of spring training. They used words like "smooth" and "ballet of the infield" to describe his defensive skills. His first year in Toronto—his first complete season playing, because Cleveland had kept sending him down to the minors—Griffin won Rookie of the Year, the coveted Jackie Robinson title.

When a young man from San Pedro got his hands on Major League Baseball money, he almost always did something for his family, and especially his mother. But in Griffin's day a signing bonus wasn't enough. Griffin did not see money until Toronto; once he had his first full season there, he built a large house for Mary Griffin on Carty Street in Consuelo. Later he put some earnings into a long gray stone house with a fountain in Rico Carty's newly developed neighborhood in central San Pedro.

Over an eighteen-season major-league career, Griffin became known as a reliable hitter, a fast enough runner to score numerous triples, a nearly unstoppable base stealer, and a smooth-handed, award-winning infielder who played in several World Series for both Toronto and the Dodgers and then went on to be an infield coach for the California Angels. In between seasons he played for the Estrellas. He seemed to relish his winters back in San Pedro: his comfortable house, the music, and the discos—including the one he bought by the waterfront. He even enjoyed going back to Consuelo, where his mother still lived.

Griffin projected a different kind of image of a Dominican in the major leagues. He was known as a leader and a peacemaker, a player with the kind of temperament that holds ball clubs together. He always made a special effort to help rookie players adapt to the team. Griffin always insisted that this wasn't new for Dominicans and that Rico Carty had helped him. Among his prized baseball souvenirs was an autographed photo of the Beeg Mon. But the American press seemed not to notice that Griffin contradicted the stereotype: for them he was simply another Dominican. In a 2001 interview, *Sports Collectors Digest* even used Juan Marichal's old moniker, calling Griffin "a Dominican dandy."

Baseball became a serious enterprise all over San Pedro wherever there was poverty, which was almost everywhere. Epy Guerrero found another smooth shortstop in Barrio Restauración, the one-story tin-roofed neighborhood of crumbling pavement behind the outfield wall of Tetelo Vargas Stadium. Tony Fernández was one of the street urchins who shimmied up palm trees to watch the Estrellas play and to occasionally grab a fly ball for later use. Some would even bring a net to grab the flies. Fernández played informal games along the side of the stadium with a sock, or a real ball if he could snag one. Today boys still play sock baseball in the same spot.

Fernández also found work tending the stadium grounds, which made a boy well positioned to get balls. The Estrellas called him "Cabeza," head, because they thought his head was too big. In reality, like a lot of Dominican kids, his body was too small. But Fernández's head was also a great asset: he had an understanding of the game that went far beyond his years.

Everyone knew Cabeza, and several scouts had their eyes on him. He tirelessly practiced fielding ground balls and other infield skills. But the scouts' interest cooled when they learned that Fernández had bone chips in one of his knees, a disabling condition: while injuries are part of the game, no one wants to start off with an injured prospect. Guerrero, who always had surprising ways to grab promising players, took Fernández to a hospital in Santo Domingo and paid for the operation. After his recovery, Guerrero signed him.

Fernández had a seventeen-season major-league career, one season less than Griffin. Fernández was not only a great fielder but a solid hitter, known for his triples, and he was a smart and swift base runner. He was famous for a strange but impressive maneuver, the kind of flourish for which shortstops become popular: he would leap to catch the ball and, while still in midair, toss it underhanded to first base.

Julio César Franco grew up in Consuelo playing with socks and milk cartons. His father's name was Robles, but Julio—like Alfredo Griffin and many other Dominicans—chose to use his mother's name. His father worked in the Ingenio Consuelo, pulling the carts that loaded cane into the grinder for 230 Dominican pesos a month. In those days the peso was worth almost a dollar. Later he got a better job as a welder earning 450 pesos a month, an excellent sugar-mill salary.

"It was everybody's ambition to make the majors," Franco recalled. But among the boys he grew up and played with in Consuelo, Franco was the only one who succeeded. There were a lot of games, especially on weekends, but very few programs in which a teenager could get training in baseball's many basic skills. However, he did manage to find a program run by a man named Antonio García, whom everyone knew as simply "El Chico." El Chico was known in Consuelo as a stern disciplinarian. He educated the San Pedro teenagers in the very American rules of the major leagues, including being on time. They would play two games a day. One week the games would be in Consuelo; the next week they would be held in downtown San Pedro, and the Consuelo players would walk miles to get there. The first game would start at nine a.m., and after the game there would be lunch at the home of someone who lived nearby—a player or a coach—before the second game at three p.m. In the early 1970s, food was inexpensive in San Pedro because it was an agricultural community. After the second game they would all walk back to Consuelo.

Most players didn't have gloves; when it was their team's turn at bat, the fielders who had them left their gloves at their positions so their counterparts could use them. The "rich" kid of the neighborhood was Carlos Rymer, not because his family was really wealthy but because he had relatives in New York who sent equipment. All of the players would use it, but if Carlos got mad he would take his equipment and leave, shouting, "Game over!" Rymer signed as a pitcher with the Atlanta Braves, but more than thirty years later Franco could not conceal his boyish glee when pointing out that Rymer never made it out of Atlanta's minor-league system. Then again, none of his other childhood teammates did either. Few do.

By Franco's time, Major League Baseball knew about San Pedro and the scouts were out looking. "If you were an outstanding player," he recalled, "word got around and you got recognized."

Franco "got recognized" by another legendary Dominican scout, Quiqui Acevedo. Acevedo was ready to sign him to the Philadelphia Phillies when Franco was seventeen. He was to stay in a hotel in Santo Domingo and begin his baseball training. But Franco's mother thought that he was too young to drop out of school and start his career. Yes, it was an opportunity, but he would not have an education, he would be taken away at a young age, and the odds were against his ever getting to the major leagues. Families in San Pedro were beginning to understand that most boys who got signed would not succeed.

But after three months, Julio's older brother, Vicente, persuaded their mother to let Julio go to Santo Domingo and take a chance at stardom. She agreed, only on the condition that Julio be brought back home every weekend. And so Franco signed with the Phillies for $4,000, which was only slightly less than what his father earned in a year on his good salary. Like most young Macorisanos who first get their hands on some Major League Baseball money, he gave it to his mother.

Franco trained at the University of Santo Domingo, "the oldest university in the Americas," he proudly pointed out many years later. George Bell, a lean but broad-shouldered and muscular kid from the Santa Fe sugar mill in San Pedro, was also there, as was Juan Samuel from Barrio Restauración, where Tony Fernández grew up. All were signed by Acevedo to the Phillies.

George Bell was born in a neighborhood near the Tetelo Vargas Stadium, but he grew up in Santa Fe, where his father was an engineer on a locomotive that carried the cane from the fields to the mill. In the dead season he worked in the mill as a mechanic. The Bell family, like Julio Franco's in Consuelo, had a modest but above-average income; in San Pedro they were considered middle-class. Bell's father's salary of 360 pesos a month—minimum wage was 90—was the envy of most Santa Fe workers. The sugar mill provided them with a three-bedroom house for their family of seven. Franco's mother sold food to sugar workers out of her home.

George Bell was pure *cocolo*. His father's father was from the little British colony of Anguilla, where he had lived with a woman named Bell from the volcanic island of Montserrat, also British. According to family legend, Anguilla had so little that when Franco's paternal grandfather went to Santo Domingo to buy a machete and saw that the island was bigger and wealthier than his, he took a job cutting cane in San Pedro. His son, George's father, took George's paternal grandmother's name. George's mother's family was from Nevis, and George grew up speaking that uniquely San Pedro English with an accent that is part West Indian and part Spanish.

Bell said of his childhood in Santa Fe, "We played ball—any kind of ball." His father's first love was cricket. "I remember when I was eight years old, my dad took me to a baseball field to see a cricket match. He and his friends played a lot of cricket and a lot of golf." There was a golf course in Santa Fe for the sugar executives.

The boys of Santa Fe played a game they called cricket with a sock ball and four players in two-man teams: one to bowl and one to bat. The bowl was underhanded or sidearm, and there was an old license plate on the ground that served as a wicket. If the bowl hit the plate, you were out. There were three outs to a side. If you hit from one side to the other, it was a run. They played twelve-run games. A variation on this game, called *plaquita* and sometimes two-man baseball, is still played by the youth of San Pedro—*cocolos* as well as Spanish Macorisanos. They carve their own wooden cricket bats with machetes, the all-purpose tool of the cane fields.

When playing baseball, George always got hits and always won. He also boxed a little in the neighborhood—"Baseball and boxing were the only sports," he noted—and with his exceptionally strong body, athletic reflexes, and aggressive personality, it could have been said that he was a natural fighter. But Bell didn't like boxing as much as he liked baseball, and since his father played for and managed the sugar mill's team in Santa Fe, George grew up with it, starting as a batboy.

In the 1970s, television came to San Pedro, which meant the opportunity to watch American baseball broadcasts. The notable increase in top-ranked San Pedro players in the 1970s and 1980s was due to many factors; one was the fact that this was the first generation to grow up watching major-league games. If someone in the neighborhood had a television set, everyone would come over to see the game. In 1971 the Bells got a TV.

When George was fourteen years old, his family moved to a larger house in San Pedro. Just as the streets in Santo Domingo were a little tougher than those in San Pedro, the streets of central San Pedro were a little tougher than those of Santa Fe, Consuelo, and Angelina: if a teenage boy wandered into a different barrio, he would be jumped and beaten. There were no guns or knives, and Bell would say years later that it was not as dangerous as a poor neighborhood of New York, but he learned early on to stick to his own barrio, not go out alone, and concentrate on baseball.

In San Pedro, talented young players found other talented young players. Fifteen-year-old Bell came to know Tony Fernández, the kid with the great hands and a bad leg who was always hanging around Tetelo Vargas Stadium practicing fielding ground balls. Increasingly, San Pedro was a place to play baseball. Out in the cane fields or in the center of the city, there were baseball diamonds everywhere. On weekends, boys would play nine hours a day. According to Bell, about two of those hours were spent arguing about plays. But that, too, was baseball.

On weekends, instead of fighting, San Pedro boys who loved baseball would take on the next barrio in a series of five three-inning games. Each team contributed twenty pesos, and the losing team would go to the street stands and buy oranges, tropical fruit, ice cream—whatever treats they could find—and the two teams would have a party. To give themselves an incentive not to waste time bickering, the teams would give twenty pesos for the umpire to hold. If he decided that the boys were arguing too much, he could keep the money.

Bell's special talent was hitting. When he was twelve years old, he was paid to hit on a team for sixteen-year-olds. As he got older he played for the Ingenio Santa Fe team against Julio Franco at Consuelo. Bell played second base, third base, and outfield. He loved third base, his father's position, but it demanded more fielding skills than he had. However, he was also drawn to the outfield, where his hero, Rico Carty, had played; in fact, Bell grew up to be a similar player: primarily a hitter. San Pedro was not just about shortstops.

Pedro González watched Bell play for Santa Fe, thought he was an interesting prospect, and brought him to a program in San Pedro. But it was Quiqui Acevedo who signed him with the Phillies for a $3,500 bonus.

Young Sosa was only five feet, nine inches tall, and very thin, and Acevedo wondered if he was ever going to develop a major-league body. Julio Franco, George Bell, Juan Samuel, Jose Moreno . . . by 1980, they had all been shipped off from their training program in Santo Domingo to American ballparks—along with dozens of others who would never make it to the majors. Juan Samuel was another Macorisano who would make baseball history by being awarded the Rookie of the Year title; in fact, he was the first player in history to reach double digits in doubles, triples, home runs, and stolen bases his first four seasons in the major leagues and was only one triple short of doing it again his fifth year.

Those four—Franco, Bell, Samuel, and Moreno—all had stellar major-league careers, even though leaving their island and living in America was not easy for any of them.

It was a bit easier for George Bell than the others because he was comfortable in English, but he was ill prepared for life in Helena, Montana, in 1978 when the Phillies sent him there. When the electricity went off he was not surprised, because electricity regularly goes off in San Pedro; but when the lights did not come back on, someone had to explain to him about paying an electric bill.

While a black man was fairly unusual in Helena in 1978, Bell said, "I didn't have the problems of black Americans because I was a Latino. Helena girls liked the way I spoke Spanish. The Latinos were not treated like the blacks. I walked down the streets, went into stores, people were nice, and the countryside was beautiful."

"It was okay for George Bell," said Julio Franco. "He spoke English and he was in Helena. I was in Butte. There were Latin guys in Helena but not Butte. In 1978, I went to spring training in Sarasota, Florida. There were Spanish-speaking people around. There was a pool and a Ping-Pong table and a pool table. It was really nice. Then they said we were going to Montana. I didn't even know where Montana was, but I looked out a window and saw snow on the mountains. I didn't even own a coat! It was freezing cold there."

In what was becoming something of a cliché for Dominican ballplayers, Franco often resorted to eating Kentucky Fried Chicken because it was easy to order. However, he also bought food and cooked in the dormitory where he was living. There was one Spanish-speaking player who knew English, a Puerto Rican named Carlos Cabassa. He taught Julio to speak English and then things got a little easier. But one of the players went to a local disco one evening, "and the cowboys beat him up and then we weren't allowed to go there. We learned never to go out at all."

Sammy Sosa was born in a shack on a well-trimmed unpaved street in Consuelo. The small, crumbling, toffee-colored structure still stands, a different family occupying it, around the corner from F Street where Julio Franco was born in a house about the same size, number 14, which was why Julio always wore that number. Like many homes in the Dominican Republic, these had only occasional electricity and running water that was not drinkable. Sosa's father drove a tractor, clearing harvested cane fields. It was not as good a job as the ones inside the mill, but it was much better than cutting cane. Sammy's mother, like George Bell's, earned money cooking and selling food out of her home.

When Sammy was six, his father died of a cerebral hemorrhage. Sammy's mother tried hard to support her three children. They moved to Santo Domingo and then back to central San Pedro, where Sammy wandered the streets with a shoe-shine box, competing with hundreds of other poor kids in search of customers.

Sosa's brother Luis was a boyhood baseball fanatic, but not Sammy. His heroes were not Juan Marichal and Rico Carty but Sugar Ray Leonard and Marvin Hagler. Like Alfredo Griffin and many other boys, he had fought a great deal on the streets in Consuelo. When he got to central San Pedro, he discovered a boxing school and started working out on the bags and sparring. His mother convinced him to give it up.

When Sammy was thirteen, an American businessman in whose shoe factory he worked took a liking to him and brought him a gift from the United States: a blue glove that cost a hundred dollars. In his eighteen seasons in the major leagues, Sosa always played with a blue glove. He joined a youth organization team that played in a park named after Rico

Carty. With his powerful throwing arm, he could accurately fire the ball to basemen to tag out runners. He hit home runs. Some of the local experts watching these games did not believe he was only fourteen. Sosa had power but no skills, and predictably every hit went to deep right field. But a coach named Héctor Peguero began teaching him how to change his leg position and swing a little early to hit the ball just before it arrived so that it would pop off to left field, a technique known as pulling the ball.

When Sosa was fifteen years old, Acevedo signed him to the Phillies and hid him away in Santo Domingo for training with some forty other prospects, most of them older, some on their way to America. Acevedo brought Sosa's mother to Santo Domingo to negotiate the signing bonus. According to Sosa's autobiography, the negotiation process gave her the sickening feeling that she was selling her own son; demoralized, she accepted the first offer, which was $2,500.

Acevedo began training the boys and fattening them up at the university in Santo Domingo. They practiced and worked out from nine a.m. until three or four in the afternoon. "They fed us, washed our clothes," said Julio Franco about Acevedo's training program. "We all ate a lot. We were very skinny. Four times a day as much as you wanted. But we were running all day. Then we ate. Then we went to sleep."

Sosa was in the last group of prospects whom Acevedo signed to the Phillies. Acevedo had a falling-out with the organization and these last players never got their bonuses, nor did the Phillies send for them. They were simply dropped—a bitter disappointment for an impoverished Dominican teenager who had thought his life was about to be changed by Major League Baseball. The Atlanta Braves, Rico Carty's team, were very interested in San Pedro at the time and signed some of the best of this group. But Sosa was still young, only sixteen, and undeveloped.

Sosa went back to working with his old team and went to every scout and every tryout he could find. It was the 1980s and San Pedro was full of scouts, especially after the previous wave of rookies: Bell; Franco; Samuel; the shortstop Rafael Ramírez from Angelina, whom Pedro González had signed to the Braves; and Pedro Guerrero, the Dodgers' popular first baseman from Santa Fe. But no one was interested in scrawny Sammy Sosa. Sosa remembers Pedro González taking a look at him and saying that he didn't sign "undersized players." González denied this story in his sometimes unmusical Cocolo, saying, "That's bullshit." He argued that he would never dismiss a player for being too small, pointing out that he had signed Rafael Furcal, who, at five feet, nine inches, was one of the smallest players in the major leagues.

For two months Sammy played at the training camp Epy Guerrero had set up in the bushes just inland from Santa Domingo. Guerrero had said he liked Sosa; Sammy hoped Epy would sign him. He never did. Sosa spent a year in this desperate limbo while George Bell and Julio Franco were becoming stars. But a new scout in the Dominican Republic, Omar Minaya, was looking for Dominican talent for the Texas Rangers. Minaya offered Sosa a signing bonus of $3,000. Sosa asked for $4,000 and they settled on $3,500. Sosa would be saved. According to Sammy—not always a reliable source—he gave $3,300 to his mother and bought a used bicycle.

The Dominican players all had different temperaments, but they had one thing in common: they were determined to make it, because there was simply no other option. George Bell said, "Being cocky, I always knew I would play in the majors. I knew I could do it. I could see a breaking ball from a fastball. I just knew. I could see it."

Julio Franco put it another way: "My feeling was I have to make it. It's all I've got. I mean, you leave school and that's all you've got. Of course, that was also true of the many more who didn't make it."

PART TWO

DOLLARS

La esperanza es la muerte de la muerte.
La esperanza es la esperanza
de reanudar la juventud del pueblo.

Hope is the death of death
Hope is the hope
to restore people's youth.

—Pedro Mir, "Concierto de
Esperanza para la Mano Izquierda"
("Concert of Hope for the Left Hand")

CHAPTER EIGHT

The Fourth Incarnation of San Pedro

The oldest and most timeless part of San Pedro, Punta de Pescadores, never had a single reincarnation. Just before the bridge leading to the town along the mangrove coast of the Río Higuamo, slightly upriver from the port on the opposite side, was a little village of pastel one-story houses on unpaved roads by the river's edge. In Ernest Hemingway's novel *The Old Man and the Sea*, the Cuban fisherman Santiago bravely goes to sea in his small open-deck boat to hand line for billfish as big as his craft. That way of life was still alive in twenty-first-century Punta de Pescadores. This was one of the rare San Pedro neighborhoods that did not produce Major League Baseball players. It produced fishermen.

They fished in deep-welled nineteen-foot open boats, the old ones made of wood, the newer ones of fiberglass. It was essentially a rowboat, but with outboard engines mounted on the back. They had to go a long distance to catch fish—farther all the time as fish became scarcer, because too many were being caught and because of pollution.

Gasoline for the outboards was expensive, and the only viable fishery within rowing distance had been steadily vanishing since the 1990s. From their muddy shore, fishermen rowed a few hundred yards and dragged a net over the side. They would slap the water with the oars to scare the fish and drive them into the net. These small freshwater fish did not command a high price, but when they were plentiful, a full net—which the fishermen wove together by hand—would quickly pay for the $600 in nylon line used to make it.

This fishery was dying out because it was downstream from Cristóbal Colón and a plant owned by CEMEX, the Mexican cement producer, both of which dumped pollutants in the river. A fisherman named Edwin said of CEMEX, in good New York English, "They kill everything. There is no fish left." Tony Echavaría, the mayor, recognized the often-cited problem: "CEMEX is a problem because of pollution, but it is very important to the local economy."

CEMEX provided fourteen thousand jobs. The entire San Pedro sugar sector was now providing only two thousand jobs, and many of those for only half the year. Also, CEMEX brought supplies through the port, one of the few port activities left. They even provided one of the better youth baseball programs developing teenage major-league prospects.

Meanwhile, Edwin complained that although the price of gasoline was rising, the fishermen were forced to go farther every year to find fish. Their engines were small—usually only forty horsepower—but still burned twenty-five gallons in a day of fishing, which meant the first 140 pounds of fish that was caught only paid for the gasoline. Some days they caught less than 140 pounds.

Edwin grew up fishing from Punta de Pescadores but went abroad, becoming a Dom Yor, as Dominicans refer, not altogether kindly, to those who move to New York. He lived in Queens with his father, a former fisherman, until, as he put it, "I did something bad and was sent back." The reference to "something bad" was not awkward English but a touch of satire that made Dominicans laugh about the patronizing nature of U.S. policy. The U.S. government warned Dominicans with the ultimate threat: if you don't behave, we will make you go back to your hometown.

Drug convictions most often led to deportation, but Edwin did not want to explain or give his last name. However, he came back with investment money and owned five nineteen-foot fishing boats.

Edwin fished the only profitable way left here, by taking his boats sixty miles out into the Caribbean. A line was planted with an anchor in 1,500 fathoms of water at one end and a buoy with a palm tree at the other. The palm, known as the *balsa*, provided shade, which attracted small fish, which in turn drew larger fish. The fisherman dragged a heavy handheld line with a baited hook through the shaded area and tried to hook a four-foot-long sharp-toothed, sleek, and silvery king mackerel, which Dominicans call a *carite*. Or the yellow fish with the huge foreheads and tender flesh that are sometimes five feet long and weigh more than fifty pounds, known here as *dorado* and sometimes in the U.S. as dolphin fish—except by the squeamish and politically correct, who prefer the Hawaiian name, mahimahi. There are also hefty yellowfin tuna, large sharks, and six- and seven-foot-long marlin.

Landing these fish on a small boat in open sea with a hand line takes considerable strength and stamina, and the battles may last ten minutes or longer. Some of these fish are strong enough to haul these boats; some are stronger than the forty-horsepower engine.

It is a culture of the-one-that-got-away stories, which was also the basis for Hemingway's novel. Edwin and his friend Ramón Fernández, known in Punta de Pescadores as Sanbobi, once hooked what they estimated to be a thousand-pound blue marlin. It was clearly longer than their boat. Sanbobi hooked it on a steel cable and was so jubilant that he could not stop laughing and joking. The more somber Edwin, operating the boat, just said repeatedly, "That's a lot of money out there." But Sanbobi had the giant by a steel cable, and so he kept laughing as he struggled to bring it in until finally the marlin did the impossible and snapped the cable, swimming free.

Both Sanbobi and Edwin had for the time being given up on deep-sea fishing because of the cost of gasoline and instead were finding smaller fish closer to shore. But there were no fish in the mangroves, the rooty growth along the banks of the Higuamo where oysters used to grow before the pollution killed them. Sanbobi still believed he was better off than his father, who was a worker for the Cristóbal Colón mill. Of fishing he said, "It's cash every day," in contrast to his father's seasonal employment.

The fishermen went out in the morning. In the afternoon the action switched to the other side of the river in downtown San Pedro, where the fish were taken to market, most of them stored at extremely low temperatures in walk-in freezers—a precarious business in a country known for power outages. The fishermen putt-putted back from sea and up the river with about five fish, four to seven feet long, tying up at a concrete landing with corrugated metal roofs. The fish were gutted and then hefted onto a large basket made of steel concrete-reinforcement rods and hung on a scale. Prices varied depending on the fish. A gruff man playing dominos on the dock explained dryly, "Fish are all different. Women are all the same." The men all laugh.

Everything—gutted fish, shelled conch, and bags of clawless tropical spiny lobsters and crabs—was immediately dragged into the freezers, their floors covered in bloody ice. Fresh fish is not a commercial concept in the tropics.

The best place to eat fish in San Pedro was the Robby Mar, which started in 1989 on the river next to the fish market. It had a pleasant white tableclothed terrace with a view of the river and its dense, tangled mangroves. Neither stuffy-pretentious nor downscale-ugly, which are the two usual choices, it would have been popular with tourists, but tourists did not turn up very often for a meal in local restaurants because the price of a room in a resort hotel included all meals. The tourism industry did not want tourists straying away from the resorts: something might happen to them, and that would be bad for tourism.

Without tourists, Robby Mar, located near much of the city government, did lunches for government officials, who—baseball players aside—had the best jobs in San Pedro. On some days half of the restaurant was taken over by the town fire department—some twenty men and women in white uniforms with dazzling arrays of metals and battle ribbons on their chests. After a few guavaberries, everyone just had to hope that no fires started during lunchtime.

The restaurant specialized in local seafood with a long menu that included some rare specialties and some very popular San Pedro dishes, such as *congrejos al ajillo*.

> Grind garlic in a food processor with salt and oil. If you have olive oil, it's much better. Boil crabs, take out meat, cook with a little butter and add garlic sauce. The same recipe can be used with fish.

But this whole world might be ending: the San Pedro of fishermen and waterfront, the original San Pedro before baseball, sugar, and even poets. Sanbobi gave Punta de Pescadores at most twenty more years. "Kids just aren't becoming fishermen anymore," he said. It is a trade that has gotten more and more difficult. It was different when the only alternatives were baseball and sugar. But now there were a few choices in between. Or at least it seemed that way.

San Pedro de Macorís entered the twenty-first century in the town's third reincarnation. Originally it was a rural fishing town, then it turned into a booming sugar center, then it became the wretchedly poor failed sugar town of the Trujillo years, when baseball was the only respite from the mills and the only way out for a lucky few. Then came the fourth reincarnation, in which San Pedro had a slightly more developed economy and baseball was no longer the only alternative to sugar, just the only good one.

Sugar was still there, but it was now secondary to employers such as CEMEX and César Iglesias, an old San Pedro factory making soap, flour, and butter that had eight thousand workers.

The Porvenir mill was off a street in central San Pedro. It used to be in the northern rural area like Consuelo. But the town—which, like the country, tripled in population in a generation—grew around Porvenir just as it may eventually grow past Consuelo. That is what is happening in the Dominican Republic: more and more rural areas are being taken over by the shacks of urban sprawl. Already a grid of dirt roads with modest concrete houses with corrugated metal roofing had spread north of Porvenir.

The mill itself, Porvenir, "Future," was a shack, albeit a large one five or six stories high but mostly slapped together with the ubiquitous Caribbean building material, corrugated metal. It was dark inside, but hot white rays of sunlight shot through seams in the metal skin, slashing across the huge dark space at dramatic angles. Workers who stood on top of a two-story-high tank for cane juice could look longingly at a ball field where young signed prospects trained for the Pittsburgh Pirates.

The tall, dark shed housed monstrous nineteenth-century cast-iron machinery: two-story-high cogwheels with menacing teeth for cane crushing; wood-burning furnaces for cooking the juice, stacks of chopped trees at the ready; tall cane elevators; and huge conveyor belts.

All this for what was now four months of operation a year. Some of the better jobs lasted six months. Some workers earned 20 pesos an hour to clean machines and others 800 pesos a month to supervise. Some workers had nothing to do at all. Porvenir was controlled by the ruling Dominican Liberation Party, the PLD, and party members in good standing could get paid to do absolutely nothing. And some of those jobs were year-round. Killing time, unlike cane crushing, is not seasonal. And so some workers were at the mill in the dead season, showing up every day, sitting around, sometimes gratefully wearing purple hats, the party color, with a picture of Leonel Fernández on them because they did have reason to say *"Gracias, Presidente."*

Guards stood at a chain-link gate manipulating a thick chain and a padlock, letting people in and out as though the era of Trujillo were still alive and well at the sugar mill. A woman worker wanted to go out, explaining that she had a family emergency, and the guard told her that if she left she would not be let back in until the next day, thereby forfeiting a day's wages.

In a good year, when there was not much rain, Porvenir produced forty-two tons of sugar in its four-month operation. In Brazil the waste from crushed cane, biomass, fueled cane ethanol production to meet most of the country's energy needs. But in the Dominican Republic, which did not produce ethanol and ran on expensive imported oil, a little biomass was sold to paper mills and the rest was just burned as scrap.

Twenty-first-century Consuelo still looked like a village: most streets were unpaved, and two-story buildings stood out. The mill in Consuelo, more spacious than Porvenir, was set in an immense area of weed-covered lots and, like Porvenir, was covered in corrugated metal several stories high. The mill was fenced off and surrounded by a dirt road. Along the other side of that road were green wood-shuttered Caribbean houses originally built for the upper-echelon mill workers, fine old houses rotting in the tropics. The families of those mill workers still lived in these homes, although most of the residents didn't work in the mill anymore.

Inside, one of the crushing machines was stamped *Farrel Foundry and Machine Co., Ansonia, Conn., 1912*. After the 1950s, parts were no longer available for these monsters, stories high, with teeth, shafts, and belts. Now Consuelo had its own machine shop with lathes and other machinist's tools where parts were made to keep these antiques running. Nor did they depend on the vagaries of Dominican utilities: Consuelo had its own power plant. A generation earlier, this had been the leading San Pedro mill, and once the *zafra* began, there could be no stopping, night or day, for eight months. But now the company struggled to stay running for four months.

At a small street bar, just a shed by the side of the road, two men were having coffee—good strong Dominican coffee that tasted as though half the sugar of Consuelo had been dumped in it. People in sugar towns eat sugar. They start sucking on cane stalks as children and develop a sugar-craving palate.

The man behind the bar spoke Creole because his father had come to Consuelo to cut cane from Haiti. The only other customer spoke English because his father had come to Consuelo to cut cane from Saint Kitts. He had been a sugar maker, sometimes called a chemist: the man who supervised the actual boiling and making.

Did that job pay well?

"No, the only job in a sugar mill that pays well is owner."

Despite their different languages, they understood each other and asked a question that was still frequently asked in San Pedro: Why wasn't sugar profitable anymore? "I don't know what happened," said the one who spoke Creole.

"I know," said the other in English. "There used to be money in sugar."

There was not much money in sugar anymore, and so there were not many jobs in it, although Consuelo now had 45,000 residents—which was more than all of San Pedro had when there was a lot of money in sugar. Much of Consuelo was still a village of small one-story pastel houses set close to each other, gardened with tropical plants and shrubs. Some of the few paved streets even had sidewalks. It was a tidy, orderly town where people took pride in their homes despite the fact that there really wasn't any work. They had not been living any better when there was.

One of the leading economic activities in this neighborhood, a short distance from the main town, was to drive a *motoconcho* and charge passengers to cling precariously behind as the scooter sped over and around potholes. The noisy two-wheelers swarmed around Consuelo like flies on old meat.

Fortunately, most families in Consuelo had relatives outside of the country who shipped them money. This was not unusual. It was estimated that more than ten percent of the Dominican population lived in the United States. Large-scale immigration began in 1966, when Balaguer, with the help of U.S. troops, got back into power and began killing supporters of Juan Bosch and the left. It continued at a rate of about 150,000 a year. Dominicans often speak disparagingly of these Dom Yors, sometimes calling them *encadenados* (people in chains) because of the New York street fashion of wearing gaudy gold chains. But communities like Consuelo could not survive without them. In New York and around the United States, establishments whose only business was wiring money to relatives in the Dominican Republic sent several million dollars every day.

One of the important mills of the Dominican Republic's sugar-based economy had been Santa Fe, which was now closed, although people still lived in the surrounding shacks, where sugar workers had been housed. Narrow dirt alleys separated the shacks, and garbage heaps were everywhere. Children played on them. Bit by bit, the mill was vanishing. The unemployed sugar workers who still lived in Santa Fe, George Bell's old neighborhood—many of whom were of Haitian ancestry—made up for periodic shortfalls in cash by stripping some of the mill and selling it as scrap metal. "Haitians," one Macorisano grumbled, showing that old attitudes endured. "The Haitians strip everything. Soon they will start chopping down all the trees for charcoal. You look in Haiti: there's not a tree left standing except at the Dominican border."

A Macorisano who had been away for only a decade would immediately notice the difference on returning to his hometown. He would drive in from the capital on a wide, well-paved four-lane highway built in 2006 to enable tourists to get from the airport to the beach resorts of Guayacanes and Juan Dolio. The coastline leading into San Pedro offered a Caribbean Sea like blue agate, sheltered by coral reefs that made fine-sand beaches. Juan Dolio and especially Guayacanes were originally fishing communities where the fishermen launched their open boats from the beach—some under oar power, others with outboard engines.

Typical of Dominican history, there are two competing versions of the origin of the name Juan Dolio. It is at least agreed that no such person ever existed. It either is a bastardization of the term *juego de lengua*, tongue twister, or—the more logical and therefore less preferred version—comes from *juando*, or conch, one of the many pastel shells in a variety of intriguing forms that wash up on the beach.

In the 1980s, when there were not many Dominican resorts, weekend recreation spots were built here for affluent people from the capital. A ferry ran between Santo Domingo, San Pedro, and Puerto Rico. A highway wasn't needed until the resorts began to attract better-paying foreigners. It has been Dominican policy to develop beach resorts with fast access to and from a nearby airport so that visitors see as little of the country as possible. The Santo Domingo airport, located halfway between the capital and San Pedro, would be close enough. To get to the hotels, the visitor had only to turn off the highway and travel for a brief stretch through a pretty, wooded zone via a washed-out narrow two-lane road that Dominicans used to drive on to get to the hotels. The road became full of such enormous potholes that the speed bumps placed before each hotel entrance seemed unnecessary.

While the streets of San Pedro were choked in traffic, the new four-lane highway leading to it was usually lightly traveled because it was designed for more traffic than tourism created. Most of the tourists did not even rent cars. Those who did steered around slow, lumbering buses and buzzing motor scooters, the primary methods of transportation for most Dominicans. The scooters were so underpowered that they often used the wide shoulders of the highway. Only a few affluent Dominicans, many of them baseball players, sped by in their SUVs.

When it was *zafra* time, that became evident by the cane trucks swaying down the highway, flatulent with black smoke, and by the smoke clouds puffing out of the two tall stacks of Ingenio Cristóbal Colón just outside of town. Some things never change. But upon exiting the highway and climbing the pockmarked pavement of the bridge over the Río Higuamo—still wide and muddy, with thickly grown tropical banks, the white steeple of the cathedral visible in the distance—the traveler encountered something surprising at the entrance to town.

Here was a poor and crumbling neighborhood known as Placer Bonita that had produced numerous major-league players, including the pitcher Josias Manzanillo, infielder Juan Castillo, and pitcher Salomón Torres. In the middle of this dilapidated old barrio was what appeared to be a huge stage announced by high steel arches. It was a sculpture commissioned by the city from artist José Ignacio Morales for almost seven million pesos—which, thanks to a bad exchange rate, was only slightly more than $200,000 but was nevertheless a serious expenditure for a Dominican town.

In this work—erected in 2006, the same year the highway into town was built—the artist seemed to exhibit a documentarian's urge to collect all the important images of San Pedro and display them on this spacious platform in no particular order. There was a pen and inkwell for San Pedro the city of poets, and of course two baseball players, a cane cutter, and the actual steam locomotive from a train that once hauled carts of cane to the Porvenir mill. There was also a strange dancing figure with a feather headdress known as a Guloya, a popular symbol of *cocolo* culture.

But for all the exuberance of this display, there was also a touch of realism: climbing up the platform were giant land crabs that seemed about to eat the cane cutter, the baseball players—everyone. At sunset, when the shadows are long, it becomes clear that San Pedro really is full of land crabs that, for unknown reasons, cross the roads at that time of day, ready—like mold, humidity, mosquitoes, hurricanes, and a thousand other tropical menaces—to devour this town.

The different reincarnations of San Pedro were apparent along the city streets like rings in the cross section of a tree. Downtown was a mix of architectures, all made homogeneous by the same palette of turquoise, pink, yellow, and apricot. There were old pre-sugar-boom, rural Caribbean wood-shingle houses with fretwork above the doorways. The sun parched the brightly painted wood of these houses, some of which listed slightly, while the darkness inside made them look abandoned. But they were designed to keep out sunlight, and their simple architecture with pitched roofs was conceived with an understanding of the climate and so they last forever, surviving sun and rot and hurricanes.

The fine old late-nineteenth- and early-twentieth-century buildings from the days of the sugar boom, with high arched doorways and ornate cornices and charming balconies, had not fared as well. A few of these buildings were well preserved; others were worn but surviving; many were gutted; some were roofless; and some were no more than a miraculously preserved façade in a vacant lot.

The cathedral was perfectly maintained, and so fresh and bedecked with bobbles and swirls that it looked as though it would melt in the tropical heat. It was the tallest, whitest thing around, the steeple looking almost electric in the hard sun with a black afternoon storm sky in the background. And the yellow City Hall still looked as decorated as the gooey piped cakes displayed under glass at the pastry shops.

And there was modern concrete, the innovation San Pedro is proud to have introduced to the Dominican Republic. Since that first concrete structure went up, many more followed, including four big chain department stores, office buildings, apartment buildings, and, inexplicably, numerous shoe stores—none more than a few stories high.

The port, where seaplanes once landed and sugar once was shipped but was now barely used, filled a long swath of riverfront with abandoned hangars and warehouses. The Parque Central, or Central Park, on the other hand, was still the social center it was intended to be. Between street vendors, sidewalk musicians, people taking a break and those with simply nothing to do, this square of palms and local tropical trees and plants was never empty.

Across from the park was a popular restaurant, Amable, which specialized in *pasteles en hojas* and *batidas de lechosa*. With its plastic chairs and tables, it looked like a fast-food restaurant except that it was decorated with San Pedro paintings and sculptures. Macorisanos would tell you with their local pride that the *pasteles* were a local specialty. They were either mashed cassava root or ground bananas filled with meat and steamed in banana leaves. In fact they were tamales, a food invented in central and southern Mexico by an indigenous people—anthropologists disagree about which one—long before the arrival of the Spanish. After the Cubans got tamales, they brought them—as well as sugar and baseball—to San Pedro, where they became part of local life. *Batidas de lechosa*, papaya milk shakes with lots of sugar, probably did not originate locally, either, although the word *lechosa* for papaya is authentically and uniquely Dominican.

The clearest expression of a unique San Pedro culture is the *cocolos*, who are sometimes heard singing their Afro-Caribbean music in the Parque Central. The *cocolos* also maintained a dance troupe, which was what was being honored by the statue of the man with the feather headdress on the crab-infested platform at the entrance to town.

The troupe was led by Donald Warner Henderson, nicknamed Linda, a mischievous little seventy-six-year-old man with glasses, a West Indian lilt to his English, and a wry sense of humor. His father was from Antigua and his mother Saint Kitts. Both came to San Pedro for work in the cane fields at age twenty-four. Linda's father cut cane on various estates, but Linda himself was a tinsmith by trade and noticeably proud that he had never worked in the cane fields.

The *cocolo* dances of San Pedro came from Antigua, Nevis, and Tortola and were passed down through families. Linda's father had danced traditional dances in Antigua. In the British West Indies they would dance on Christmas Day. "Christmas belongs to us and Christmas eve belongs to Dominicans," he explained. "On Christmas eve we serenade and Dominicans eat and drink."

The *cocolos* also perform their dances on February 27, the national holiday—which, interestingly, celebrates independence not from Spain but from Haiti, which withdrew its occupation forces on February 27, 1844.

The most colorful and famous dance costume, the Guloya, featured in the sculpture at the entrance to town, is misunderstood by the non-*cocolos* of San Pedro. Guloyas are Goliaths who combat Davids in a different *cocolo* dance. The dancers with feather headdresses are Indians for a dance called Los Indios Salvajes in which *cocolos* dress like Indians and dance around waving tomahawks—just one of many aspects of Caribbean culture that Americans would find politically incorrect. But the Spanish didn't leave any Indians to protest. The wild Indians seem to wear as many colors as they can find, with their beaded masks with long black pigtails, beaded costumes with capes, tall peacock feather headdresses, and painted tomahawks.

Many other dances are in their repertoire, including one, believed to be of English origin, in which a man goes out to gather wood for a fire, then comes home to find his wife with another man, whom he chases with a stick. Traditionally, none of the dancers are supposed to be identified until evening, when the masks are taken off. But in reality many of the *cocolo* dancers sit around in their beads without masks, getting so drunk before the dance begins—traditionally on guavaberry, but shots of rum work well, too—that they are well exposed before they ever get their masks on.

Cocolo music is African and is performed using a snare drum, a larger drum, a wooden flute, and triangles. The dances are clearly African as well. *Cocolos*, who have such a distinctive presence in San Pedro culture,

are always the stars of these fiestas; but the other Dominicans also celebrate, often wearing bull masks and chasing people in the crowds. Women
do wild things with toothpicks spiking out of their hair, and some men
wear fetching gowns. In fact, if you look closely in the bars, which spill
out onto the streets, many of the women could use closer shaves. Macorisanos of Haitian origin crowd close together in the street for African slow
dancing. No one gets more out of a small, slow movement than a Haitian
dancer. There is always a Fidel Castro or two and a few Zorros on horseback. Young people come in from the *bateys* on horseback. It's surprising
that the fast and loud, buzzing motorbikes and merengue blasting from
trucks don't panic the horses, but Dominican horses, like Dominican
people, are used to noise.

Cocolo food is Eastern Caribbean, which is also a bit African and has
had a huge influence on San Pedro. They eat salted fish—not the imported salt cod of their English islands but cured local fish—as well as
pigeon peas, which come from Africa; calaloo, the broad leaves of a tuber,
which are cooked like a spinach soup; and *fungi*, the Eastern Caribbean
corn dish. Although corn is one of the few indigenous pre-Columbian
Caribbean foods, the name for the dish is African. On some islands it is
funchi, and if okra—which is also African—is added, it is called *coo-coo*.
Rincón Cocolo, a restaurant of a few tables in a small room painted green
in downtown San Pedro, specialized in these dishes, most of which are
unknown in the Dominican Republic outside of San Pedro.

Gladys María José was born in San Pedro in 1923. Her father was Haitian and her mother was from Dominica. Her mother died when she was
very young. Her father came to cut cane and stayed illegally, making up
the name José for her because he was afraid that with his foreign family
name she might be deported. She was the cook at Rincón Cocolo and
she gave this recipe for *fungi*:

> Take cornmeal and put it in a pot with salt over low heat. Then wet
> flour with cold water. Then gather up the wet flour and put it in the

pot that has the cornmeal. Stir fast so that it doesn't make balls. Add
a little butter and stir it in.

Cocolo cooking, like drinking guavaberry and playing *plaquita*, has become a part of San Pedro life adopted by the rest of the population. Almost
every housewife in San Pedro makes *pescado y domplin*. The *domplin*, or
dumplin, pronounced "doompleen," is the typical British Caribbean dump-
ling served from Jamaica to Saint Kitts: a heavy little ball made from flour
and water. If a town can have its own dish, this would be San Pedro's. Most
Macorisanos do not know that *domplin* is from an English-language word.

Linda was born in a neighborhood called Miramar, meaning "see the
sea," which is literally true. Because San Pedro's waterfront was on the river,
the side facing the Caribbean Sea was an undeveloped back barrio where
poor people, many of them sugar workers, lived. Miramar has produced
a number of major-league players in recent years, including catcher Ángel
Peña, infielder Fernando Tatis, pitcher Lorenzo Barceló, and outfielder
Luis Mercedes. They played on the streets. Tatis described tearing up
blankets to make balls: "We tore blankets in strips and rolled them tight
and sewed them together. We loved baseball so much, we would play with
anything." Miramar is no longer poor. In the 1960s, in the push to make
San Pedro more tourist friendly, a broad boulevard was built by the oceanfront where a rocky coral coast leads to a perfect, bright Caribbean Sea,
blue for miles on a good day. Like the longer seaside boulevard in Santo
Domingo and the one in Havana, it is called the Malecón.

A whole other town grew by the Malecón. There was a huge and sump-
tuous school of hotel management, clean and well-presented private
schools, government buildings, well-kept modern apartment buildings,
and gardened, one-story, California-style ranch houses. It became an
expensive neighborhood. Even water and electricity cost more, and few
could afford to live there. Much of this neighborhood was oddly deserted.

The clean and well-paved streets were empty. In an otherwise bustling town, this center was devoid of cars: even the ubiquitous scooters and motorcycles of the rest of the town, and the rest of the Dominican Republic, were absent. There were not even pedestrians.

Tourism settled into the beaches outside of town. Only a few tourists came in for a brief walk around the park and a look at the cathedral. The Malecón was for locals: a quiet stretch of oceanfront by day with a few coconut or sugarcane vendors. Past the coral rocks and the palm trees was a postcard-perfect vista of a turquoise and cobalt-blue Caribbean Sea interrupted only by a few local touches, such as the rusting carcasses of ships wrecked in storms and, perched dramatically on a rock above the sea, an outhouse, because a lot of Presidente beer was consumed at night along the Malecón. After dark it was *the* place, with merengue exploding from phenomenally powerful speakers that rattled the windows in the nearby hotel, the only attempt at a business- or tourist-class hotel in town. The music came from many clubs, one of the most popular of which, the Café Caribe, was owned by Alfredo Griffin. The sad *bachata* ballads were for earlier hours. At night, merengue was still the music.

Macorisanos came every night until late, on foot, on scooters, by car—whatever they had—and cruised the Malecón, the women dressed in tight, sparkling fantastic clothes contrasting with a lot of exposed skin of every color, the men drinking and looking. If you had a car, you could do the "Malecón crawl," driving five or ten miles an hour, checking everything and everyone out.

Traveling north from downtown most hours of the day, the traffic was crammed into unmarked lanes—as many lanes as would fit. Mixed in with ailing buses coughing black smoke, trucks, and cars were carts pulled by those lean and fearless Dominican horses.

There were traffic lights, but they didn't always work. The rule was to drive up to them and see if anything happened, then the bravest started through first. The system worked so well it made you wonder if towns really need traffic lights.

Anyone with a car who stopped at a traffic light was quickly swarmed by *tigres*—local boys who washed windshields and demanded pay. They were a little gentler than the *tigres* of Santo Domingo, and they tried to do a good job on the windshields before the light changed. They were hardworking, enterprising youths earning pennies on a hot afternoon, looking for some way to survive other than crime. Another possibility was to work the Parque Central or the Malecón with a shoeshine kit, as Sammy Sosa did as a boy. But with the popularity of canvas sports shoes, that was getting to be an even tougher business. Another possibility was to go to the rural outskirts and get some cane, oranges, plantains, or other produce to sell on the street.

On Calle 27 in San Pedro, the neighborhood Rico Carty brought electricity to when he built his own house, a row of mansions sprang up. A large Mediterranean-style house that somehow ended up looking more like a Pizza Hut was the home of George Bell. Alfredo Griffin's house was there. Joaquín Andújar also had a large house, but either out of modesty or for reasons of security, it was hidden behind a wall. The neighborhood used to be known as a baseball player's ghetto, but Bell and Andújar lost their houses in divorces. Still, the houses stood as a reminder to young *tigres* of what a major-league career could do for them.

Nearby, on Calle Duverge, was a sprawling two-story building with balconies, an ornate gate, and seemingly the largest satellite dish in San Pedro—the house Sammy Sosa built for his mother. Also nearby was Plaza 30/30, a small, three-story, horseshoe-shaped, turquoise-colored shopping center with pricey shops built by Sammy Sosa in 1996. Actually it said PLA   30/30, because the sign had lost its ZA. The name referred to Sosa's 1993 season, in which he hit thirty-three home runs and stole thirty-six bases. Two years later he hit thirty-six home runs and stole thirty-four bases in the same season. As of 2009, there had been fifty-two "30/30" players—those who have hit at least thirty home runs and stolen at least thirty bases in a single season—starting with Ken Williams's thirty-nine home runs and thirty-seven stolen bases in 1922. Despite the arbitrariness of the figures, it is considered a distinction to be a 30/30 player, because home runs are the ultimate baseball test of strength, usually hit by large, burly men, and base stealing is the ultimate test of speed, usually performed by smaller, lithe men. Few players have both the speed to steal bases and the strength to hit home runs. But Sosa's record of having done it twice does not even stand in San Pedro, since Alfonso Soriano, born in the sugar-mill barrio of Quisqueya, debuting in 2002 for the Yankees, did it four consecutive seasons. In 2006, Soriano hit forty-six home runs and stole forty-one bases, becoming one of only four 40/40 players. In fact, the same year he hit more than forty doubles, so he became the first 40/40/40 player in major-league history. This statistic, which is cited more often in San Pedro than anywhere else, demonstrates nothing as much as baseball's unending thirst for statistics and records.

Nevertheless, Sammy Sosa was the first player in San Pedro to have a shopping mall named after his statistics. There was little doubt about whose shopping mall it was, since in the center, where the bougainvilleas grew, was a fountain and in the fountain stood a full-color statue of Sosa at bat. The statue wasn't recognizable as Sammy, but it wore a number 21 Chicago Cubs uniform. Also in the mall was a discotheque named the Sammy Club Disco.

Many of the streets of San Pedro were unpaved, or the pavement was so badly crumbling that they were in the process of unpaving. Like all Caribbean towns, San Pedro smelled of overripe fruit and burning charcoal. More English language—the language of both *cocolos* and baseball— was heard here than in other Dominican towns. Many of the stores had English names, such as the downtown salon called the Hair Gallery.

San Pedro's commerce spilled onto the street from the kind of one-story Latin American concrete architecture that tried to avoid drabness by being painted in the industrial color palette used in the making of Popsicles. In the end, most of these newer buildings resembled dirty bubble gum. The metal grating on every door and window made the houses look like smiling teenagers with their braces showing. The gratings were to lock out criminals. Street crime, robberies, break-ins, and muggings in this century became an unprecedented problem everywhere in the Dominican Republic. It was worse in Santo Domingo, but it had become serious enough in San Pedro for Mayor Echavaría to consider it his leading problem.

Young people were not finding a way to earn a living. The problem shifted from unemployment to underemployment. In recent years, inflation soared and the currency plunged, and most of those who found work still did not have enough money to meet their needs. It used to be, in this area of agriculture, cattle ranching, ubiquitous small-scale farming, and fishing, that even a poor person ate because food was cheap. Now, for the first time, people were struggling to buy enough to eat.

The Dominican government provides few safety nets for the poor. Juan Bosch and José Francisco Peña Gómez had called for such programs but never had a chance to implement them. Once in power, Leonel Fernández, Juan Bosch's protégé, abandoned such ideas and instead developed an infrastructure for foreign investment, declaring that he was making the Dominican Republic "the Singapore of the Caribbean." He garnered some popularity by stabilizing the economy. Because Fernández was barred by law from a second term, the opposition under Hipólito Mejía came to power on the promise of social programs and did manage to increase spending on education and social services, including the country's first government-financed retirement program. Wanting to do more, he used his legislative majority to end the term limit, and this allowed Fernández to come back and defeat him, using his next presidency to build still more infrastructure, such as new highways, but without the growth in social programs or the economic stability he had achieved in his first term. A poor Dominican still had to live by his wits to survive.

Traffic moved slowly around potholes, past *tigres* and uncertain traffic lights from the statue at the entrance to town past the Tetelo Vargas Stadium, which, like the Catholic churches of old, was never closed. The almost gridlocked street curved past all the low-ceilinged chicken restaurants, their large-screen televisions showing baseball games. Plastic chairs scattered on the street with the smell of fried chicken, plantains, yucca, and rum. The street then wound by a sprawling fenced-off landscaped area. It was the campus of the Universidad Central del Este, which, since its founding in 1970, had become one of the biggest changes in San Pedro.

For only 9,000 pesos a semester, a little less than $300, a student could become a teacher. To become a doctor cost only 6,500 pesos a semester, about $200, for the first two years and then 12,500 pesos a semester for another two years. Only four years and $1,600 for a medical degree may seem like a bargain to an American, and in fact Americans attended the medical school. But this was a great deal of money to be able to set aside from most jobs in San Pedro.

It would take most of a year just to earn one semester's tuition working near the university in the "free zone." The original 774,000-square-yard zone, established in 1971 under the same Balaguer development program as the university, soon filled, and a second zone was built. The plan was to allow foreign manufacturers, mostly of clothing but also some jewelry, shoes, and low-technology industrial products, to bring in parts duty-free, have them assembled by inexpensive Dominican labor, and ship them out. The Dominicans didn't get much for this, but it didn't cost them much, either. The Dominican government spent little more than $50,000 to build the zone. The companies have been mainly American. Anyone who breathed a word about unions or organizing for better wages would be quickly locked out, and so American manufacturers were provided with very cheap labor and Macorisanos were offered jobs that paid barely a subsistence salary. Once the Dominican peso went into free fall against the dollar in the 1990s, Dominican labor cost Americans less than fifty cents an hour. In the first four years of the twenty-first century, the peso fell again, losing about half its value. In dollar terms it made Dominican workers a bargain, but they had to put in ten- and eleven-hour days to earn enough to survive. It didn't even create a significant increase in San Pedro port traffic.

The free zone and tourism were cited by Echavaría as "the two main pillars of the San Pedro economy." Tourism jobs also meant long hours and low wages. A man named José was born in 1959 in a small farming town in the interior of the eastern region. His father owned a very small plot of land on which he grew bananas and a few other crops. They worked hard, but life was cheap and they had enough to eat. In 1980, José left the town and came to San Pedro because he had heard that jobs were available in the free zone. He got a job with an American shoe manufacturer. After twenty years he had worked his way up to supervisor and was earning 800 pesos a week, about $100 a month, which was a high salary for the free zone. "It was very bad pay," José remembered.' "But it was so cheap to live then."

However, prices started to go up and José's salary didn't, and by the year 2000 he was finding it very hard to live on his income as a supervisor for the American shoe company. So, despite the fact that he had only a grade-school education, he taught himself how to speak English in order to get a job in that other pillar of the San Pedro economy: tourism. He got a job as a porter in a beach resort hotel and earned 1,400 pesos a week. But that 1,400 pesos did not go as far as the 800 pesos at the free zone had ten years earlier.

José shrugged. "What could I do?" he said. "I came from a very small town. There was no baseball. I never had the chance to play it."

———

Ángel Valera de los Santos, an octogenarian, had been working in City Hall since 1948, when it was a much smaller city with only a few thousand people and few cars.

"Sixty years ago, San Pedro was much more prosperous but there were far fewer opportunities," he said. "Sugar was the economy. There was no tourism or free zone. There was César Iglesias. But now the wealthy families have all moved to Santo Domingo, where there are more investment opportunities. They all moved when sugar died."

Many new jobs had been created in San Pedro: driving a *motosconcho*, working in one of the big stores, such as Jumbo or Iberia, or in the free zone, or in tourism. Politicians liked to boast of the jobs they had brought in and the economic development they had fostered, but in truth most economic development in San Pedro de Macorís meant only the creation of underemployment.

But there was baseball.

CHAPTER NINE

The City of Baseball

In the handsome City Hall, on the second floor, was a room marked "Departamento de Cultura." It was a cramped little room with tiled walls. The dimensions and lack of windows suggested that it might have once been a closet. There was enough space for a desk, a file cabinet, and three chairs. Benancio Rodríguez Montaño, a thin, four-foot-tall elderly man with sunken cheeks and no teeth, was in charge. On the rare occasion when a visitor came to the Department of Culture, he would show them to a seat, pour a cup of strong, sugary Dominican coffee, and remain standing, which usually brought him to the visitor's eye level.

Questions about baseball irritated him. "Everyone says this is the city of baseball players, but before that it was the city of poets. There was Gastón Fernando Deligne, Pedro Mir, and here, there is me," he said proudly. "I am a poet too. Look, I was improvising just this morning." Then he took out a dog-eared envelope covered with writing and recited in cadence his latest sixteen lines about loss and vanishing culture in a style vaguely reminiscent of Gastón Deligne.

He may have been right about the loss of culture—"the rose lost from the garden"—but it was clear to most anyone that San Pedro de Macorís, the city of poets, was now the city of baseball.

Not everyone in San Pedro was desperately poor. Most of those who weren't were baseball players. They were easy to spot because they looked a little larger, a little better fed, and more muscular. If he was gangly, he was probably a shortstop. If you shook hands and his hand was large and powerful and the skin as coarse as a leather glove, he was probably a pitcher. They spoke American English and, in fact, they looked a little like Americans. This was why any large American in San Pedro was frequently asked, "Did you play baseball?" If you said yes—and most Americans have played a little baseball while growing up—invariably the next question was "Did you sign?"

The idea of playing baseball simply for fun had become a rare notion in San Pedro. In the hundreds of fields around town, many variations, like softball, *plaquita*, and cricket, were played for fun. Some played *molinete*, a Cuban variation on softball in which the underhanded pitch can travel more than 100 miles per hour. But even this was getting a little serious. *Molinete* in San Pedro had corporate sponsors, and the players were paid professionals.

Once baseball players started going to the U.S. and coming back with the money to buy mansions and SUVs, baseball was no longer about fun: it was about salvation, the one option that could work. Of course, most of the players around town had not made the major leagues, but many had made enough money somewhere in the game to start a business or take some kind of small step up.

It was no great trick to pick out those big, strong, American-trained and, more important, American-fed ballplayers. In the supermarket there was Ervin Alcantara, age twenty-seven. A few years earlier he had been practicing in a San Pedro field when a scout noticed him; in 2003 he was signed to the Astros. He played minor-league ball until 2007 and then was released. Now he was playing with the Estrellas. Since he never made it into the majors, his salary in the Dominican League was not very high, but it was still a lot better than a salary in the free zone. Also—and this seldom gets said—it was a lot more fun.

Everywhere in San Pedro, baseball connections were to be found. Ramón Pérez Tolentino, a pastry maker with a little shop in Consuelo, lovingly displayed in glass cases his work with white fluffy swirls and bright-colored jellies. He used to coach Manny Acta. Acta never made it to the majors as a player, but as manager of the Washington Nationals he became the first Macorisano to manage a major-league team and also the youngest manager in the majors. His old coach, the pastry maker back in Consuelo, now ran the Consuelo chapter of the Manny Acta Foundation, which supplied baseball equipment and training to young Dominicans.

Danilo Rogers was a *cocolo* who grew up in downtown San Pedro. His grandfather was from Anguilla and had come to San Pedro to work at Ingenio Consuelo. He became a "mixer," a technician who made white sugar. Danilo played ball and signed with the Atlanta Braves, playing left field on the A and Double A teams. He never made it to the majors, but he put away enough money to start a pleasant, airy restaurant serving Dominican food. His specialty was *mofongo*, a very Dominican dish, although, typically, the Puerto Rican sugar people brought it here. It is made from mashed plantains, fried in fat and garlic. Anyone who complained that *mofongo* is too heavy satisfied the Dominican definition of a gringo. Here is Danilo's recipe:

> Fry plantains with pork, beef, chicken, whatever you want to do it with. Also *chicharón,* the fat layer under the skin of pork. Crush the *chicharónes* and plantains in a pilón, a Caribbean mortar and pestle for mashing bananas, with butter, garlic, salt and pepper.

Young baseball players in San Pedro were fit, serious, and clean. Theirs was a disciplined youth. Their games, which took place every day all over town, were played with great seriousness. When a coach demonstrated a move, the boys would imitate it like ballet dancers learning a new step. This was not playing, it was working. Nevertheless, they were amusing games to watch, because the players had a thrilling combination of talent, determination, and undeveloped skills. A fly ball soared to center field and the center fielder, for no apparent reason, dropped the ball. But he had a good arm and threw quickly to shortstop. The shortstop, with bad hands but quick reflexes, also dropped the ball but quickly scooped it up and then tossed it to third base. The swift runner, who had been sprinting hard but was thrown a little off his step because he never expected to be running this far on a routine fly ball, was tagged out at third. One out—the same result had the center fielder caught the ball in the first place, but much more interesting.

There were a lot of scouts in San Pedro, but there were also a lot of baseball games to watch. Dany Santana, a native Macorisano who scouted for the Tampa Bay Rays, estimated that there were between thirty and forty baseball fields in town that he regularly dropped in on. One way an ex-ballplayer could make money was to buy a small plot of land, build one or two baseball diamonds, and rent them out. If he spent some money and put in dormitories, a gym, and some other facilities, he might be able to rent it out to a major-league franchise for a high price. But there was a market for lesser facilities as well.

Santana often scouted Astin Field, a ballpark of major-league dimensions, measuring four hundred feet from home plate to the center-field wall. During games or even practice, boys waited in the papaya trees around the walls, just as they did in the palms around Tetelo Vargas Stadium, for a foul ball or home run. The owner, Astin Jacobo, Jr., like many ballpark owners, was an ex-player, signed by scout Rafael Vásquez.

Vásquez was a legend in San Pedro. Before he was a scout, he had been a pitcher from nearby La Romana; in 1976 he threw twelve pitches for a Pittsburgh Pirates scout and was signed immediately. His rise was phenomenally swift. In the Rookie League in Bradenton, Florida, he struck out five batters in a row and was immediately sent up to a Class A team. It took him only two years from signing until he played on a major-league team, the Seattle Mariners. But his major-league career lasted just one season, in which he pitched in only nine games for the Mariners, first as a starter and then as a reliever; then he was sent down to Triple A, never to rise again. What made him famous in San Pedro—what the name Rafael Vásquez meant to Macorisanos, lovers of Macorisano baseball trivia—was that he was the first Dominican pitcher ever to get a win against the New York Yankees.

Vásquez went on to be a scout for the Kansas City Royals, for whom he signed Jacobo, who did not become a star, either. But Astin Jacobo was a famous name—perhaps more famous in the Bronx, where he was born, than in San Pedro. His father, Astin Jacobo, Sr., was from Consuelo, and like many people in Consuelo was a cousin of Rico Carty, whose paternal last name was also Jacobo. Astin Sr. scouted for the Houston Astros, but he was also one of the men who tried to organize the workers in Consuelo and consequently had to flee Trujillo. In the 1970s, the worst period for the South Bronx—when gunfire ignited fires that burned down whole blocks, and many buildings were abandoned—he settled in the Crotona neighborhood. There Jacobo, known as Jacob, became an activist in a troubled and impoverished community, saving buildings, getting City Hall involved, turning abandoned lots into gardens and baseball fields. There is still a street and a baseball field named after him.

His son owned the field in San Pedro, and on most days there was baseball practice there and almost always a few scouts taking a look. On the concrete block of seats behind home plate was written "Scouts Only."

Dany Santana often went to Astin Field to watch a lean fifteen-year-old pitcher with a hard fastball and a nice breaking ball. Good breaking balls were unusual for young San Pedro pitchers. In his first two years with Tampa Bay, Santana signed twenty-eight players but distinguished himself with pitchers including Cristófar Andújar, Joaquín's son, and Alexander Colome, also from San Pedro—a closer who at the age of sixteen was already throwing a 97-mile-per-hour fastball.

When his young pitcher went to the mound, Santana took up position behind the backstop with a stopwatch. This was unusual. Scouts usually stood in that spot with a handheld radar gun the size of a hair dryer to check the speed of the fastball. But Tampa Bay scouts were influenced by Eddy Toledo, the veteran scout who signed twenty-seven major leaguers, mostly for the Mets, before switching to Tampa Bay in 2006. Eddy never used a radar gun and frequently said, "I have two eyes: one is to watch arm movement, the other is a radar." Many organizations emphasize the speed of pitches—especially in the Dominican Republic, where many pitching prospects have only a fastball and a changeup. But Tampa Bay scouts under Toledo were more concerned with the fluidity and speed of the pitcher's movement than the actual speed of the ball after release. A pitcher with a fast movement was difficult to steal bases on, and they believed that good arm movement was a harbinger of good future development.

This youngster had a very good movement. It was also apparent without a radar gun that his fastball had considerable velocity.

Then Santana spied a young outfielder he didn't know.

"How old are you?" he asked the boy.

The boy began to glow. He was fifteen years old and a major-league scout was talking to him.

"Are you from San Pedro?"

He was. This was good because, being a Macorisano himself, Santana believed San Pedro players were a quality brand. Furthermore, the boy was from Santa Fe. Santana liked that because a lot of good players had come out of Santa Fe. So he patted the boy on the shoulder and sent him back to the outfield, the player's stride showing new bounce and his black skin heating to a shade of mahogany.

This was how Santana liked to work: identify talent at fifteen, watch him develop for a year and a half, sign him at sixteen and a half. It would be safer to sign prospects at twenty, but then the organization would not be able to play a hand in their development. Besides, by law all boys who are over sixteen become available for signing on July 2, and that is the day most of the good prospects are bought up by one organization or another.

If a prospect is of age and not signed on July 2, he could be signed at any time of year, so when a scout found talent in a player who was over sixteen, he signed him quickly. That past winter Santana had seen a boy in a field in Barrio México, not far from Tetelo Vargas Stadium. Santana said he "reminded me of Tony Fernández, the way he used his glove." He asked him to run and the boy hunkered down and performed a fast sprint. Then he asked him to show him how he swung the bat. The boy went into a batting stance and did a few swings for him. Santana signed him immediately with a $26,000 bonus, an average bonus at the time.

The age limit had been established in 1984. Before that, it sometimes seemed that scouts were snatching children from their homes. Epy Guerrero boasted of signing thirteen-year-olds. Not that this was a good way to treat children, but on the other hand, it took a scout of rare skill to recognize a player's potential at the age of thirteen. In 1986 it was recounted in *The Washington Post* that a terrified family reported their son missing and the Dominican commissioner of baseball located him hidden away by a scout in the training camp of a major-league team.

It is part of the tradition of Dominican kleptocracy, this idea that Major League Baseball could come here as did the Spanish, as did the sugar companies and do whatever they wanted to do. It is an image that neither the Dominican government nor Major League Baseball wants. And so, periodically, regulations are made. The age-sixteen-and-a-half rule helped lessen the unfair treatment of teenagers. A better minimum age would have been eighteen so that prospects finished high school education before leaving. But most baseball players, except big hitters, have their best years when they are in their twenties. This is when they have the most speed running bases, the most agility for fielding, and the best arms for throwing and especially pitching. Most players take about four years to develop for the majors. Few Dominican players had finished high school when they went off to their professional baseball careers, but for that matter fewer than one in three Dominicans had a high school education anyway. When a sixteen-year-old boy signed with a major-league organization, he had little education and no other skills: succeeding in baseball became his only chance. An occasional Rafael Vásquez did it in much less time, but then he washed out in one season. A few, like José Reyes, did it in only three years and went on to be stars. But when Major League Baseball signed a prospect, they calculated that it would take four years to get him into a major-league game. Some players, like Alfredo Griffin, find their rhythm that first year. Others take a year or two more to start realizing their full potential.

So signing a player at sixteen meant that he would probably hit his athletic stride at about the age of twenty-two. Physically they might be ready to reach full potential at age twenty if they could be signed at age fourteen, but sixteen was still workable. Another factor in the equation was the widespread and unproven belief, both by Dominican and American baseball people, that Dominican boys took longer to mature.

These teenagers who gambled everything on Major League Baseball signed a contract, got a signing bonus, and appeared to be on their way. But statistically their complete success remained very unlikely. A few hundred Dominicans are signed in a year, and probably only about three percent, maybe a dozen players, will ever play in a major-league stadium. And there is very little money in baseball between the signing bonus and the first major-league season.

First they are taken to the club's training ground in the Dominican Republic: the academy. From there they play a series of exhibition games known as Dominican Summer League. This is a last look before sending them to the United States. If they do well and are not released, they are then shipped to the States, usually to a remote, rural place, because that is where minor-league baseball is played. Sometimes they are brought to spring training first, but then they go to the Rookie League. Then, if they advance, they go to a Class A team. Sometimes, before getting there, players go to a subdivision, Class A Short Season. If they do well, they are moved up to Class A. From there they advance to Double A, unless they are released first. From there, things get even tougher. The last level, Triple A, is not far behind major league—except for the size of the stadium, the salaries, the perks. Triple A is full of major-league players. It is where major leaguers are sent to work out their problems or to get in some practice games while recovering from injuries. Some but not all major leaguers get back to the big leagues. A few new recruits get called up from Triple A to the major-league team. Some of those fail under pressure and are sent back down, but at least those few get to say they were in the major leagues. Most don't even get to Triple A.

The job of handing new prospects their signing bonus checks fell to a Dominican employee of Major League Baseball, Aaron Rodríguez. "What I love about it," said Rodríguez, "is that the first thing most kids do with their money is improve their parents' house. If it was wood it becomes blocks, or they paint it. But I always tell them to save a part of it. I tell them, 'You are not big leaguers, and this is the biggest amount of money you are going to see until you get in the major leagues, and you may not get to the majors.'"

They earned nothing while training at the academy. Dominican Summer League paid $600 a month, which was better than the sugar mills or the free zone or a resort-hotel job but not life changing. Even when they got to the U.S., minor-league players earned little. Not until the majors was there another chance at significant money. Usually the lecture was not necessary. Most of the young Dominicans bought something for their family. In many cases, a signing bonus alone is enough to change an entire family's future.

Alberto Medina worked as a welder on the big machines in Consuelo for sixteen pesos a day. His father was a field supervisor earning four pesos a day. Medina said, "If a kid gets a signing bonus of $25,000, that's a million pesos! He isn't poor anymore."

In the first few years of the twenty-first century, $25,000 was an average signing bonus, already ten times as much as Rico Carty, George Bell, and Sammy Sosa were paid.

In 2008, 423 young Dominicans signed major-league contracts and were paid a total of $41,057,000 in signing bonuses. Both the number of players signed and the total amount of bonus money steadily increase from year to year. On July 2, 2008, under intense competition, a sixteen-year-old pitcher from Puerto Plata, Michael Inoa, received a $4.5 million signing bonus from the Oakland A's. He was a six-foot-seven-inch right-hander throwing faster than 90 miles per hour. Height is increasingly valued in pitching, especially after the impressive career of Randy Johnson, who was six feet, ten inches tall and threw 100 miles per hour. A taller pitcher has long arms and releases the ball significantly closer to home plate, giving the hitter a split second less to identify the pitch. But also being longer and higher, he can get more torque on the throw because he is coming down from a higher position, which is why the pitcher's place was raised to a mound in the first place.

Some of the scouts compared Inoa to Randy Johnson. But Johnson was taller and he was left-handed. Left-handed pitchers are more valuable because they are rare. A six-foot-seven-inch right-handed pitcher from San Pedro had recently made it into baseball record books. On August 22, 2007, Daniel Cabrera, pitching for the Orioles, let a three-run lead slip past him and the Texas Rangers went on to win 30 to 3, the worst loss in Major League Baseball history since 1897.

The Inoa bonus created a whole new level of daydreams among Dominican teenagers. Real wealth could be attained without a career, with only a signing bonus. Part of the reason was the rule concerning sixteen-year-olds. Every year there was a new crop of players who were to become available on July 2. All the scouts knew who they were before that date and had decided how far they were prepared to go in order to get which player. In 2008, Inoa was the one they were talking about most. The Red Sox had given more than a million-dollar bonus to a pitcher the summer before, and the talk was that the club that wanted Inoa was going to have to ante up even more.

This kind of climate has done much to boost signing bonuses well over the $100,000 level, and they keep going up. In the 1990s, with bonuses increasing, scouts began thinking that there was more money in signing bonuses than in a major-league paycheck for scouting. Herman Martínez, a player from San Pedro who had turned scout, said of scouting, "You don't get rich, but you can live on it." But then a better opportunity started to appear, and Martínez, like many other scouts, left scouting to start a baseball school.

The idea was not originally Dominican. After the draft was established in the U.S., men known as bird dogs began earning a living by training promising youth for the draft. In the Dominican Republic they became known as *buscones*, from the Spanish verb *buscar*, to look for. A *buscón* looked for promising youth, sometimes no more than twelve or thirteen years old, and worked with them every day for years, feeding them, training them, teaching them what they needed to know until they were ready, then got them a major-league tryout. When one of their boys signed, they got a percentage of the bonus. The percentage was not fixed: it was typically a quarter and sometimes as much as a half of the bonus.

Not only was there the possibility of earning more money as a *buscón* than a scout, but to the way of thinking of some scouts, *buscones* were having all the fun. In the days of Avila and Guerrero, a scout scoured the wild Dominican countryside, sometimes sleeping in a jeep because there were no hotels. Now someone was leading them to prospects. The *buscones* were the ones who got to *buscar*.

One of the first *buscones* in San Pedro plowed up the garden in front of his house to use as a training field. Soon they were occupying bigger fields and parks, renting or buying spaces. Bringing in millions a year, signing bonuses had become the biggest business in San Pedro.

Apollinaire Batista, like many Consuelo natives, was the son of a Haitian cane worker. Batista was a *buscón*. He supplied all his own equipment, trained teenagers until they were ready to be seen by major-league scouts, and arranged tryouts. If they signed, he said, he took five percent of the bonus, which was an unusually small cut. After the player was signed he found a new prospect, so that he was always working with a small group. He liked to get them at the age of twelve so that he had four years to develop them and they could be ready the moment they were old enough. The younger a prospect, the more money he fetched. So *buscones* wanted to present all their players as young as possible. But they also had to make sure they were ready, because a second or third tryout gets harder to arrange. Batista had players who were not ready until the age of twenty, which meant a significantly smaller bonus. "You can't show them until they are ready," he pointed out, shrugging.

The boys worked out in the morning and went to school in the afternoon. Batista's goal was to get every boy that he took on signed to a major-league organization. In his best year he got five boys signed. Francisco de los Santos, a seventeen-year-old right-handed pitcher who threw faster than 90 miles per hour and also had a good changeup and several breaking balls, was signed by the Mets in 2008. His bonus was $25,000, which was a considerable amount of money in Consuelo, even though by 2008, the year of the $4.8 million pitcher, $25,000 indicated only a modicum of excitement on the part of the Mets. Bartolo Nicolas, a young outfielder, signed with the Blue Jays for $20,000. Once those two were signed, Batista had another seven ready to show to scouts.

One of the reasons scouts have so many fields to look at in San Pedro is that there are so many *buscones*. Like *cocolo*, *buscón* is a word that may or may not be pejorative, depending on who says it and how. Astin Jacobo, Jr., proud of his late father's name, did not like to be called a *buscón*. He said the word carried the connotation of "hustler," which he insisted he was not. He took thirty percent of bonuses, which was by no means the highest percentage but was among the higher ones. On the other hand, he had one of the better-equipped programs.

"Thirty percent sounds like a lot to an American," Jacobo said in his New York English. "But I have to provide clothing, schooling, food, housing, a woman to cook them food four times a day, and a staff of eight. I have $7,000 a month overhead, plus balls and bats. I lose four balls a day: they get hit out to the street and kids grab them.

"It costs me between 350,000 and 450,000 pesos in two and a half years to get a player signed," he added. But those pesos would only be about $14,000 in the U.S., and while a drafted American player does not come with all the nutritional, medical, educational, and developmental issues of a Dominican player, because of the difference in economies, it still costs Major League Baseball considerably more to develop a player in the U.S.

For Jacobo, there was no better place in the world to develop baseball players than his father's hometown. "I've been all over Latin America. This is the best town I have ever seen for baseball, because we have every kind of player here. You could come by a field on a Saturday morning and you might see a few major leaguers out playing with sixteen- and seventeen-year-olds."

The academies were the logical outgrowth of Rafael Avila's backyard operation in the 1970s. But by the twenty-first century they had become sprawling, sophisticated operations. Every major-league franchise operated an academy. Most of them were in the southeast, either in San Pedro; La Romana, a few miles to the east; Boca Chica, a few miles to the west; or a few miles farther west toward the capital. An academy was a place where a major-league organization could feed, train, and educate Dominican prospects, addressing all their special needs at Dominican costs, rather than those of housing, feeding, and preparing them in the United States. That higher cost of operating in the States was why clubs did not hesitate to give up on their investments and release players who were not living up to their expectations before sending them up to the States. The Dominican Summer League was established as a kind of pre–

Rookie League—a last proving ground before paying to bring prospects to the United States.

An academy also gave an organization a scouting base in the Dominican Republic. In the 1970s and 1980s it became apparent that the teams that had operations in the country were getting most of the best Dominican talent.

But the other purpose of academies was to serve as holding tanks while Dominican players waited for their visas, a safe place where the teenagers' sleeping, eating, and other habits could be controlled.

To many Americans, especially New Yorkers, it seems that Dominicans can easily get visas to the U.S., because so many have. The Dominican Republic, with an estimated total population of ten million, has sent more immigrants to the United States than any other Latin American country except Mexico, with an estimated population of 103 million. But it is not easy to get a visa, especially for poor people. The U.S. Embassy requires a $100 fee just to have an appointment to discuss a tourist visa, and the majority of Dominicans do not have the $100.

Major League Baseball generally gets its players a special visa for people who have proven to be exceptional in their field. But newly signed prospects are brought in as temporary seasonal laborers, like farmworkers, whose visas expire at the end of the season. To get these visas, it has to be established that the worker is not taking a job away from an American worker. The U.S. government limits the number of such visas. After the 2001 attack on the World Trade Center and the creation of a Department of Homeland Security, these visas became even harder to get. Until the player got his visa, he was kept at an academy, where his life and training could be carefully regulated and he could be further screened. Obviously, an organization is not likely to release a pitcher with a $4 million bonus or even one who received $500,000. But a few $20,000 or even $50,000 players got weeded out for visa problems.

These boys at the academies, whose future seemed so bright when they received their bonuses only weeks before, were under tremendous pressure. The usual practice when releasing players, whether in the Dominican Republic or in the minor-league system in the U.S., was to simply inform them that they were released without giving any explanation. Sometimes they were released for what was deemed "bad behavior." What would happen today to a Dominican Babe Ruth, Mickey Mantle, or Ted Williams, all famous in their day for bad behavior? If the Dominican player was released in the U.S., he would be given a return ticket to Santo Domingo. With the termination of the job, the temporary work visa expired.

Exactly what the ball clubs were looking for was always a little mysterious. The scouts, the academies, the organizations, were looking for someone who would make a great Major League Baseball player. When considering a sixteen-year-old, however, this usually required some guesswork.

Traditionally, what everyone in baseball wants are the "five-tool players." Baseball requires an unusually varied list of skills, and it is extremely rare to find someone who does everything well. Only a handful of major-league stars have been five-tool players. Playing ability has been reduced to five basic tools: a good throwing arm, speed at running, skill in fielding, the power to hit home runs, and the ability to hit consistently, which is measured by batting average.

Dario Paulino, who grew up in San Pedro and in 2007 became the coordinator of the Atlanta Braves' academy in San Pedro, said, "That's what we look for in every player: a five-tool player."

But there were a lot of less tangible things that scouts and trainers wanted to see. Dany Santana said, "The first thing I look for is . . ." and he pointed at his head. He quoted a favorite Eddy Toledo saying: *"No puede pensar, no puede jugar"*—If you can't think, you can't play. "If you are young and smart, you can improve quickly," Santana noted. Coming from a stable home with some education came to be considered an important asset for Dominicans, even though many great Dominican players hadn't come from such homes. The organizations wanted boys who could learn how to speak English and get along in the United States.

Dominicans, especially Macorisanos, generally lived their lives confined to a small world. They didn't travel and, despite the enormous number of both local and national newspapers, knew little about what went on in the outside world. During World War II, it was said that the average Dominican knew almost nothing about the war. Most sixteen-year-old Macorisanos had seldom left San Pedro. They may have gone a few miles east to La Romana or north to Hato Mayor, both agricultural areas. If they were signed by an organization with an academy a few miles east in Boca Chica or a little farther in Santo Domingo, that alone was a huge adventure.

Rafael Vásquez said, "I look for a good arm, how he runs, how he talks to other people. Is he a good guy with a good family?"

Asked what he looked for, Eddy Toledo said, "Athleticism and a passion for the game. It's hard to find now. In the past, people loved the game more than now. Kids used to play baseball because they loved the game. Now the top priority is to be rich and famous, and not because of a passion in their hearts."

As bonuses went up, the teams grew more cautious. They used to simply pay what the scout recommended. Then they started sending someone to take a look and decide if the player merited the investment. There was a growing feeling that the amount of money paid was adversely affecting the players.

Toledo did not like big bonuses. As of 2009, the biggest bonus he ever got was $43,000. He said, "If you give a poor kid $300,000, this is the first rock in the way of his development. He's not hungry anymore. I am very worried about giving kids big money, because they don't try hard anymore."

But this was inevitable as the power of Major League Baseball to change a Dominican life became ever more dramatic. Bonny Castillo, known as Manny in the U.S. when he played Major League Baseball in the early 1980s, coached newly signed prospects for Tampa Bay in the Dominican Republic. He said, "When I was playing, $15,000 was my best-paid year. I make more money now as a coach than I ever made as a player. The minimum wage got to $35,000 and now it is $400,000. If you make $400,000, you come home a rich man if you only play four or five seasons. You get in the big league, you've got it made."

Toledo's example of what he liked was signing José Reyes for the Mets. Reyes, who exuded a love of baseball in the way he played, got a $13,000 signing bonus. "José Reyes was a special case," said Toledo. "I signed him in Santiago at a restaurant lunch with his family and friends. When he left and walked toward the parking lot, I said to someone, 'Look at that. There's a specialness you can see. It's like a halo.'"

But Toledo admitted that he did not often see halos. So he looked for how easily the player moved to see if he was a natural athlete, and he looked at the kind of body the boy had and imagined what it could look like with the addition of protein and conditioning. If it was a pitcher, he looked for long arms, big hands, and broad shoulders. He pointed at a tall, thin young pitcher throwing on the mound with long arms and legs. "He's got a perfect body," he observed. "A lot of room to fill out." And then he shouted with great enthusiasm, "That kid could tie his shoes standing up!"

He and a lot of others also looked for aggression—aggressive pitchers and aggressive batters. Eddy Toledo recalled spotting Mets superstar pitcher Dwight Gooden as a boy: "I said, 'He's Bob Gibson. He competes, the aggression is there. His body is just not finished.'"

José Serra, scout and Latin American supervisor for the Cubs, said, "The secret of scouting is that, more than anything, he has to be a kid who wants to be something special." The Cubs' academy was in a huge complex out in the fields on a dirt road off the highway between San Pedro and Boca Chica. The complex housed academies with dormitories, workout rooms, staffed dining rooms, and other facilities for four different major-league teams, and was expanding in the hopes of drawing one or two more. As the scouting became more intense, success depended less on secrecy and more on outbidding competitors, and to adjust to this new reality, the organizations were increasingly clustering together in these large multiteam complexes rather than hiding away in small individual camps in the fields. This particular complex was built by former ballplayers, including Junior Noboa, a Dominican from Azua in the desertlands of the southwest, the poorest part of the Dominican Republic. Noboa, in an unspectacular eight years on various major-league teams, hit only one home run and never commanded huge paychecks. But he understood that for very little money he could buy a plot of undeveloped tropical brushland, clear it, build a few simple concrete buildings, landscape some baseball diamonds, and rent it for handsome prices to major-league organizations.

Others followed. In San Pedro there was increasingly tough competition among ex-players, including George Bell, who had bought plots and were looking for major-league organizations to rent them. Salomón Torres, a native Macorisano, was most remembered for his first major-league season, 1993, when in the last game he gave up three runs in as many innings and cost the Giants first place in the division. In San Pedro he was also remembered for losing control of a fastball in 2003 and hitting fellow Macorisano Sammy Sosa in the head and shattering his batting helmet. But Torres also took a part of his major-league earnings, cleared a cane field on the edge of San Pedro, built diamonds and dormitories and offices, then rented it to the Atlanta Braves and the Texas Rangers. He called it Baseball Towers, a play on his name, Torres, which means "towers."

The compound was gated, with an armed guard—one of those ubiquitous sleepy men with a beat-up pump shotgun who stood watch at most gates in the Dominican Republic. Inside it was prim and clean vanilla concrete buildings with red and blue trim, pristine interiors, and sparkling tile floors, all surrounded by careful groomed gardening—nothing too lush, but it is easy to grow things in the tropics. Of course, the grounds, like all grounds in the Dominican Republic, are grazed by chickens—free-range chickens, the national dish. Rent was $35,000 a month, food and maintenance included.

There were four manicured diamonds, two for the Braves and two for the Rangers. The Braves' academy, which moved to Baseball Towers in 2006, had twenty employees. Dario Paulino, coordinator of the Braves' academy, said, "This is the first step in the Braves' system." It was used as a Latin American center: signed prospects from throughout the region were brought to San Pedro.

Some academies sent players to a language school to learn English. The Braves had their own English teacher at the academy. Other courses were also taught so that the players, most of whom had dropped out of school to sign, could finish their high school education.

"The teams are trying to make them believe that they are intelligent people who can learn," Paulino said. "A lot of players don't make it because they can't speak English.

"Most of the players here are illiterate," Paulino continued. "They were too poor to go to school, though some have been to university. If they have never been to school, it is easier to teach them in the field. They are using a glove and you tell them it's called a glove."

The first phrase of English learned by many San Pedro teenage boys is "I got it!"—grammatically questionable but important words to know if you are ever going to catch a fly ball in an English-speaking game without a collision.

"Then, when we feel they are ready," said Paulino, "we send them to school." Many of the San Pedro programs use a locally produced book titled *English for Dominican Baseball Players*. It explains phonetically such critically important instructions as "Du nat drap de bol" as well as terms like the verb *ejaculate*—something all boys everywhere are told to avoid before a game.

The young ballplayers, even those from San Pedro, sleep at the academy in bunk beds, eight boys to a room. The rooms are kept spotless, as though ready for military inspection, with shoes neatly lined up under the bunks.

The academies all have gyms with weights for bodybuilding and trainers to guide the boys. Gary Aguirre, trainer at the Braves' academy, said, "Many of these Dominicans, because of cultural background and nutrition, are undersized. I try to build them up." The teams were considering a variety of protein supplements, such as energy bars. Aguirre added, "They are sixteen and seventeen when they sign and they have a very high metabolism. They can burn 1,500 to 2,500 calories a day, sometimes more." They were fed three, four, and sometimes five times a day and encouraged to eat copiously. Most of it got burned off in exercise.

Typically, the Braves' academy in San Pedro had about forty-five to fifty young, signed prospects at a time. This included some from other Latin American countries, but as in most academies a few American boys were also sent there to get some additional practice.

It all unfolded rhythmically. The big signing was July 2. Dominican Summer League ran through mid-September, then Instructional League began in October and ran until December 12, when players were either sent to farm teams in the U.S. or released and sent home. In the Braves' camp, out of the forty-five or fifty prospects, about thirty-five would move on to the U.S.

The program was designed to teach players by providing games for them to play. José Martínez, a Cuban who played and coached for the major leagues, now worked as special assistant to the Braves' general manager. "You have to play these kids until you have them figured out," he said.

Sometimes one organization would sign so many players that they needed to create two teams. In 2006, the Braves had two Summer League, teams. José Tartabull, the manager of their instructional league, said it was "for kids who need more swings or have issues of development to work on." Tartabull, a Cuban who played in the major leagues in the 1960s, was famous in Boston for throwing out Chicago White Sox center fielder Ken Berry at home plate, saving the 1967 American League pennant for the Red Sox.

Tartabull believed that Latino players had a much easier time in the major leagues than they did in his day because the academy system slowly integrated them into baseball as they came up: "Everyone thought you were trying to get their job. Today players help new guys. Back then they wouldn't talk to you."

They still don't always. No one at the end of a distinguished career enjoys seeing a kid of any nationality brought in to replace him. In a classic example, the Baltimore Orioles superstar shortstop Cal Ripken, Jr., was moved to third base so that the young Manny Alexander could try out at the shortstop position. Alexander later complained that Ripken would not talk to him. The older star, a huge, towering man, just stared at Manny with his ice-gray eyes.

But Dominicans were becoming more accepted. Things had changed a great deal in a few decades. Dominicans were getting to Rookie League ball in the U.S. speaking a little English and having been trained in the fundamentals of the game. Older players, like Rogelio Candalario, the son of a Consuelo sugar maker, remembered how they learned baseball with little instruction: "It wasn't like now. There was no organization. I trained myself. We used to watch American major-league ball on television and try to do what they did."

The Angels also had their academy in San Pedro, on the city's east side, in the rich ocher soil of the sugar fields that stretched to La Romana. Up the dirt road, in lush tropical growth that men hacked clear with machetes, was the fenced-off, spacious compound with two big diamonds and no guard, a striking change in a country where almost everything had an armed guard.

The facility was owned by the Universidad Central del Este in San Pedro. The Angels had been using it on and off since 1992 but full-time since 1998. This was an older, more threadbare facility than Baseball Towers, with a smaller dining room, one big room for bunk beds, worn tile floors, and no landscaping around the diamond—just a very serious baseball program. Rough-hewn and without the corporate feel of the Braves' academy, it had red paint peeling from the shutters, and no air-conditioning. But it was clean—again with an almost military sense of orderliness.

Major League Baseball, which regulates academy conditions, did not require frills like air-conditioning. Aaron Rodríguez, who inspected the academies for Major League Baseball, said he mainly made sure there were no dangerous conditions, such as holes in the outfields, and that the kitchens were clean and provided nutritious food.

The Angels had six scouts around the Dominican Republic. When they found someone they wanted to sign, they called Charlie Romero, a lean, fit black man from La Romana who was the Angels' program coordinator at the academy in San Pedro. Romero then traveled to where the prospect played and had a look before the player was signed. He usually signed between fifteen and twenty Dominicans in a year.

At the Angels' academy, baseball began at eight in the morning with organized ball games. Then they spent the afternoon working on fundamentals, such as fielding ground balls and baserunning. They were served three meals a day and two snacks. It was mostly Dominican food— rice, beans, chicken—but it was considered part of their education to slowly introduce a few American foods, such as hamburgers for lunch and pancakes for breakfast. Romero said, "Most of our kids go to the States, and when they come back—wow—they put on twenty pounds. It's the training and the nutrition."

English was taught five days a week at the Angels' academy, and twice a week the boys had to play entire games during which everything on the field had to be said in English. "We have to teach them English, and how to open a bank account, and baseball fundamentals," said Romero.

Some were quickly sent up to U.S. farm teams. Others were patiently developed there in the cane field, sometimes for four years.

"Some kids—as soon as you put them in the field you can spot them—haven't played twenty games in their life," said Julio García, Latin American field coordinator for the Cubs. He blamed this on *buscones*. "They find a kid with a good body and say, 'Do you want to be a Major League Baseball player?' They teach them throwing and hitting fundamentals and get them a tryout and take between twenty-five and thirty percent of the signing bonus. My job gets harder because they don't have playing experience."

This was the main point of the academy system: to give them experience playing games. But also they worked on developing specific skills, especially with pitchers. The Braves organization was the first to emphasize pitching, but now most of the franchises do. José Serra of the Cubs said, "Baseball is about pitching. The Braves decided that a long time ago." But the young pitchers at the Cubs' academy are seldom allowed to throw more than fifty pitches.

A young pitcher is easily destroyed, so they are not encouraged to do a lot of breaking balls, which can damage a young arm. José Martínez of the Braves said, "Most of the time, pitchers are asked to throw only fastballs. It builds up strength and doesn't strain ligaments like other pitches."

A third or more of the players signed by the Cubs are pitchers. Julio García, a big cigar-smoking Cuban of charm and insight—as long as he was kept off the subject of Cuban politics—said, "We sign pitchers because the arms down here are incredible. My boss came down and told me after watching training that it would take months to see that many arms in the States."

They have them throw mostly fastballs and changeups. A changeup is a hard pitch to master. It looks like a fastball but the speed is reduced. If the delivery is slow, the batter will see that it's a slow pitch and hit it far. The motion and speed of the arm must be identical to those when the pitcher throws a fastball. A fastball is held across the seams with a space between the ball and the palm, which causes the wrist to whip it faster on release. A changeup is the same throw but with the ball snug against the hand, which causes no wrist action on release and a backspin on the ball that slows it down. It used to be called a palm ball. If an academy can take a young pitcher with a hard fastball and teach him a truly deceptive changeup, he can be a dangerous pitcher. But it is not entirely enough. Garcia said, "We let them throw occasional breaking balls. They are hard on the arm, but it's a fine line, because you have to throw breaking balls to develop them."

Along the road to Consuelo was a compound with a guarded gate. Inside was one of the better-appointed academies. Started in 1991, San Pedro had the only Japanese camp in the Dominican Republic, the Hiroshima Carp Baseball Academy.

There were some clear disadvantages for a young Dominican in signing with a Japanese club. Asked what the Japanese signing bonuses were like, Yasushi Kake, assistant general manager, a husky, gray-haired Japanese man, said, "I can't tell you. It's a secret." Then he mischievously put his hand over his mouth and pretended to whisper, *"Muy barato"*—Very cheap—and he laughed.

There were some advantages to the Japanese system, money not being one of them. A top Japanese salary is $200,000—minuscule by the standards of the major leagues, but better than the American minor leagues— and when a player signed with a Japanese team, his chances of making it to the top were much better. There was only one level of minor-league ball between a signing and the major-league teams. And the Japanese released very few players once they were signed.

But there were tight controls on letting foreigners in. Each team was allowed only six foreigners, and there were only twelve teams. Typically, there were about twenty-five foreigners playing in Japanese baseball. It could be a route to American Major League Baseball. Alfonso Soriano at age seventeen, with no good offers from the Americans, signed with the Hiroshima Carp and played well. He might not have gotten to the major leagues had it not been for Gordon Blakely, a Yankees vice president, who learned that the pitcher Francisco Delacruz was going to be available from the Japanese. He went there to see him play but also noticed the Dominican shortstop.

This might have been a tantalizing story for other young Macorisanos thinking about the Japanese academy, except for the fact that, once the Yankees discovered him in Japan, Soriano found that it was extremely difficult to get out of his Japanese contract. In the end he had to officially resign from professional baseball to get out and become available to the Yankees.

The Japanese do not want to be another stepping-stone to the American major leagues. Kake said, "They leave us for the major leagues for the money, but more than that for the prestige. It's a big problem."

Nevertheless, the Japanese in search of Dominican talent signed an average of five or six players a year.

Charlie Romero was asked why so many ballplayers were produced in San Pedro. He smiled and then sighed. "I ask that question to myself all the time. They have even done studies on it. No one can come up with a real answer. It's like Brazil, where you always see the kids kicking a ball. Here the kids are always throwing something. Or catching, or hitting."

But the answer may lie in Romero's own story. He was raised in a *batey* not far from the Angels' academy, a village of a few hundred sugar workers who all worked for a mill owned by the American giant Gulf+Western. His father was a cane worker from Antigua. "I was poor," said Romero, "but I really enjoyed my childhood. I had a responsible father who made sure there was food on the table every day. Growing up in a *batey*, most kids work at an early age. When they are ten, after school and during school breaks boys work in the fields to make some money. They do cutting and planting. You have to plant them one at a time; a row was about here to the wall. [He pointed about 350 feet to the end of the outfield.] In the early 1980s they were paying twenty-five cents a row. Working in a sugar field is one of the worst jobs you can do. You just make enough money to survive; there is no saving and going to Hawaii on vacation. That's not going to happen. But we didn't know anything else."

Two things led him to a better life. He had a father who insisted that his four children finish high school; he did well and skipped a year and finished at age sixteen. And he took up track and field. A fast sprinter, he ran the hundred-yard dash and the quarter mile.

When Romero was seventeen years old, Epy Guerrero saw him run and asked if he wanted to play baseball. By the following September he was signed with the Blue Jays. He was trained in the fundamentals, although he remained essentially a one-tool player: a great base runner. While still in the minors he tore a ligament in his knee and never made it to the majors.

Romero reflected, "Most of the Dominican kids who have made it to the majors have come from the *bateys*. These kids really work. You don't want to go back where you came from, so you give a little extra."

CHAPTER TEN

Three Three-Brother Families

The Struggling Pitcher

Police in the Dominican Republic, like most other Dominicans, are poorly paid and are always hungry. They supplement their meager incomes by periodically stopping cars and in a soft, sweet voice asking for a tip or, sometimes, a fine, depending on which line they think the customer would be most moved by. Who could say no knowing the homicidal tendencies of the Dominican police force? And they were usually satisfied with a few pesos.

One afternoon in San Pedro, the police stopped a large, shiny black SUV—a Mitsubishi Montero. That was their mistake. They must have been out-of-town cops, because even though the windows were smoked glass and they could not see who was inside, everybody knew that in San Pedro a Montero was the car of choice of *peloteros*, especially former major leaguers. The driver lowered the window, and one of the policemen started his talk and a passenger said to him, "Don't you know who this is?"

The policeman stopped in confusion and the driver, a large, powerfully built man with a deep, soft voice, said, "I'm José Canó."

The policemen were still confused, and so the passenger helped them: "The father of Robinson Canó."

"Robinson Canó!" The two policemen nearly saluted and the conversation quickly turned, as it often did here, to baseball.

To be someone in the Dominican Republic, you didn't really have to be someone, you just have to have somebody in your family who is someone. One of the important advantages of being someone was that the police would leave you alone.

José Canó, with considerable talent and even more determination, had struggled mightily, and he had traveled a very long distance. But really it was his son, Robinson, who made him a someone. But that was something he had earned too.

Canó was from Boca del Soco, the mouth of the Soco River. Of the numerous rivers in San Pedro, the Soco is one of the few that are not tributaries of the Higuamo. Its mouth is on the other side of San Pedro. The river is a beautiful, wide, curving tropical river with blackish-brown water and banks overgrown with thick greenery. Unlike the Higuamo, there is little built on those jungle-thick banks: looking around the bend from the mouth suggests a Conradian journey to the heart of darkness. In reality, though, the Soco wanders down from the heart of sugar, the cane fields, and the cattle farms in the center of the island.

To cross the Soco and get to the little fishing village on the other side, Macorisanos had to cross a narrow two-lane metal bridge of the kind of minimal construction that the U.S. Army Corps of Engineers tossed off overnight.

Vendors lined up by the side of the road selling the small, black, white-fleshed fish caught in the brackish waters of the channels. What had become the big item along this roadside was crabs—very ugly land crabs with boxy black and gray bodies and protruding eyes. They sold them in strings of twelve.

Across the river was a series of sheds and ramshackle houses around a large square field, a cricket field. It was a *cocolo* neighborhood with a good number of Haitians as well. It had been a neighborhood of fishing and crabbing even before the *cocolos* and the Haitians arrived.

Andre Paredes, twenty-six years old, had been doing this since the year 2000, although he was at least the third generation in his family to catch crabs in Boca del Soco. Every year more people wanted crabs, which at first he thought would be good for business. But the result was that more and more hungry people came to Soco to dig crabs and sell them by the side of the road. Now there was more demand but fewer crabs. This was true of the fish in Soco also: more people wanted to buy them, so the prices went up, so more people fished until there were fewer fish to catch.

The crabs burrowed straight into the ground for about a foot and then turned at a sharp right angle. A crabber looked for a crab hole and then dug a second hole with a machete. If this was done right, the crab would now find itself in a tunnel with two exits. Sometimes the crabber could just reach down the hole and grab the animal. Or he could stick a hook down to grab it. If the crab ran, it would come out the other hole and the crabber could still get it. In the dry season there was one crab to a hole, but in the wet season three or four would be found in the same hole. There were several theories on why. One popular and implausible theory—Dominicans usually prefer the implausible—was that they huddled together in the rainy season because they were afraid of thunderstorms.

A good crabber used to catch five or six dozen in a day around the village of Soco. But then too many crabbers came and the crabbers had to hike for miles over rugged terrain into the mountains to find crabs.

The locals in Soco eat crabs, often in coconut. Cooking with coconut was a *cocolo* idea that had become typical of San Pedro. This was the recipe of Raquel Esteban Bastardo, who was married to José Canó's cousin. Squeezing the liquid out of coconuts is still common practice in San Pedro, although few Americans would have the patience.

Grate coconut and squeeze out the milk until it is completely liquid. Add garlic, big and small *ajies* (long chartreuse peppers that are not very hot), and ground oregano.

Mix the coconut milk with the seasoning and a little oil and vinegar. Wash the crab in clean water and take out the meat. Add it to the coconut milk mixture, add 3 spoonfuls of Maggi chili pepper sauce, and let boil 15 or 20 minutes, but be careful not to let the meat fall apart. (Nestlé makes a series of Maggi sauces that are very popular in Latin America, including the chili pepper sauce for this recipe.)

The Canós were fishermen, the only alternative to being crabbers in Soco. The fishermen lived in Boca del Soco, on the eastern side of the river. José's father would get him up at two every morning, and they would row their deep-welled, open-decked wooden boat out into the river. A man stood on either end of the boat, holding a net. They dragged a net while rowing, which demanded tremendous skill because the rowers had to maintain an even speed to keep the net extended behind the boat. At noon they would row in and sell whatever had turned up in the net. Some days the ten hours would not yield a single fish.

An exceptional day on such a boat might land one hundred pounds of fish, which today would earn them about $125, a fat paycheck in San Pedro. But that rarely happened. Half that much was more likely. There were fewer and fewer fish near shore. Most locals blamed this on too many fishermen. But in North America, studies of climate change show northern species moving toward the arctic, subtropical species moving toward temperate areas, and tropical species moving toward the subtropics. What will that leave in tropical waters? Today, to get a good catch, fishermen have to mount little fifteen-horsepower engines on their boats and go to sea to a fishing ground seven hours away. They stay there in the calm Caribbean Sea for five days to catch enough fish to make it worth the cost of gasoline and ice.

In good weather Soco seemed empty, a quiet town of women and children, because the men were all off fishing. It was a village of unpaved streets and small Caribbean wooden houses, some of which seemed to have been slapped together out of scraps. Other houses, such as one handsome little dwelling on a corner, freshly painted a bright blue, were constructed a little better. That was the house of Canó's mother, and as everyone in town knew, the Canós had money. But it wasn't always like that.

José remembered his father, a catcher, as a good ballplayer. But he never made it into professional baseball. Life would have been different if he had, because he was trying to support his fourteen children on fishing. Three of the fourteen tried to go into baseball. Charlie Canó was a shortstop who signed with the Dodgers but never made it past the minor leagues. Another brother, David, was never signed at all. Then there was José.

He started playing on the dirt streets of Soco when he was five years old. His was a typical San Pedro story. He and his teammates had socks for balls, sticks for bats, and no gloves at all, but socks are not very hard on the hands. There was no diamond. When a car came they had to stop the game, but in Soco that didn't happen often.

This was San Pedro and there were scouts everywhere, and one day a scout from Florida watched José playing shortstop and walked up to him and said, "How would you like to be a major-league ballplayer?" At that moment his life changed, although it did not all work out the way he had imagined.

He was signed to the Yankees at age eighteen, a little late, with a signing bonus of $2,000. Two years younger and he might have gotten twice as much. But the bonus was all right, because it was 1980 and ballplayers did not expect big bonuses; the important thing was that he had leaped the first hurdle to his major-league career. He had not yet gotten fed and trained in America: although he was tall, he weighed only 145 pounds. The scout had been impressed with his throwing arm and signed him as a pitcher, calculating that in the U.S. they could bulk him up to give him more power.

Soon José was in Bradenton, Florida, with $2,000 in his pocket, richer and farther from home than he had ever been. He went to a shopping mall and bought small presents for his parents and thirteen siblings, and his signing bonus was spent.

He could say three things in English: "Yes," "Thank you," and "I got it!" José remembered, "We would go to the restaurant and point at something on the menu, not knowing what it said and not liking it when we got it. We loved Big Macs and especially Whoppers with cheese. Man, we loved those Whoppers. But we would order Whoppers at McDonald's and Big Macs at Burger King. We could never get them straight. Then we learned how to call Domino's and order a pizza, but we only knew how to say one kind, 'pepperoni with double cheese.' So that is what we always got."

He did not get along with the manager of his farm team, a short Cuban who, according to José, "treated Dominicans like shit. He would grab me by the collar when I did something wrong and shout, 'Do you know what your're doing?' I complained to the scout who signed me."

After one month José was released. That was the end of it. His career was over at age eighteen, only weeks after it had started. "They never gave me a chance," he said. "I didn't know you could get released so quickly. I was crying. All they said was 'We are going to release you.' No explanation. They just give you a ticket home."

The day he was released, the team was playing an away game and the other players were on the bus. He had to get on the bus and say good-bye to his teammates. Some of them told him that this was not the end of his career, because he was young and had a good throwing arm. But José knew that organizations were wary of players who had been released.

Back in Soco his father said, "Don't worry. We are going to work." His father was a fisherman and knew what hard work was. The next morning he woke José at five, not particularly early by their fishing standards. They both got on his motor scooter and rode a few miles. Then José was told to get off and start running home. His father followed along on the bike. In this way, every day before breakfast José ran two miles or more in the dark, when it was still cool enough to run.

Being a catcher, José's father could work with his son on his pitches, which they did three days a week. Four months later he was signed by the Atlanta Braves, and at the age of nineteen he was pitching for a Single A team in Anderson, South Carolina.

Now he was an American-fed ballplayer, no longer a thin 145 pounds but a large, powerful man who stood six feet, three inches tall and threw hard, with a good breaking ball and a good changeup. For the next two years he pitched in the farm system, all the time enduring pain in his right throwing arm. No one would ever know how painful it was. Canó just endured it in silence: he was not going to complain about it and risk getting released again. He couldn't count on getting picked up a third time. Finally, when he could not endure the pain anymore, he told management and they sent him to a doctor. But the doctor could find nothing wrong and recommended three weeks' rest. They released him and he was back in the Dominican Republic.

He would not let his story end there. He played in the 1985 Dominican League for the La Romana Azucareros and his arm felt good all winter. He started to wonder why his arm hurt in America but never troubled him when he pitched at home. He pitched well and the Houston Astros offered him a contract, but there was no signing bonus: it was clear by then that he was a risky property. Canó had no objections; he just wanted to play and get his shot at the majors. He was getting older and it was now beyond a question of pay. He had to be able to come home a member of the club, a major-league ballplayer.

He pitched well in the 1987 season but still didn't tell anyone how uncomfortable his arm felt. He was sent to the Florida state league, where he won twenty-five games and lost three, a phenomenal record. He was throwing a fastball at 97 miles per hour. There was talk of him going to the big leagues. In 1988 he made it to the Houston Astros, a big leaguer at last. But it was discovered that he needed shoulder surgery, and so he didn't pitch that season.

Finally, on August 28, 1989, at the age of twenty-seven, José Canó pitched his first major-league game. This was his moment to show the world how good he was. Facing the Chicago Cubs, he pitched so well that they kept him in for the entire game, which he won. Complete games had become a rarity. Major-league teams have on their rosters batteries of middle relievers, setup men, and closers. A pitcher who gets to the seventh inning has done well. Nine innings is just too hard on a pitcher's arm, especially a power pitcher like Canó. But he did it. If he had been twenty-one instead of twenty-seven, it might have been the beginning of a promising career.

The next game he started in, he lost. He was used a few times as a reliever. He played in six games in all with a win-loss record of 1 and 1. And then his career was over. The following year he injured his back; the season after that management watched him in spring training and decided to release him.

Canó started playing for the Azucareros in the Winter League and with the Mexican League in the fall. He played for a few years in Taiwan. But he never got back to the U.S. He was careful with the money he earned in baseball. He bought a house and a building that he rented out for income.

José had four children, two sons and two daughters. The daughters he sent to college. But he had other plans for the boys. He named both sons after major leaguers: his first son after Jackie Robinson and his second after himself. From an early age he taught them baseball. José thought he was just being like every San Pedro father. "Every father looks at the big leagues and says, 'My son could be one of them,'" he said. "The kids play twenty-four hours a day. Kids here get up in the morning and they work, and if they have free time they play baseball; and if they watch television they don't watch cartoons, they watch baseball."

When Robinson was a small boy, José would take him to the park to play baseball and passersby would say, "Look at that kid! He's going to be a big leaguer." But Macorisanos are always on the lookout for the next big leaguer.

José wanted his oldest son to be a pitcher, but having seen how his father had struggled—the constant pain, the arm and shoulder packed in ice—Robinson just didn't want to do it. By the time he was sixteen, his father realized that he was a natural left-handed hitter—too good a hitter to be a pitcher. In the American League, pitchers don't even bat, but even in the National League, they are only in every fourth or fifth game; relief pitchers play only a few innings.

Robinson finished high school and, like his father, signed with the Yankees when he was eighteen years old. Twenty-one years later it was not the same game. Instead of $2,000 to spend in a shopping mall, Robinson signed for $150,000, which by then, though better than average, was not even considered a huge bonus. Bidding was not competitive. There was not a lot of interest in him because he did not run well.

He called his father at eleven at night to tell him he was signing and the size of the bonus. Robinson told him, "You don't need to worry about money. I'm going to have a lot of money. I'm going to be a big leaguer."

The family already had a house, so Robinson bought himself a car and saved the rest of the money. Not as tall as his father, he, too, was a skinny boy until he went to America and got built up, which put power behind his smooth swing. He played his first game in Yankee Stadium in 2005 and was immediately a batting star, hitting over .300. He was not a slugger who constantly hit home runs; however, he did hit more than sixty in his first three years (his father in his only season hit two, but that was respectable for a pitcher). Robinson was a consistent hitter getting on base, driving in runs. In 2008 he drove in the last run to be scored in historic Yankee Stadium before it was torn down.

His prediction about money came true: in 2008 alone he earned $3 million—considerably less money than a few of his teammates made, but a phenomenal mountain of wealth in San Pedro. He was likely to amass a fortune by the time his major-league career ended. But in some ways he remained a small-town kid from San Pedro, living quietly in Fort Lee, New Jersey, shunning the life of a Manhattan celebrity enjoyed by some of his teammates.

Robinson was an emotional player, given to batting slumps and slow-starting seasons. He probably would have felt very isolated in an earlier generation. Charlie Romero remembered, "The mail doesn't work here. When I was playing baseball, my parents didn't know how the season went until I came home in the fall. Your first year or so you are homesick. When you have a bad day, a bad game, you want to hear your mother's voice telling you it's okay. Now they have cell phones."

It was not his mother's voice that Robinson Canó heard after a bad game, and the voice was not always telling him it was okay. After one game Robinson called his father's cell phone.

"How'd you do?" José asked.

Robinson said, "One for four," or one hit in four at-bats.

"That's not good enough," José told his son. "If you can hit him once, you should be able to at least twice—maybe not four times, but at least twice. He's going to think that you won't expect the same thing, because you already hit it. So he will do it again to fool you." It is an advantage for a hitter to have a pitcher for a father.

José's other son, Joselito, was another skinny Dominican boy waiting to get American-fed. This time José was determined to produce a pitcher. Joselito showed early signs of a strong arm, mastering breaking balls when he was quite young. And he was left-handed.

But, like his brother, Joselito had watched his father suffer and did not want to be a pitcher. He was not yet fifteen years old when this lanky boy showed a gift for smooth-handed fielding, a powerful throwing arm, and the kind of flowing swing that can't be taught. Plus, he could bat from either side of the plate: he was a natural switch-hitter.

José had a number of business interests around San Pedro, including a little club, Club Las Caobas, named for an unpaved street next to the field where the Porvenir softball team played. It was a round, fenced-off, open-air dance space with a bar—a breezy place to go in the evening and play dominos and drink and dance. On the back wall, dominating the club, was a larger-than-life-size mural of Robinson Canó at bat in Tampa spring training.

José was also a *buscón*. He ran the José Canó Baseball Academy, which worked out every morning before school. From its founding in 1999 through 2008, the academy got twenty players signed. Canó spent $1,500 a month keeping his academy running in an old ball field in Barrio México near the Tetelo Vargas Stadium. Over the outfield wall, in the distance, the twin smokestacks of the Cristóbal Colón mill could be seen. He periodically went to New York to visit his son and pick up used balls and other discarded equipment from the Yankees.

José not only trained his players, he taught them. One of the things he told them was: "If you have five pesos to buy something, make sure it's food."

"Salami," suggested one of the young players.

"Salami is not food. Neither is cake," he said.

Among the most promising prospects at this academy was Joselito Canó, because of his talent as well as his good family background. Major League Baseball had come to like the idea of Dominican baseball families. It had started early and well with the Alou brothers. The Canós had become a San Pedro family that had made it—at last.

Three Chances at Shortstop

Along one side of Ingenio Porvenir was a swayback one-story neighborhood on an unpaved street. It was referred to as a *batey*, which it had once been, but it was no longer surrounded by cane fields, only housing. Still, it was where sugar workers who labored long hours inside the mill were housed, in order to be next to their workplace. Most of the residents were *cocolo* and still spoke a West Indian English–Spanglish.

The neighborhood was within walking distance of the sea, although it was a serious hike. There the locals set nets, which they called fish bags. They left them for a few days, then salted down their catch to make salt fish, a West Indian staple. In the fall the local *cocolos* raised pigs in the urban neighborhood to eat at Christmastime. They made a strong but smooth distilled corn alcohol and aged it by burying it in the ground, and for Christmas they made strong guavaberry.

"Everybody gets drunk for Christmas," declared a man known in the neighborhood as Ñato. His favorite recipe was a dish he called English steamed fish. (When *cocolos* used the term *English*, they meant the English-speaking Caribbean.) This was his recipe, in his own words:

> You take a fish, any fish, cover with salt for two hours with garlic inside. Mash onions and potatoes and put it in a pan with this much water boiling [he puts about a quarter-inch of water in a pot], cover it, let it boil, put in the fish, twenty seconds on one side, twenty seconds on other side *¡Ayi! ¡Bueno bueno!*

The best-known house in the *batey* was a turquoise-painted part-wood-and-part-concrete shack with a corrugated metal roof belonging to Ñato, whose real name was Felito James Guerrero. His mother was from San Pedro and his father from Antigua. Ñato's father had come to San Pedro to cut cane at the age of seventeen but managed to get a better job inside the mill as a mechanic; when he died in San Pedro, an elderly man, he had been back to visit his family in his native Antigua only once. It was a typical San Pedro *cocolo* story.

The dark three-room shack where Ñato lived smelled of liniment. A steady stream of teenage baseball players, one with a strained thigh, one hit by a ball on the elbow, lined up there. This was where coaches and managers sent players with physical problems. Sammy Sosa came to him when he was just starting. In 2008, while playing for the Estrellas Orientales, Robinson Canó came by with a problem.

Most of the people in the neighborhood worked for Porvenir half of the year and sold fruit on the street or did whatever else they could to earn money during the dead season. Ñato had seen baseball as his way out and struggled as a second baseman and a catcher. But no one signed him. As a boy a boxer had taught him to work on injuries and give massages, and he started doing that for boxers in the off-season. Then he started helping the *cocolo* cricket players of the neighborhood and even some basketball players. But it was inevitable that Ñato's business, being located in San Pedro, would mostly involve working with baseball players. In 2000 he stopped working for Porvenir to do his therapy full-time. He charged about ten dollars for a two-visit treatment.

Around the corner from Ñato's home, on a street whose pavement was so crumbly that it, too, would soon be unpaved—stood a small yellow concrete house with white wrought-iron gates. It was in the shadow of the tall smokestacks of Porvenir, and facing the sign thanking the president for the new *zafra*. The Corporáns lived there. There was no need for Alcadio to thank the president because—after working most of his life for Porvenir and reaching the level of supervisor—he no longer had the strength for a new *zafra* or anything else. A sinewy but frail man who seldom spoke, he stumbled around the house's cramped rooms with his heart condition: a warm, friendly man but exhausted, worked nearly to death at the sugar mill.

The house was a small rectangle with a corrugated metal roof, pleasant from the outside in its lemon yellow. The floor was a concrete slab painted with considerable artistry to resemble green marble. The rectangle was divided with Sheetrock into rooms and, like so many San Pedro homes, the doorways had curtains for doors. A television with powdery images was on most of the time. Alcadio glanced at it with no real interest. There was a stove, a refrigerator, a stereo, and running water some of the time.

In a tiny kitchen Alcadio's wife, Isabel de los Santos, made food for an enormous extended family with eight children, their spouses, and their children. A favorite, as in most Macorisano homes, was *pescado y domplin.* This was Isabel's recipe for fish and dumplings:

> Grate the coconut and squeeze out the milk. Put in a pan and season with garlic, *ajies*, onions, and celery. Put the pan over fire and, once the liquid is boiling, add the fish. After fifteen minutes, remove from heat.
>
> For the dumplings, gather the amount of flour you want to use. Add butter and salt. Little by little, add water until you get a compact dough. Put a pot of water to boil. Shape dough into little cylinders and put in boiling water. Leave for twenty minutes.

Three out of their four sons were shortstops with good arms, good hands, and considerable talent—three chances at salvation for the family. The first brother signed with the Oakland A's and progressed to their Single A team in Canada, which released him. The second signed with the Diamondbacks and was released from their Single A team also. Neither one ever came home again. As José Canó observed, "They give you a plane ticket home and that's it. Some Dominicans go to the airport and change the ticket for New York. Every Dominican has someone in New York."

Isabel spoke of her sons in dry-eyed anguish: "I haven't seen one of my sons in six years. The other I haven't seen in five months. They can't work. They are illegal but they stay. They say here there are no opportunities."

"No opportunities," Alcadio confirmed emphatically.

It was a painful reality for Dominican ballplaying families. The major-league infielder Fernando Tatis grew up in Miramar without his father, who had the same name. The father had signed with Houston when the son was too young to remember. He was released from Triple A but never came home; the son first saw his father in 1997 when he signed with the

Texas Rangers and went to the United States. His father came to a game and introduced himself.

The Corporán family had one shortstop left to save them: Manuel. In 1989 the Baltimore Orioles signed him, along with Manny Alexander. They each got a $2,500 signing bonus, but while Alexander bought his bed, Manuel bought the expensive medicine his father needed, and used what was left over to buy food for the family. "I love my parents," he said. "They gave me the best they could."

For two years Manuel played shortstop for the Orioles in the Dominican Republic; then, without warning, he was released. "I don't know what happened," he said, his eyes almost tearing, fifteen years later. It was over. He never even made it off the island. "I had a dream," he said. "I would play baseball in the major leagues and earn money for my family. They are poor people. My father can't work. My mother has no work and I was going to buy them medicine and everything they needed."

Manny Alexander was sent up and had a major-league career. He never became a superstar, but he could return to San Pedro an ex–major leaguer and a man of affluence. Manuel, on the other hand, cleaned machines at Porvenir for twenty pesos an hour, which was less than a dollar. Seeing the hopelessness of that, he worked for five years in the free zone as a quality-control inspector of blue jeans. He had gotten married and had two children to support, so he worked extra hours, but he could earn only about 900 pesos, which, as the peso declined against the dollar, ended up being around $30 a month. "I wasted five years of my life in that place," he said.

He started working as a coach for José Canó, training teenage prospects for a share of their signing bonuses. He worked with them every morning and seemed to enjoy the work. But the brother who didn't play baseball and worked as a mechanic seemed to be better off than the shortstops. One of their sisters managed to put her son through the local medical school. So there was hope.

"I'm still here," said Manuel, still lean because he never got American-fed, but tall and fit. "I'm still alive. I have a life. And I have two sons who are going to be big." His son Alexis, still small at thirteen—he hadn't had his teenage growth spurt yet—already had a good swing and was developing his hands in the family trade: playing shortstop.

"Are you going to be a pro?" he was asked.

"Yes," he said matter-of-factly. Manuel and the entire family were hoping, but they knew that this was a dream that could vanish without warning in an instant. Manuel had come to see life differently. "They say a man who has no money is nothing, but I don't believe that. If you are a good person and you work hard, you are not nothing."

The Education of a Center Fielder

The highway east from Porvenir that goes out to the cane fields of La Romana is intersected by dirt roads. This is suburban sprawl Dominican style: a maze of uncharted, unpaved roads on which new houses—small concrete blocks with sheets of corrugated metal for roofs—have been built, painted turquoise or sky blue, with shrubs and gardens around them. An American might look at such a neighborhood of small blocks with tin roofs off dirt streets that turn muddy when it rains and think this is a slum. But in the Dominican Republic, a land that lacks a middle class, this is considered a middle-class neighborhood.

In one such neighborhood, Barrio Buenos Aires, there was a typical house, a bit better maintained than some of the neighbors', with a motor scooter and a shiny SUV parked safely out front behind a steel gate on which the Cleveland Indians logo was carefully hand-painted. Both the SUV and the logo said that Major League Baseball had come to this home. This was the home of the Abreus.

Enrique was a construction worker. When he finished a project, he had to find another, and often there were weeks of unemployment in between. Senovia was the principal of a *colegio*, a private institution that offered grade school through high school. Despite the late-model SUV and large stereo equipment, theirs was a modest home with small rooms and a corrugated metal roof.

In 2007 their oldest son, Abner, a shortstop, signed with the Cleveland Indians for $350,000—more than an average bonus. The size of the bonus was important not only for the money but as a reflection of the organization's commitment. A $350,000 signing bonus indicated that the Indians were excited about this young shortstop.

But the Abreu home, aside from the logo on the gate and the things they had bought, was not about baseball: it was about education. Their little windowless living room, cooled, when the electricity was working, by wall-mounted fans, proudly displayed pictures of their sons in caps and gowns for various graduations, rather than suited up for baseball. A place of pride went to a plaque awarded to Abner for his honors performance. *In recognition of academic achievement,* it said. Abner was studying at the Universidad Central del Este but dropped out to sign.

Major League Baseball was finding out that Dominican parents were upset that their sons were giving up their educations for baseball contracts. This was partly because the families had come to understand that even though their sons had signed, they were not likely to have major-league careers. Charlie Romero said, "Baseball is such a big thing here. A lot of kids don't care about school if they can get signed. But their parents come here and say, 'He doesn't want to go to school anymore. He just wants to play baseball.'"

The Tampa Bay Rays started putting a clause in their contract stating that if a Dominican player was released, they would pay for his education through college. They could not afford the signing bonuses of the Red Sox and the Yankees, so this was a relatively low-cost way of making signing with them more attractive.

Enrique's father was a chicken farmer who dispensed medical assistance in rural areas. Senovia's father worked in the cane fields. Enrique and Senovia had bettered their lives and hoped their three sons would do the same.

But the sons loved baseball.

Enrique claimed that he was a good player, although he never signed anywhere. He played every position. "In my day you played everywhere," he remarked.

The sons caught it from the father. They started playing at the age of six. Enrique said, "For them baseball is like food. They live baseball. We love baseball. We also know it can give a better life. But we also love it. It's our life."

But this was not their plan. "We thought our children would be doctors or engineers," Enrique explained. "But they always wanted baseball." He gave a smile of resignation, but Senovia looked worried. She was sorry that Abner had dropped out of school but shrugged: "It is his big dream." She said she hoped he could still study. Enrique quickly added that while Abner was in Summer League in Boca Chica, he went every afternoon to Santo Domingo to study English. But this course was a required part of the Indians' academy program.

Meanwhile they were watching the launching of their next son, Esdra, also a star student. He began playing at the age of five in the Escuela de Béisbol Menor de Santa Fe. No rolled socks or stick bats at the baseball school in Santa Fe. They started small boys off with real baseballs and bats and gloves, even uniforms. The school ran through age eighteen. Despite what Enrique and Senovia said about education, they would not have started Esdra at this school if they had not wanted him to be a baseball player. The school was run by Herman Martínez, who grew up behind the center-field wall of Tetelo Vargas Stadium and played in the minors for the Baltimore organization. Asked what the goal of the school was, Martínez replied without hesitation, "To get kids signed to Double A teams."

He said of Esdra, "As soon as his parents told him to play, all he wanted to do was play baseball." Martínez, who was a scout at various times for the Mets, the Detroit Tigers, the Cleveland Indians, the Montreal Expos, and the Atlanta Braves, regarded Esdra as his best prospect. "He comes from a good family, well-educated people," he said. Only then did Martínez mention the strength of Esdra's throwing arm.

Lean but over six feet tall, with long arms for throwing and long legs for running, Esdra played center field with a strong right arm and was a good hitter—although, like many fifteen-year-olds, impatience often caused him to strike out.

Once Esdra was fifteen he was moved to a more advanced program, where he held his own against sixteen- and seventeen-year-olds. The program was called RBI, for Riviviendo el Béisbol en el Interior de Ciudades, Revitalizing Baseball in Inner Cities, a program devised in South Central Los Angeles in 1989 but sponsored in San Pedro by CEMEX. Having, on average, gotten two players signed a year since 2005, it was considered one of the best programs. Their practice field was the Tetelo Vargas Stadium.

The head coach was the tough and fit Rogelio Candalario, whose pitching career ended in Double A with a broken arm. Their pitching coach had coached Pedro Martínez when he pitched for the Dodgers.

Increasingly in this and other programs, when teams rated players, they did it with money: rather than talking about the great arm, the fast and smart baserunning, the beautiful and natural swing of the bat, they talked of the signing bonus. To say a player received a $300,000 bonus was a way of saying he was a good player. Increasingly in San Pedro, a great ballplayer was one who signed for a lot of money. By extension, some would say of Esdra, "His brother signed for $350,000," as though to say, "He has a good bonus in his genes."

By the spring of 2008 a number of scouts were watching Esdra. He was going to qualify for July 2 bidding and it seemed certain that there would be a number of bidders. The date of July 2 only had to be mentioned and blood would rush to shy young Esdra's face. Dany Santana was interested, but he scouted for Tampa Bay, a club that was famous for spending its money carefully. That year they were to make it into the World Series with their low-budget team. He said of Esdra, "He is fast but not as good as his brother Abner. He doesn't practice enough. He only practices three days, because he is always going to school. It's this July 2 he will be signing, but maybe not with us, because I think he may cost more than he's worth."

Santana was right. The highly organized system was driving up prices. On July 2 the Texas Rangers signed Esdra for $550,000. The Abreus, having already taken in $900,000 in signing bonuses, were on their way. But they still had one more card to play: their youngest son, Gabriel. Gabriel was a little beefier than his brothers—beefier than most Dominicans. Before he was even a teenager he had learned English, to be ready for playing in America. The young Macorisanos knew a great deal about what was needed to make it to the majors. It was a different world than just a few decades earlier when Rogelio Candalario signed with the Astros in 1986 without learning a word of English. "When the manager said something, I would watch the first person who did something and try to guess what the manager had said." But they weren't getting half-million-dollar signing bonuses in those days, either.

CHAPTER ELEVEN

The Curse of the Eastern Stars

I t was January 2008. Going down the homestretch of the season, the Estrellas had won seven of their last nine games and were firmly in first place. But the other teams were not worried. Nor were Estrellas fans excited. This was San Pedro's Estrellas Orientales, the Elephants, a team that had won only three championships in almost one hundred years—the last one in 1968, when they beat Santo Domingo's Escogido.

They needed only three more wins to clinch the playoff. But, to no one's surprise, they lost six games in a row. Now it was the final elimination match and it was on the home field, Tetelo Vargas Stadium. They had to win now or their season was over.

José Mercedes, a starting pitcher for Licey, said, "Don't feel sorry for them. They do this every year."

And in fact no one was giving them any sympathy. Tetelo Vargas Stadium was half empty. Many of those who were there were rooting for Santiago's Águilas Cibaeñas. Alfredo Griffin had been general manager of the Estrellas for the past three years. He was still a fit shortstop, a calm, soft-spoken man with few pretensions for a multimillionaire in a small town. His one indulgence was the very bright gold-and-diamond bracelet on his wrist. During his major-league career he had returned every winter to play for the Estrellas, and now as a major-league coach he came home to manage. "I wanted to manage because they are my team," he said. "I want them to win."

Not all Macorisanos have this home team loyalty. They know baseball and they like winning teams, so many root for either Licey or the Águilas. Usually Licey or the Águilas win. The rest of the time it is Escogido. The La Romana team, Azucareros del Este, the Eastern Sugar Makers, have won only once: in 1995, when it was managed by Art Howe, an ex-infielder who had managed three major-league teams.

Macorisanos believed in winning, and if the Estrellas were not winning it was their own fault. Julio García, the Cubs' academy pitching coach, complained, "Everybody here is a manager. They all consider themselves baseball experts." Not that it was any different in his native Cuba, where a spot is reserved in Havana's Parque Central for angrily tearing apart the mismanagement of yesterday's games. The spot is called the *esquina caliente*, the hot corner. There is no such spot officially reserved in San Pedro's Parque Central, but that doesn't stop Macorisanos from having a lot to say.

Dominicans are great fatalists, believing that the future is sealed supernaturally and beyond anyone's control. They talk a lot about the role of curses, what is called in the Dominican Republic a *fukú*. Americans are different, but American baseball fans understand. Everyone on the North Side of Chicago knows that the Cubs are cursed. That particular curse, the curse of the billy goat, stemming from the ejection of a smelly goat from Wrigley Field during the 1945 World Series, even sounds like a Dominican *fukú*. New Englanders knew well the curse of the Bambino that kept the Red Sox from winning a World Series for eighty-six years. And when it was revealed that a shirt of Red Sox slugger David Ortiz—it would have to be a Dominican player to make a good curse—was buried in the concrete of the new Yankee Stadium to curse them, the Yankees management took it seriously enough to pay thousands of dollars to weekend overtime workers to find it and dig it up.

Dominicans see curses at work everywhere. Trujillo used curses. Everyone dabbles in the supernatural. But not in baseball. The reverse of Americans, Dominicans see fatalistic, supernatural forces in life but only science in baseball. If the Estrellas kept losing, there was something wrong with management. Dominicans would not cling to their Indians, or Red Sox, or Cubs, and complain of Bambinos and goats. They just moved on to a team that knew how to win.

Bonny Castillo played twelve years for the Estrellas. "We find any way we can to lose," he said. "In 1985 we were in the finals, beating Escogido 3 to 1. We lost the next three games. In 1982 we led the league in runs and batting. The team batting average was .305. We beat the Águilas and made the finals." Then they went home to San Pedro to celebrate. The team's two best starting pitchers were riding together, and on the bridge over the Higuama, entering San Pedro, they pulled out to pass a bus and hit an oncoming car. Both pitchers were through for the season.

Griffin, who had been having notable success with the Angels in California, was expected to turn things around in San Pedro. And he hadn't. Griffin knew he was a disappointment. "The fans think that because I'm involved, we are going to win for sure," he said.

The problem with the modern Dominican League was not that different from the problem in the great showdown of 1937. Then it was a question of who had the money to bring in the most Negro Leaguers and Cubans. In the modern Dominican League it was a question of who had enough money to bring in the most major leaguers. And the answer was clearly Licey, a team that tried to have fifteen or more major-league players on their roster.

José Mercedes, with his roots in San Pedro, explained why he liked pitching for Licey. "Licey pays more and they treat the players well," he said. "They treat you as family. I always heard this, but this was my first season and it's true. They clinched the playoffs and they sent me a bottle of champagne."

Major League Baseball is not a stranger to such inequality. There are tremendous differences in what organizations can afford. In 2008 the highest-paid player was Alex Rodriguez for the New York Yankees. His $28 million salary was more money than the entire roster, disabled list included, of his hometown team, the Florida Marlins. But the Marlins had won two World Series, as have other low-budget teams. The consistency with which the money teams, Licey and Águilas, won the championship was difficult to ignore.

At the start of the new century the Dominican League began addressing this inequality. A draft, similar to the major-league draft, was initiated in which the losing team had the first pick of available players. Griffin was among the many who thought that this would even out the results. But in the first six years of the draft, either Águilas or Licey won every year.

It was growing harder to get major-league players. The major-league clubs did not like their multimillion-dollar properties risking injury in the Dominican Republic in the off-season. It had happened too many times. Everyone remembered 1971 when Rico Carty, at the height of his skills, was out for a year from an injury playing for Escogido. The clubs started limiting the participation of their players. "When I was in the majors," Bonny Castillo complained, "they let us play. They're probably protecting their money." Attitudes change when a few million dollars have been invested in the player.

Griffin claimed that the reason the Estrellas went on a losing streak at the end of the season was that they had lost their best players, including two San Pedro natives, Daniel Cabrera and Robinson Canó. Griffin had to use Cabrera judiciously because the Orioles would only allow him to pitch five games for the Estrellas. Now, at the end of the season, his five games were used up. Canó, one of the Estrellas' most reliable hitters, could no longer play because the Yankees had allowed him to play in only ten games.

To Macorisanos this was not an acceptable explanation for their six-game slide at the critical end of the season. "It's just an excuse," said José Canó. "One player doesn't decide a team." And it was true that there were numerous other major-league players on the Estrellas, including Fernando Tatis. Griffin, it was felt, had not done what he had to do to win, although there was some disagreement around town about just what that would have been. The general feeling was that he had failed to assemble a good enough team.

Dominican League teams wanted the major leaguers not only because they wanted to win games but also because they wanted to earn money and these were the players who drew the crowds, especially when they played in their hometowns. Another reason why the crowd did not turn out in Tetelo Vargas Stadium for the critical game was that neither Cabrera nor Canó was playing.

Although the pay was low by Major League Baseball standards, star quality was important. When Griffin was a player, the Estrellas wouldn't use him regularly until he won Rookie of the Year. Julio Guerrero, the very tall, lean, broad-shouldered pitcher from Porvenir, in his best year made Triple A for the Pirates for three weeks. That was enough to get him a salary of 40,000 pesos a month from the Estrellas the following winter. But when he dropped down from Triple A, the Estrellas paid him less. A top salary for a major leaguer was only about 300,000 pesos—about $10,000.

Mercedes said, "When I was playing in the major leagues, I didn't even think about the money here. But any kind of baseball—you have to love baseball to play it."

"But I'll tell you something," said Bonny Castillo in spring 2008. "Young players improve when they play winter baseball. Ervin Santana is having a better year for the Angels this year because he pitched for Licey last winter. He threw thirty innings. Young players need added experience."

Young major-league players, not all of them Dominican, came down to the Dominican Republic to play winter baseball and improve their game.

In the Dominican Republic, time is an approximation. So even though the baseball games started late, many fans did not get there for the first inning. The poor were more punctual. The cheap seats, benches along right and left field, were filled at game time, but the better center seats, which could be as high as $6 or $7, only filled gradually during the course of the early innings.

The worst seats in Tetelo Vargas were in the press box. It was an enclosed room with a long window with rumbling air-conditioning. Being sealed off in air-conditioning gave the press a sense of superiority, and they sat in there drinking rum and beer and arguing about Middle Eastern terrorism. It was hard to concentrate on the game from the press room because, unable to hear the pop of the bat or the snap of the pitch hitting the mitt or the screams of the crowd, the people in the press box were not involved.

Noise was part of Dominican baseball, as with most things Dominican. Estrellas fans were equipped with incredibly loud green noisemakers. Vendors sold them. Estrellas fans wore green. The women wore it in such tight clothes that they appeared to have green skin. The women were dressed in their most spectacular and revealing outfits because the games were televised and in between plays the cameramen liked to zoom in on women who caught their eye. If you were done up right, you could get on television. That, too, was Dominican sports. The sports pages in the newspapers always featured cheesecake photos of women, with no further explanation offered.

When the Estrellas scored, the sound system trumpeted jungle-stirring elephant noise. Someone in an Estrellas uniform with an elephant head was on the field dancing merengue at propitious moments. Vendors sold homemade confections of wrenching sweetness. Between innings there were cheerleaders in skintight white and green with suggestive hip movements and a lot of skin showing in many different shades.

The Estrellas would have to win this game or be eliminated. Then they had to win the next game to come to a tie and force yet another game, which they would also have to win to be in the playoff. There was no room for mistakes now. Any loss in the next three games and Las Estrellas would once again go down in defeat.

As the Águilas came onto the field, old friends among them came over to Griffin and they hugged. Given the situation, Griffin seemed remarkably calm. He explained, "There is so much pressure in playing a game seven of a World Series that, once you've done that, you never feel pressure anymore." Griffin was on three World Series–winning teams.

Griffin started right-hander Kenny Ray, mainly a relief pitcher, who had played with Kansas City but in recent years was struggling with injuries to his arm. The Águilas started with Bartolo Colón, a hometown hero in their Cibao region who started for Griffin's own Angels, for whom he had won pitching's highest honor, the Cy Young Award, in 2005. Despite this seemingly unequal match, Ray pitched well, and with some good hitting the Estrellas had a 4-to-3 lead in the middle of the game. Elephant sounds were heard. Then the Águilas scored four runs. But to the trumpeting of plastic horns, the Estrellas came back with two more runs. The Estrellas had their last chance in the eighth inning, when they were down by only one run, 7 to 6. They loaded the bases with only one out. Then they did a typical Estrellas maneuver: they hit into an inning-ending double play. Another disappointing year for the Estrellas Orientales.

CHAPTER TWELVE

San Pedro's Black Eye

When George Bell was a teenager playing in Santa Fe, he fell while avoiding a flying bat and hit his right eye on the corner of a bench. The discoloration under his right eye never went away, and so Bell always looked as though he had just been in a fight and gotten a black eye. When he was a player, the press constantly asked him about his black eye. This was in part the image of a Dominican player—a brawler—but it was also who George Bell was. Once when he was playing for the Blue Jays in Toronto's Sky Dome, he delivered an unmistakable gesture with his middle finger to some 50,000 booing fans. Bell was booed a lot, and he always said that it was bigotry directed against him because he was a Dominican. But some of the fans said that it was because he was a bad outfielder. He often failed at critical plays and was booed for that. Eventually, over his angry protests, he was taken out of the field and made a designated hitter who only stepped in to bat for the pitcher. Batting was what made him valuable.

Boston Globe columnist Dan Shaughnessy once wrote, "Baseball fans hear the name 'George Bell' and they think of tantrums, bumps with umpires, confrontations with pitchers and public pouts." He went on to say that Bell would "never get the recognition he deserves as long as he wears the badge of the Loco Latin." The "Loco Latin" badge has kept many Dominicans from getting their due, but Bell was particularly insensitive to this problem. Bell played baseball as a contact sport. Not only was he known for running over catchers and even basemen—an accepted practice to make them drop the ball—but he was also notorious for "charging the mound." If he was hit by a pitch, he ran up to the pitcher's mound and threw a punch at the pitcher. At least once he tried out the karate kick he had learned in karate school back in San Pedro. In his autobiography, *Hard Ball*, published in 1990 when he was still a player, he attempted to explain this behavior:

> Some games the fans get angry because they can't understand the way I act, but part of my game, along with hitting homers and driving in runs, is fighting back. If I hit a home run with two men on and the next time up the same pitcher knocks me down, I'm going to get up and charge the mound. I don't care whether it's a home game and the place is sold out, or we're in Cleveland and no one is watching, or the game is the TV Game of the Week. If a pitcher tries to intimidate me, I'm going to go out there to kick his ass. That's the way I grew up playing the game.

Eighteen years later, in a 2008 interview in La Romana, Bell—now a middle-aged man—hadn't softened in the least. "Every time I got hit I would kick their butt," he stated.

You mean literally?

"Fuck yes. They are trying to intimidate you."

Bell felt justified because he believed, as Pedro González had before him, that pitchers were hitting him intentionally because he was a Dominican. He would hear angry fans shouting pejorative comments about Dominicans. He always remembered a restaurant in Milwaukee in 1989 that refused to serve him and two other Dominican players.

"I understand," Bell said. "You don't like to get beaten by a foreigner, and I was a good hitter and I was black. It's all part of the mix."

But what was disturbing to other Macorisano players was Bell's claim that charging the mound was something he learned in San Pedro—that it was the San Pedro way of playing baseball. A later generation of San Pedro players developed a sense that baseball had become something extremely valuable that they had to handle with considerable care.

Fernando Tatis, asked about Bell's assertion that his aggressiveness was the San Pedro way, said, "Some people play like that and some people don't. I don't. I think you have to respect the game. It is what is going to give me and my family a better life."

The better *buscón* programs emphasized that such antics are unprofessional and not good for them or for baseball.

George Bell was not the only San Pedro player with the Latin-hothead reputation. Pitcher Balvino Galvez, born on a *batey*, would have been infamous had his career lasted longer. He threw a hard fastball, often while sticking out his tongue. His control of the pitch was flawless, but the pitches started drifting when he had the pressure of runners on the bases. He pitched only one season in the majors, 1986 for the Dodgers. He then had a career in Japan, where he was known for his tantrums, more than once expressing his anger at an umpire's call by throwing the ball at him. Galvez almost made it back to the majors in 2001, when he was slated to join the starting rotation of the Pirates. But at spring training he got into an argument with the pitching coach, Spin Williams. Galvez threw down his glove, stomped into the clubhouse, and without saying a word packed up and flew back to the Dominican Republic. He was immediately released, never again to play.

Joaquín Andújar was infamous for his erratic behavior. He once removed himself from the mound, complaining that his crotch itched, and after one game went badly he demolished a toilet with a baseball bat. In 1985 he took off after an umpire in a World Series, had to be restrained by his teammates, and started the following year suspended for ten days.

Then there was a drug scandal that might explain the erratic behavior. In between the Chicago World Series fixing scandal of 1919 and the steroid scandal of the twenty-first century, the biggest scandal to shake baseball was the 1986 investigation into widespread amphetamine and cocaine use among important major-league players. During the investigation Andújar confessed to using cocaine.

Even in retirement back in San Pedro, Andújar maintained his reputation. Alfredo Griffin kindly said that it was just that "Joaquín has too much blood." When Griffin was building his new house next to Andújar's in 1986, the pitcher dropped in, had a tirade about the carpet being too dark, shook everyone's hand, and left. Even people in San Pedro thought he was a little crazy. Bell once said, "A lot of North Americans, some Dominicans as well, say that Joaquín is *muy malo*, a bad guy. But I know he's honest." Nor did Andújar have any objection to Bell's public persona. Andújar repeatedly described himself to the American press as "one tough Dominican" and was fond of characterizing himself as "born to be macho," which to American readers seemed more true than interesting.

Juan Marichal remained the only Dominican inducted into the Hall of Fame, although several good prospects waited in the wings. To be elected, a player must be retired for five years. Entry is voted on by only the members of the Baseball Writers' Association of America who are currently working and have been active writers for at least ten years. To be inducted into the Hall of Fame, at least seventy-five percent of the members have to vote favorably. The number of voters varies, but in 2009, for example, this meant receiving a minimum of 405 votes. Few players are assured entry. Babe Ruth and Ty Cobb easily made it their first voting year with over ninety-five percent. But Cy Young barely made it with seventy-five percent. Lou Gehrig, Joe DiMaggio, and Hank Greenberg were all turned down the first time they came up for a vote. So it is difficult to predict this process, but the most likely Hall of Famer from San Pedro, according to his records, would be Sammy Sosa.

And yet if Macorisanos were asked who was the best ballplayer they ever produced, it is unlikely many would say Sosa. They would probably say Tetelo Vargas. Sosa was not a five-tool player. Early in his career, when he was stealing twenty-five bases each season, he was a three-tool player, but mostly he was an extraordinary hitter who in 2007 became only the fifth player ever to hit more than six hundred home runs. He also drove in more than 140 runs year after year. He was the leading home-run hitter in baseball in two different years, he had the most home runs in a four-year period in history, he was the only batter to hit sixty or more home runs for three consecutive seasons, and he was famous for the record-breaking season of 1998, when he beat the long-standing sixty-one home-run record of Roger Maris, the most celebrated record in baseball, by hitting sixty-six—only to be beaten by Mark McGwire, who hit seventy home runs.

Yet at the opening of the Winter League in San Pedro in 1999—at the height of his record-making career—when Sosa threw out the first ball, people booed. Then others cheered, but he was clearly booed first. The reason was that San Pedro had been devastated by a hurricane and Sosa had made a great show in the American press of hurricane relief, but Macorisanos were not believing it. The mayor at the time, Sergio Cedeño, said, "He asked for money to help the people of San Pedro de Macorís. That's what we are asking—where's the money?" In the U.S. also, Sosa's much-trumpeted charitable work was called into question. But for baseball fans, other questions were to arise. By 2004 the onetime Chicago superstar was being regularly booed in Wrigley Field, and his T-shirt was so unpopular in the Wrigleyville Sports store near the field that it had been marked down thirty percent.

In 2002 the steroid scandal was beginning to overtake baseball. Steroids were found in the locker of Sosa's home-run competitor, Mark McGwire. The other home-run king, Barry Bonds, denied using steroids but had tested positive several times.

That left one home-run champion, Sosa, for whom a grandstand was more than just where he sent the ball. With his customary bravado he took to saying that if baseball started testing for steroids, he wanted to be first in line. In an interview, *Sports Illustrated* columnist Rick Reilly asked him if he meant it, and he said emphatically yes.

Then Reilly asked, "Why wait?"

"What?" said Sosa.

Reilly, thinking that Sosa could clear the air and give a lift to baseball by proving that he, at least, had come by his home runs honestly, wrote down the telephone number and address of a diagnostic lab that could test him only thirty minutes from Wrigley Field, where he was playing for the Cubs.

Sosa became enraged, accused Reilly of trying to "get me in trouble," and stopped the interview, calling Reilly a "motherfucker." Reilly said that the lesson for sportswriters was to always ask the steroid question at the end of the interview.

The public and many sportswriters began suspecting Sosa of steroid use. Anabolic steroids are drugs related to testosterone, a male hormone. *Anabolic* comes from a Greek word meaning "to build up." The drugs were first developed in the 1930s and are used today to treat patients suffering from bone loss and to counteract deterioration in cancer and AIDS patients. But steroids can also be used to build up muscles, and consequently strength, in athletes. The risks are many, including increased cholesterol, high blood pressure, infertility, liver damage, and heart disease. Some studies indicate a physical altering of the structure of the heart and personality changes, including extreme aggression. Since the 1980s the possession of anabolic steroids without a prescription is a crime, in the United States. Not only were baseball players who used them committing a crime, but they were violating the rules of Major League Baseball. Like the Olympics committee, the National Football Association, and basketball, hockey, and most other sports organizations, Major League Baseball considered steroids to be an unfair trick to enhance performance and had banned their use. A baseball player who used steroids was considered a cheater.

Sosa, once a fan favorite for his ready smile and his maudlin talk of remembering the poor, had other problems. In 2003 he was at bat for the Cubs in the first inning against Tampa Bay, a notoriously ineffective pitching team that year. But Sosa, the home-run king, was having a bad year. It was June and he had hit only six home runs—none in the past thirty-three days. Sosa took a swing; the pitch shattered the bat and sent a ground ball to second base. The alert catcher, Toby Hall, gathered the broken pieces and showed them to the umpire, who promptly ejected Sosa from the game. The pieces revealed that the bat had a cork interior.

It is not clear if corked bats are an advantage. They make the bat lighter for a faster swing, but Robert K. Adair, a Yale professor who authored *The Physics of Baseball*, claimed that because cork is a softer substance, it may actually slow down the ball. But corked bats were used by hitters who believed they sent the ball farther, and Major League Baseball had banned their use. Players caught using them were officially cheating. Baseball rules state that a bat must be a solid piece of wood.

The following day, seventy-six bats were confiscated from Sosa in the Cubs locker room while a game was still going on; the bats were all X-rayed and found to be "clean." Sosa had claimed that his use of the corked bat the day before had just been a big mistake, that he had accidentally pulled out a bat that he used for home-run exhibitions. Major-league officials said they believed his story and cut his eight-day suspension to seven days. But the fans and the press felt Sammy Sosa had been caught cheating. *USA Today* sports columnist Jon Saraceno called Sosa's explanation a "highly implausible defense." *USA Today* conducted a poll in which sixty percent of respondents said they didn't believe Sosa and thought he had used the corked bat intentionally. The press wrote variations on the "Say it isn't so, Joe" line to "Shoeless" Joe Jackson after the 1919 World Series had been found to be fixed. The *New York Post*, with their traditional love of tabloid headlines, ran the story with "Say It Isn't Sosa," a line that was being used by Chicago fans. Jackson, by the way, got only two votes when his name was brought up in the Hall of Fame in 1936. Baseball writer Roger Kahn in the *Los Angeles Times* linked Sosa to Pete Rose, a player who has not been voted into the Hall of Fame because he was caught betting on baseball.

Things got worse for Sosa. In 2004 it became clear that the Cubs organization wanted to trade their onetime star, and the fans wanted them to also. The relationship reached a low point when they fined Sosa $87,400 for arriving late and leaving early for the last game of the season. Being late to work is one of those things that is not—not ever—supposed to happen in baseball, and sneaking out early is also unacceptable. Sosa tried to claim he left in the seventh inning, but the security videotape in the player parking lot showed that he had actually left in the first. His teammates were furious.

Fairly or unfairly, in both the U.S. and San Pedro in the last years of Sosa's career, a cloud of suspicion hung over the once smiling hero from Consuelo, and it remained there even after his 2007 retirement. In 2009 lawyers leaked to the press that Sosa had been shown positive for steroids in a 2003 test that Major League Baseball gave on condition that the results remained secret. Such a cloud can do a lot of damage to a player's reputation. It can keep a significant number of sportswriters from voting positively for a Hall of Fame candidate.

There is already a growing sentiment among some sportswriters, old-time players, and fans that it is not fair to compare modern players' records with old-time players' achievements, even without performance-enhancing drugs; steroid use further complicates the issue. How can a Roger Clemens be compared with Bob Feller, Juan Marichal, or Sandy Koufax, when Clemens pitched only six- or seven-inning games every four or five days and the earlier pitchers had to keep their arms in shape for complete games every three days? In 1965, Sandy Koufax pitched a complete game seven of the World Series on two days' rest, a feat that would be unimaginable to today's pitchers.

How do you compare the home runs hit in one season by McGwire or Sosa with those hit by Ruth or Greenberg, when the earlier hitters played 154-game seasons in which to make their records and modern hitters play 162 games?

Then, when it is added to the mix that Clemens and Sosa may have also used steroids, and that McGwire did, the old-time players, fans, and, most important, the sportswriters start to get angry.

Baseball had its share of scandals in the U.S., but in the Dominican Republic—where it dangled millions of dollars in front of underfed, impoverished teenagers and their desperate, often uneducated families— occasional incidents of corruption could not be surprising.

In 1999 there was the marriage scandal. Signed major-league prospects from the Dominican Republic were taking money from local women to say they were married so they would be eligible for U.S. visas. The only problem was that the U.S. consulate started noticing that suddenly a lot of young players, especially from San Pedro, were married. They uncovered the scam and denied visas to players who had been caught. One of the players who lost his visa this way was Manny Alexander, but he pleaded that he was just trying to help out his cousin, and the State Department gave him back his visa. Alexander had other problems. In 2000, while playing for the Red Sox, steroids and syringes were found in his car. When he played for the Yankees, he was accused of stealing items from Derek Jeter's locker and selling them to memorabilia dealers.

The signing prospect, an uneducated teenager from a small town, had a dizzying array of people swirling around him, mostly looking for part of his fat check. Players' agents signed them up even though it would be years before they needed an agent. Scouts and *buscones* were ready with ideas.

In May 2008 the White Sox fired their director of player personnel, David Wilder, and two Dominican scouts, Victor Mateo and Domingo Toribio, charging that they had conspired with *buscones* to pressure prospects into paying them a part of their signing bonuses. The White Sox turned the case over to Major League Baseball, which quickly turned it over to the FBI. Before any results of the investigation were made public, it became apparent that such corruption was not a uniquely White Sox problem. It was not clear exactly how they managed to get the prospects' money, but the scam was clearly based on how easily intimidated the desperately poor are. It could have all been stopped by the prospects or their families speaking up, but few wanted to make trouble because it could result in a release. It could not be done without the knowledge of the prospect, who is paid directly by Major League Baseball. Yet players were not coming forward to lodge complaints.

A scout could approach a *buscón* and tell him an amount that he could get his boy, and suggest he talk the family into taking less so he and the scout could share the extra. The *buscón*, often trusted and liked by the young prospect, went to the family and told them that he could get a larger bonus if he was willing to leave a cut for the scout. Or he might tell them that they had to pay a cut or there wouldn't be any deal. Desperate for the deal, the family usually did what they were told. No matter how big a bite they lost, they would be getting more money than they had ever seen, with the possibility of even greater paychecks in a few years.

Buscón Astin Jacobo said, "I've been around this sport all my life. Yes, there are some bad guys in baseball, but there are a lot more on top than on the bottom. Yes, sometimes a scout comes up to me with a deal, but I've got my father's name to protect and my son who is trying to be a ballplayer. But this is not the first time I've seen shit in baseball. Scouts came up to you, the old-timers, and they say, 'Listen, I like the kid, but he needs to be seventeen, not twenty. Here is five hundred pesos.' They used to do that a lot—not all the time, but a lot."

Because of the increased value of a younger player, false birth certificates were a common occurrence. In 2003, Alfonso Soriano told Yankees general manager Brian Cashman that he was not born on January 7, 1978, as stated when they signed him, but in 1976. Often false identity papers do not even have the correct name. Adriano Rosario from San Pedro, age nineteen, a hard-throwing right-handed pitcher who signed with the Arizona Diamondbacks in 2002 for a $400,000 bonus, was actually Ramón Antonio Peña Paulino, age twenty-two. Rafael Pérez, manager for Major League Baseball's Latin American office in Santo Domingo, was quoted as saying that they should have been more suspicious because everyone called Adriano "Tony." Rosario later claimed that he perpetrated the fraud under pressure from Rafael Mena, a well-known scout in San Pedro. As Astin said, it was often the scout who pushed for a changed age. Then the scout sometimes demanded part of the player's bonus to keep from exposing the fraud. It was not difficult to handle a frightened teenager trying to negotiate a life-changing deal.

False papers were not only lowering ages to make players more valuable but also raising ages to make players eligible. A boy named Adrián Beltré from Santo Domingo worked at the Dodgers' academy, where scout Ralph Avila and others spotted his remarkable speed and strong arm. In 1994 the Dodgers signed him with a $23,000 signing bonus—a good bonus for that time, considering that the Dodgers were not competing for him. In 1999, with Beltré now playing third base for the Dodgers, Major League Baseball—which was investigating illegal signings in the Dominican Republic—discovered that Beltré had been only fifteen years old when he signed. The Dodgers were fined $50,000 and banned from scouting, signing, or running an academy in the Dominican Republic for one year, although they did find loopholes to keep the academy open. Two months later, in February 2000, the Braves were fined $100,000 and banned from the Dominican Republic for six months for having signed shortstop Wilson Betemit when he had not yet turned fifteen. Pitcher Ricardo Aramboles was illegally signed by the Florida Marlins when he was still fourteen years old. After the 2001 attack on the World Trade Center in New York, visas came under closer scrutiny and more than three hundred cases of age fraud were found.

One of San Pedro's ugliest baseball scandals came in 1997, when a scout, Luis Rosa, who worked in San Pedro, was arrested not only for illegally taking cuts from players' bonuses but also for demanding sex from fifteen young prospects at the Giants' San Pedro training camp by Porvenir. The initial complaint was filed by a twenty-year-old right-handed pitcher, Yan Carlos Ravelo, who said, "Luis Rosa took advantage of our poverty and our desperation for an American visa to make us his slaves."

Luis Rosa was not a small-time scout. He had signed Ozzie Guillén, Roberto and Sandy Alomar, Juan González, Iván Rodríguez, and many other Dominican major leaguers. In a country where homosexuality was usually an unspoken taboo, this was a messy case written about in *The New York Times* and other foreign newspapers. While Rosa maintained his innocence, the case was a tremendous embarrassment involving some of the biggest names in Dominican baseball. Rosa had been working for the San Francisco Giants, a pioneering team in introducing Dominican players to Major League Baseball: Juan Marichal and the Alou brothers had starred for the Giants. Juan Marichal had to deal with the case because he was now the Dominican government's secretary of sports and recreation. Joaquín Andújar testified on behalf of the boys.

By 2008 the steroid scandal was full-blown and there seemed little escaping it—not in the Dominican Republic, not even in San Pedro de Macorís. What was most awkward for San Pedro and Dominican baseball in general was that one of the leading arguments that Sammy Sosa was a steroid user was the fact that he had been so small when he signed and then he became such a large burly man. This was true of so many Dominican players. Was it really a sign of steroid use?

"Everybody who comes to America to play this game in the minors is always skinny," Sosa argued. "When they get to the major leagues they start eating good and doing things better. If you eat better and work out better you are supposed to gain some weight." He said that he filled out when he got to Texas because he was eating so much better. "What'd he eat," quipped Rick Reilly, "Fort Worth?"

It was a disturbingly familiar story in San Pedro, and became even more embarrassing once it was revealed that Sosa really had built himself up with steroids.

In the Dominican Republic, steroids are sold cheaply and without prescription in most pharmacies. Also, in the Dominican Republic there are many talented young players whose chances of getting into the millionaire club are impeded by the slightness of their builds. Add the fact that most of these youths had an entire family counting on them, and this was a scenario for steroid abuse. In the year 2000, a *New York Times* reporter went into a dozen pharmacies—some in San Pedro and some in Santo Domingo—and found only two that were not willing to sell some version of testosterone without a prescription. This is not surprising, since there is very little effort to control the sale of pharmaceuticals in the Dominican Republic. In fact, investigations of steroid abuse in Major League Baseball have found that the drugs are often obtained in the Dominican Republic. Major-league players often talk among themselves about how those who go down to the Dominican Republic to play winter ball gain easy access to steroids. In 2009, when New York–born infielder Alex Rodriguez confessed to having used steroids, he said he obtained them from his cousin in the Dominican Republic. In San Pedro the most easily obtainable steroids are ones designed to be used by veterinarians on animals, usually horses.

Major League Baseball responded in 2004 by testing in the academies. That year eleven percent of the signed players in the Dominican academies tested positive. Clearly the practice was widespread. Talks on the serious health risks involved in using these drugs became a standard part of the curriculum in the academies. Also, prospects understood that they would be tested when they went to the academies and that steroid use would be exposed, putting their careers at risk. Test results after 2004 showed the practice steadily declining and leveling off in 2007 and 2008 to slightly more than three percent of signed players testing positive for steroid use.

Macorisanos and Dominicans have reason to worry. The American press eagerly picks up any whiff of such scandals, because in America the idea that there is something less than proper about all these foreign and wild "Latins" getting into baseball has considerable resonance. *Foreign* is generally not a positive adjective in the United States. In 1987 pitcher Kevin Gross got caught illegally creating an odd movement in his pitch by means of a sticky substance that he hid in his glove. Accused of slipping a foreign substance on the ball, he denied the charge by protesting, "Everything I used on it is from the good old U.S.A."

The fact that more and more players are not from the good old U.S.A. is not popular in America. This author wrote a cover story in *Parade* magazine in July 2007 about baseball in San Pedro de Macorís and the magazine received more than one hundred letters from readers. Most complained that there were too many foreigners, too many Latins, or too many Dominicans in baseball. Baseball, after all, was an American sport and the top players should be American. In the nineteenth century, the great American poet Walt Whitman, definer of things American, called baseball "America's game," said it had "the snap, go, fling of the American atmosphere," and even compared it in significance to the Constitution. While Major League Baseball is seeking to internationalize the game, many Americans want to keep it uniquely American.

Much of the criticism comes from African-Americans. It is undeniable that the number of black players has declined precipitously just as the number of Latino players, the majority of whom are Dominican, has risen. After Jackie Robinson, the number of African-American players steadily climbed until 1975, when it reached twenty-five percent: one in four major leaguers. By 2005, black Americans represented only 9.5 percent of major-league players. At the same time, almost one in three major leaguers was foreign born. That number seemed certain to rise. Dominicans alone made up about a quarter of all minor leaguers.

Not only fans but some African-American players have been outspoken about this, most notably the great hitter Gary Sheffield. Sheffield claimed that Major League Baseball was favoring Latin players because they could be acquired more cheaply and were easier to control. "Where I'm from, you can't control us," said Sheffield. "You might get a guy to do it that way for a while because he wants to benefit, but in the end, he is going to go back to being who he is. And that's a person that you're going to talk to with respect, you're going to talk to like a man."

That Latinos are easy to control would come as a revelation to anyone who had worked with George Bell or Joaquín Andújar. But it was true that Dominican ballplayers came to the U.S. with a terror of being released and shipped back to the cane fields. Ironically this was the exact same logic that had made the American sugar companies prefer imported *cocolos*, thinking that fear of being shipped back would make them easier to control than Dominican laborers. As for getting Latin players more cheaply, even Dominicans, including Sammy Sosa and Manny Alexander, publicly acknowleged—complained—that drafted American rookies got more money than Dominican prospects. That was certainly true of Sosa and Alexander. But top Dominican prospects in the twenty-first century were landing signing bonuses that strongly suggested that baseball's interest in Dominican players was not about getting them cheaply.

A careful study of the evidence suggests that Major League Baseball is looking abroad for talent because it is faced with declining interest in the

U.S. When asking what has happened to African-American baseball players, it should not be ignored that nearly eighty percent of players in the National Basketball Association are black, as are two-thirds of the players in the National Football League. Major League Baseball has made a considerable effort to attract African-Americans, but without much result. In black neighborhoods around America, baseball programs are closing down because of a lack of participation.

No one is certain why this is happening. It is sometimes suggested that it is because the route to a high-paying position is considerably faster for an NFL or NBA player than for a professional baseball player. Football and basketball do not have minor leagues. They bring their players up through college programs, and college stars seamlessly move to being high-paid professionals without putting in a few low-paying and humbling years in the minors.

But there is a broader problem. Americans in general are losing interest in baseball. The fans are getting older and older, and young people are dramatically less interested. Hundreds of Little League programs have closed.

Fred Cambria, a former pitcher for the Pittsburgh Pirates, who has coached major-league and college players and often runs clinics for urban boys wanting to develop baseball skills, said, "I see the Latino player being dominant for the upcoming years. They are great athletes, they work hard from an early age." He was not saying that African-Americans would not work hard but that they were poor people who found more economic incentive in other sports. "There's no scholarships for baseball players in colleges, so they go to the revenue sports—football and basketball," he explained. "You get a small amount of scholarship money and you have to divide it up, and a black kid needs a full ride. So now there are not enough heroes for them to look up to in baseball."

Cambria sees the urban programs struggling. Revitalizing Baseball in Inner Cities (RBI) was supposed to develop urban baseball players. "RBI is trying to get African-Americans to play, and it's very very difficult. Inner city programs are closing," he said. But it is not a problem only with African-Americans: Americans in general seem to be losing interest in baseball. Cambria lives in the largely white, middle-class Long Island town of Northport, where, he said, "ninety percent of the kids play soccer or lacrosse and the baseball diamonds are empty."

Major League Baseball now has thirty teams and needs 750 active players. They also need more fans and more television contracts in the world to bring in the revenue to pay all of these enormous salaries. Major League Baseball has become a huge international corporation. There is even a division called Major League Baseball International that focuses on expanding baseball in the world.

None of this is good news for Dominicans. When a few innovators such as the Dodgers and Giants and Blue Jays went looking abroad for new talent, the Dominican Republic easily dominated their attention. It still does, but now there are programs to develop players all over the world—not just in Latin America and Asia but in Australia, where the first recorded game was in Melbourne in 1857; in Germany, the Netherlands, and South Africa, where it has been played since the 1930s; and even Great Britain, although the British are not being easily lured.

Even within Latin America it is getting more competitive. Major League Baseball has become particularly interested in Nicaragua, a country that in recent years has edged out the Dominican Republic for the distinction of being the second-poorest nation in the Americas. The unassailably poorest, Haiti, seems too convulsed in its own tragedy for baseball. And inevitably the day will come when the United States government will make peace with Cuba and stop requiring Cubans to desert their country—that is to say, defect—if they want to work in the United States. Once the U.S. allows Cubans to spend their summers playing baseball in the U.S. the way Dominicans and other Latin Americans do, Major League Baseball will be awash with talent from what is probably the richest vein of baseball players in the world.

Even within the Dominican Republic, San Pedro had more competition. By 2008 only Santo Domingo, a city three times the size of San Pedro, had produced more major-league players than San Pedro, and only barely: 103 compared with 79. San Pedro had provided one out of every six of the 471 Dominican-born major-league players. But even though the pipeline—the academies and the minor-league system—was full of Macorisanos, San Pedro's share was declining. Increasingly, players were coming from the poorest region of the country, the southwest, where there was not the rich soil of impoverished San Pedro but only an arid desert where people lived in sun-parched wooden huts and struggled for food and water. Major leaguers started coming from Bani, Azua, and even—like shortstop Julio Lugo—from Barahona, one of the poorest towns in this poor country. People in Barahona needed a way out even more desperately than Macorisanos.

Still, it would be hard for a town to break the record of little San Pedro de Macorís, where seventy-nine major leaguers originated between 1962 and 2008. San Pedro has given the sport of baseball the most major-league players of any small town in the world. During those same years, New York City, with one of the oldest and strongest traditions in baseball history, produced 129 major-league players—not even twice as many—from twenty-seven times the population. And of course that included many Dom Yors such as Alex Rodriguez.

CHAPTER THIRTEEN

Fickle Judgment
from the Peanut Gallery

O n the main street of Consuelo, amid stores and other one- and two-story commercial buildings, was one large two-story house bulging and drooling white wrought-iron curlicues from its many door gates, window grates, and balcony rails. On the second story was an elderly woman in a rocking chair watching the street life below. It was eighty-seven-year-old Felicia Franco, the mother of Julio Franco, who chose to take her name rather than his father's. She had three sons. Julio was the only major leaguer. Older brother Vicente Franco was said to be a good pitcher for Consuelo in the 1960s, but he threw out his arm. He lived there with his mother. The third son never played and now lived in New York.

When Julio played in a game that was on television, friends and neighbors used to pack into the roomy house. In 1985, only three years into his long career, Julio built the house for his mother. Her husband, who was dead, could never have built a house like this. He had been a jack-of-all-trades in the mill—what the mills called, borrowing a baseball term, as a utility man.

With the typical disloyalty of a San Pedro fan, she was a die-hard Licey supporter. Her reason was simple: "They're the best. They're going to win again this year," she correctly predicted, even though the Estrellas were in first place at the time.

Although he didn't live there, the house was mostly about Julio. There was a large photo of young Julio in a Texas Rangers uniform with the team's owner at the time, a young and, as always, uncomfortable-looking George W. Bush, who had inscribed the photo to Julio: *Let's win together.* There was also an even larger photo of Julio with the elder President Bush, looking, as always, somehow in pain. They were posing in front of a washing machine as though they were doing their laundry together—which seemed hard to believe.

Julio Franco had one of the longest careers in major-league history, spanning twenty-five years from April 1982 until September 2007, when he retired at age forty-nine. He maintained an impressive career batting average of .298, getting a hit one out of every three times at bat for twenty-five years. His total of 2,586 hits was the most by any Dominican major-league player. He held a number of gerontological records. He was the oldest regular-position player—an everyday player—in major-league history, passing racist Cap Anson's record by three years. He was the last player in baseball born in the 1950s. From 2004 until his retirement, he was the oldest player in baseball and made age records on a regular basis. On April 26, 2006, pinch-hitting for the Mets, he hit a home run against the Padres, making him the oldest major-league player ever to hit a home run. He hit another on September 30 and one more on May 4 of the following year. He was also the oldest player to hit a grand slam—a home run with the bases loaded. He was the oldest player ever to hit two home runs in the same game, and the oldest to steal two bases in the same game. He would have been the oldest player to steal a base except that, in 1909, Arlie Latham, age forty-nine, came out of retirement to play one game with the Giants and stole a base. Franco tried again on June 20, 2007, at age forty-eight while playing for the Mets against the Yankees in Yankee Stadium. He got on base, beating forty-four-year-old pitcher Roger Clemens, but was picked off when he tried to steal second on him. Still, it went into the records as the oldest pitcher-batter baserunning duel in major-league history.

After he retired he returned to San Pedro not to live but just to pass some time playing dominos with old friends and his brother Vicente. He had his own house on a dirt street of new houses in a different part of town from his mother's, although nothing in Consuelo is very far away. Ask anyone in Consuelo, and he would know where Julio Franco's house was. It was a two-story pink stucco-and-stone house behind a high wall with a solid steel gate that was kept locked even on the rare occasions when Franco was there. It was a more luxurious house than most people in Consuelo had; few of the other players maintained houses there. But it was not an ostentatious mansion, because that was not the way people did things in Consuelo, even if they became rich. If you want a mansion, you have to build it somewhere else, as Sammy Sosa and Alfredo Griffin did.

When he was in Consuelo, Franco could be found in the back of the house on a red-tiled patio where a roof with a ceiling fan was held up by Grecian pillars. Julio sat there in a T-shirt and jeans, lean and fit and youthful looking at fifty, a middle-aged face on a twenty-five-year-old's body, relaxed, home at last, playing dominos with two of his best friends, Vicente and Vicente's friend Guillermo.

They slapped the domino tiles on the table hard, making the prerequisite loud clack, and kept score with chalk on the table edge.

"I come back here once or twice a year, sometimes at Christmas," Franco said. "I like to stay in Consuelo. I go to the ballpark here, the gym. I like to stay here, surrounded by people I know." Without warning he slammed a domino tile down, smiled at his brother, and started shouting, "I got him! I got him!" Julio liked to compete. He really liked to win.

No longer a player, his new ambition was to be a manager. He had a family in Fort Lauderdale, and moving back to San Pedro was nowhere in his plans.

"I could have kept playing," Julio observed, "but nobody thinks a fifty-year-old can help a ball club. They would rather give a chance to a young prospect. I understand that."

One of the reasons he would not stay in San Pedro was that in his twenty-five years in Major League Baseball he had earned millions of dollars, and everyone in San Pedro knew it.

"What I'm not going to do is give money to a guy on the street. I will give someone money for medicine, I will give money to a mother to buy milk. I'll give a kid a glove and could take him to a ball game, but that's as far as I go."

He said that he was frequently asked for money "by people who call me a friend. My real friends never have to ask me. They know I would help them if they needed it. If you had a million dollars and you gave a dollar to a million people, the million-and-first person would complain. You're not going to satisfy everyone."

Sammy Sosa's experience offers an example of this dilemma. At the height of his career he was being paid $10 million a year to play baseball, and after his home-run derby with Mark McGwire he started earning millions of additional dollars in advertising appearances and celebrity endorsements. He became an industry besieged with offers. Possibly the weirdest was from the man who wanted Sosa to send him his soiled undershirts after each game to be encased in Lucite and sold as memorabilia. Other ideas included a soft drink and Sammy Sosa Salsa.

In San Pedro, where Sosa's wealth was well known and, no matter how rich you are, you are even richer in the minds of the poor, he was constantly criticized for not giving enough. This was partly because he talked so much, especially to the U.S. press, about how much he was giving. The reason he was questioned about his contribution to hurricane relief in 1999 was that he had made such a show of giving it, and yet people felt they weren't seeing it. Mayor Cedeño claimed that Sosa had raised money in Japan to rebuild one thousand homes destroyed by Hurricane George but the money never turned up in San Pedro. Sosa said that the deal with the Japanese fell through over disputes about who would build the homes.

Sosa responded to Mayor Cedeño's accusation, saying, "Never is it enough. I want the people in the United States to know I've done the best I can to help my people. I can only do so much. I can't do everything."

Sosa always did things with big displays and a lot of noise. In his 1998 "Up with People" tour, he went to San Pedro with a lot of press and handed out gifts on the street. In 1999, Sosa, the former shoe-shine boy, took two hundred shoe-shine boys in Santo Domingo to lunch, to which Macorisanos responded that he had failed to do anything for their shoe-shine boys.

But it seemed that almost anything Sammy did turned to scandal. In 1998 he gave New York mayor Rudolph Giuliani the bat with which he had supposedly hit his sixty-sixth home run that season. Governor George Pataki got number fifty-nine. But the Baseball Hall of Fame revealed that they had both of those bats, and Sosa admitted to having gotten a little carried away with the moment. "The Mayor was so nice to me," he explained. "I didn't want to disappoint him."

In 2000, *Fortune* magazine reported that Sosa's Plaza 30/30 was assessed at $2.7 million and had been donated to his foundation for a tax savings of at least $1 million. Aside from a clinic, which was always packed with poor people and where, Sosa claimed, 150 children were inoculated a day and dental care was provided, the principal tenant was his sister, who operated a boutique, a beauty salon, and a disco but paid no rent. The magazine reported that Sosa was not putting money into the foundation and it was near bankruptcy even though his friend and onetime competitor Mark McGwire had contributed $100,000 to it. In 2001, Art Sandoval, the administrator of Sosa's charitable foundation, claimed that the entire foundation, including Plaza 30/30 and its clinic, had been set up as a tax scheme that saved Sosa millions. While legal wrongdoings were never proven, even in an IRS investigation, the damage to Sosa's image remained in the minds of many Macorisanos.

In 1999, the Congress of Racial Equality (CORE) planned to give Sosa their International Brotherhood Award but then complained that he had demanded a private jet to pick him up in Santo Domingo, fly him to the awards in New York, and then fly him to Las Vegas for a Mike Tyson fight. Also, according to CORE, Sosa wanted them to provide him with a luxury hotel suite and two other rooms for associates, buy him five ringside seats at the fight, set up a fund-raising dinner with CORE contributors, and guarantee at least $60,000 in contributions for Dominican hurricane relief. He also wanted to bring memorabilia to sell at the awards event. They could not come to terms and Sosa did not attend. CORE national chairman Roy Innis said that Sosa "has to learn how to deal with his fifteen minutes of fame." And that was exactly the problem: baseball stars are famous and they do earn millions, but only for a great moment.

For Macorisanos, Sosa had become the symbol of the idea that their players did not really come through for them. San Pedro's heroes, like those of the Greeks, had flaws. If they were seen in San Pedro, as Rico Carty was, Macorisanos forgave them. But if they were rarely seen in town, then they had turned their backs and were not forgiven.

Sosa did not live in San Pedro. Instead he built a $5 million mansion in Santo Domingo. He would often tell American reporters how much he loved his hometown and how he had San Pedro scenes depicted on stained-glass windows in his mansion. But outside the window was not San Pedro.

Alexander, a young man in Consuelo, said, "I know Sammy Sosa. I know some of his family. In '98 he built a big mansion in Santo Domingo. First he built a normal house in San Pedro, but once he built the mansion in Santo Domingo, we didn't see him anymore."

Sammy's grandmother, Rosa Julia Sosa, still lived in a three-room cinder-block house in Consuelo. When the New York *Daily News* went to interview her in 1999, she complained that she hadn't seen him in two years and asked the reporter for money.

After his retirement in 2007, Sosa abandoned his mansion in the capital for La Romana, where George Bell—who abandoned his San Pedro mansion because of a divorce—also lived. Joaquín Andújar, who also left his San Pedro mansion because of a divorce, left San Pedro entirely for

Santo Domingo in 2008. San Pedro was finding it difficult to attract its wealthy ex-ballplayers.

La Romana and San Pedro, while both eastern sugar towns, were very different. Although both had considerable poverty, the river in La Romana was filled not with nineteen-foot fishing boats but with fifty-foot yachts. Bell built a new home at the guarded and gated La Romana resort of Casa de Campo, which had white stucco villas and seven thousand acres designed by Dominican designer Oscar de la Renta. Impossible for the casual visitor or neighborhood Dominican to enter, this private compound of mostly foreigners was the ultimate in wealthy exclusion. Perhaps of even greater interest to Bell, it had two golf courses planned by the celebrated course designer Pete Dye.

Bell played golf every Saturday and Sunday. Not surprising for a man who became a star because of his hand-eye coordination and smooth swing, he was a good golfer. So was Babe Ruth. Bell had a four handicap. "I could do better," he said. "But as soon as you are good, no one plays with you, and it's no fun."

In middle age, Bell was still large, muscular, broad-shouldered, and fit—a tough-looking man with the handle of a handgun sticking up from the back of his blue-jeans waistband. He explained that he carried a gun because he didn't "want anyone messing with me." It was hard to believe anyone would, but he was a very wealthy man in a crime-ridden and impoverished land.

Bell, who had made about $2 million a year as a player, invested his money. He owned a construction company that built condominiums and a farm that used to produce dairy and then became a lemon plantation. For a while he rented it to his old team, the Blue Jays, as an academy, but they moved and he had trouble finding another team. That business was becoming very competitive. He lived a quiet life playing golf, fishing for marlin, and running his businesses.

"I don't really spend my time with other baseball players," he said. "I like to be alone. I was like that when I was playing, too. I don't like to stay out late, don't like to drink because I feel terrible the next day. I went to Alfredo's disco for the inauguration and never went back. I don't want to be out on the Malecón. I like to be home by nine o'clock. I don't like people bothering me."

Although his friend with the disco on the Malecón, Alfredo Griffin, was very different, he was one of the few baseball players with whom Bell maintained a friendship. Together they organized an annual charity golf tournament.

Mayor Tony Echavaría said of the local baseball stars, "Some make a lot of noise when they do things; others do it very quietly."

Most of the ex-players, whether they had money or not, had charitable foundations. Supporting youth programs was a favorite activity. Rico Carty had played baseball before ballplayers became fabulously wealthy, but he had a large house and a good car and lived better than most Macorisanos. And he had the Rico Carty Foundation, which was located in a beat-up downtown building. Inside the dank and dark offices, no phones were ringing and no one was working. They were playing dominoes—a tough-looking group of men. The furniture was flimsy and the doors were blackened from fingerprints. The scene was reminiscent of the local party offices under Balaguer where patronage was dispensed to supporters and punishment to opponents. One of the domino players, a burly, overweight black man with a shaved head and enormous hands, was Rico Carty.

Carty explained that the Rico Carty Foundation needed money.

What does the foundation do?

"Helps poor people," he explained. "Gives them medicine, things like that."

He wanted to be paid $500 to be interviewed. "It's not for me," he protested without prodding. "It's for the foundation."

He was offered more than $500 worth of medicine, but he insisted on cash and looked sad and disappointed when he realized he wasn't going to get it. "I've given a hundred interviews," he said in a cranky tone, "and what do I have to show for it?"

Most of the ex-players had their own ideas about helping their town. Tony Fernández had a six-hundred-acre farm on the outskirts of San Pedro that he used as a retreat for orphans, with dormitories, chapels, meeting rooms, and a baseball diamond. He also built an orphanage. Orphanages were his primary concern. He pushed the importance of education. But most of the male orphans he talked to about education were hoping to impress him with their baseball talent so they could some-day get signed.

While Fernández focused on orphanages, Soriano built a baseball field in his old neighborhood by the Quisqueya sugar mill. It was like this all over the Dominican Republic. Pedro Martínez, who grew up near Santo Domingo, built churches—one Catholic and one Baptist—in the capital.

The public likes to make heroes out of athletes, and in San Pedro, heroes who will make their poor town prosper at last. But heroics is a lot to expect from someone snatched away without education at age sixteen and handed fame and wealth at a dizzying speed while living in a world of unworldly men devoted to perfecting a boy's game. Since the public has exaggerated expectations for these ballplayers, they develop an exaggerated sense of their own importance that they find very difficult to fit into reality once they stop playing. Doug Glanville, an ex–major leaguer himself, wrote in *The New York Times* in April 2008, "Most baseball players develop a special kind of shell that forms around them as their careers unfold. It probably isn't that different from an egg shell. It's fragile, but no one is really allowed inside until the player is ready to share his secrets, or until something terrible happens causing the protec-tive layer to crack. Inside the player justifies his need to be secluded. He perceives that the court of public opinion will either build him up or tear him down. . . . So he uses this barrier to protect himself from the fickle judgments of the peanut gallery and to make it through his world."

For all their money, the best baseball players could hope for was to become what was known in the Dominican Republic as *gente de segundo,* the highest social class money can buy. It takes generations to be Dominican upper class. A lot of the big money in San Pedro still came from old sugar families like the Vicini Cabrals, possibly the wealthiest and most powerful family in the country. The dynasty was founded by an Italian immigrant, Juan Bautista Vicini, who came to San Pedro in the 1870s and was one of the early architects of the Dominican sugar boom. Cristóbal Colón was among the Vicini sugar mills. The Hazín family emigrated from Lebanon in the late nineteenth century, also got into sugar, solidified their position by close ties with Balaguer, and remained one of the wealthiest and most powerful families in eastern Dominican Republic; the Hazíns are based in San Pedro. The Barceló family started with Julián Barceló, who emigrated from Spain in 1905, and built a fortune mainly in agro-industry. They invested heavily in Juan Dolio beach hotels. Only about two dozen families own almost all of the large companies in the Dominican Republic. These are three of them. As a group they are even less known for their civic-mindedness than baseball players are.

As for baseball, Major League Baseball claimed it generated $76 million in business annually in the Dominican Republic, which would make it a leading Dominican industry comparable to tourism in the jobs and revenue it provided. Major League Baseball claimed that its Dominican players sent home $210 million in 2003 alone and that it spent $14.7 million on 30 academies that provided, directly and indirectly, 2,100 jobs, many of them in San Pedro.

Mayor Echavaría had a different way of looking at it. Even if major-league players spent money only on themselves and their immediate families, Echavaría argued, they were still investing in the town. "Sammy Sosa does a lot of things for San Pedro," the mayor said. "When he first got his contract, he built a big house for his mother, and that is an investment in San Pedro. And he built 30/30. That's an investment. Alfredo Griffin built Café Caribe, the disco on the Malecón. Most players invest here in real estate. It's for their families, but it's an investment. They mostly invest in goods and real estate." To the mayor, even a shopping spree was a welcome investment.

But he thought the most important contribution of baseball to San Pedro was that "baseball gives an activity to the poorest children and it changes their lives and the lives of their families."

George Bell wasn't completely sure about the impact of baseball. Sitting at his desk in his small office crammed with fishing tackle, a large mounted marlin, and an array of golf trophies, he said, "They give too much money and it's going to end up trouble: so much money and no education." But when he, who dropped out of school at age seventeen to sign, was asked if he had any regrets about not finishing his education, he sat back in his chair, put his arms behind his head, and replied, "Not really. I'm very satisfied with what I did and what I'm doing."

At the gate at Tetelo Vargas Stadium, the rut between the street and the parking lot is so deep that it takes great care to drive a car in without scraping its nose. But the stadium itself was one of the best-maintained properties in San Pedro and looked even newer than it was.

Most days of the year there was either some kind of a game or practice going on, with a good possibility that some kid on that field was a future major-league player. Which was why, although the stadium might have seemed empty, there were always a few serious-looking older men in the seats, some with folders or papers, sometimes one behind home plate with a speed gun to measure pitches: scouts for the major leagues.

If you had good hand-eye coordination, if you could run fast, if you could throw a ball hard, if you were extremely tall or left-handed or, even better, both, you had a chance of rescuing your entire family and becoming a millionaire. Why wouldn't you try?

Once July 2 approached, anyone with a sixteen-and-a-half-year-old boy in the family had the hope of a better life.

San Pedro is not about baseball for everyone. For some it is still the city of Gastón Deligne and Pedro Mir. When merengue star Juan Luis Guerra wrote his popular song about San Pedro, "Guavaberry," he did not even mention baseball. He sang about the Malecón, watching the sunset, meeting women, and drinking guavaberry. And it is true that it is very pleasant at the end of the day on the Malecón, looking past the rocks and the palm trees, watching the last rays of a hot sun light the bright turquoise sea, glowing against the backdrop of a dark-blue sky. It's even better while sipping guavaberry.

Macorisanos know this and appreciate it. But most of them need to be rescued. And there is only one way that will happen.

Asked that chronic San Pedro question, Why does this town produce so many baseball players? José Canó said, "Because we don't have anything else here and we aren't tall enough for basketball."

The First Seventy-nine:
Major League Baseball Players
from San Pedro de Macorís

Since 1962, Macorisanos have been entering the ranks of Major League Baseball with such frequency that between 1980 and 2008 there were only two years when at least one new Macorisano didn't debut as a major leaguer. The dates of birth and even in some cases the names given here are the official data and may not reflect the true ages and names of players.

1962

Amado Samuel

Amado Ruperto Samuel debuted in the major leagues on April 10, 1962, for the Milwaukee Braves, and played his final game on July 11, 1964, for the New York Mets, playing a total of three seasons in the majors. He was born on December 6, 1938, in Santa Fe and played shortstop, second base, and third base.

Manny Jiménez

Manuel Emilio Rivera Jiménez debuted in the major leagues on April 11, 1962, for the Kansas City Athletics and played his final game on May

27, 1969, for the Chicago Cubs. He was born on November 19, 1938, in San Pedro de Macorís. He played 214 games as a left fielder and 22 games as a right fielder. After playing for the Athletics, the Pittsburgh Pirates drafted him in the minor-league draft on November 29, 1966. He was traded to the Cubs on January 15, 1969, and he ended his seven-season career playing for the Cubs. In 1962 his batting average was .301, the highest in the American League. In his best year, 1968, it went up to .303.

1963

Pedro González

Pedro Olivares González debuted in the major leagues on April 11, 1963, for the New York Yankees and played his final game on September 27, 1967. He was born on December 12, 1937, in Angelina. He was primarily a second baseman. The Yankees signed him prior to the 1958 season. He finished his major-league career playing for the Indians. He was known for his defense, making 31 errors in five seasons.

Rico Carty

Ricardo Adolfo Jacobo Carty was born on September 1, 1939, in Consuelo. He primarily played outfield. The Milwaukee Braves signed him as a free agent on October 24, 1959. He debuted in the major leagues on September 15, 1963, for the Milwaukee Braves (the future Atlanta Braves) and played his final game on September 23, 1979, with the Toronto Blue Jays. From 1972 through 1978, he was traded by the Braves to the Texas Rangers, purchased by the Chicago Cubs, purchased by the Oakland Athletics, purchased by the Cleveland Indians, drafted by the Blue Jays, traded to the Indians, traded back to the Blue Jays, traded to the Athletics, and purchased by the Blue Jays. He played a total of fifteen seasons in the major leagues and his best season was in 1970, playing for the Braves: he was given the batting title of the National League with a .366

batting average, 25 home runs, and 101 RBIs. For his career, he had 278 doubles, 890 RBIs, and 204 home runs. He had a batting average of .300 or higher in 1964 (.330), 1965 (.310), 1966 (.326), 1969 (.342), 1970 (.366), 1974 (.363), 1975 (.308), and 1976 (.310).

1964

Rick Joseph

Ricardo Joseph was born on August 24, 1939, in the Santa Fe sugar mill. He died on September 8, 1979, in Santiago, Dominican Republic. He played primarily third base but also first base, left field, and one game as a second baseman. Joseph debuted in the major leagues on June 18, 1964, for the Kansas City Athletics. He played one season and then left Major League Baseball, returning in 1967 to play for the Philadelphia Phillies for four seasons until he ended his career in 1970.

1965

Elvio Jiménez

Felix Elvio Rivera Jiménez was born on January 6, 1940, in Santa Fe. He is the brother of Manny Jiménez. An outfielder, his first game in the major leagues, played on October 4, 1964, was also his final game in the majors. He had a .333 batting average in that one game.

1969

Rafael Robles

Rafael Robles was born on October 20, 1947, in San Pedro de Macorís. The San Francisco Giants signed him prior to the 1967 season and then gave him up to the Padres in the 1968 expansion draft. He debuted in the major leagues on April 8, 1969, for the San Diego Padres and played his final game on June 10, 1972. He played shortstop, except for one game in which he played third base. His three-season career was entirely with the Padres. He died on August 13, 1998.

Santiago Guzmán

Santiago Donovan Guzmán was born on July 25, 1949, in the Angelina sugar mill. A right-hander, he was the first major-league pitcher from San Pedro de Macorís. The Cardinals signed him prior to the 1967 season. He debuted in the major leagues on September 30, 1969, for the St. Louis Cardinals, and played his final game on April 18, 1972. In a total of four seasons, all for the Cardinals, he had a 4.50 ERA.

1973

Pepe Frías

Jesús María Andújar Frías was born on July 14, 1948, in Consuelo. He played shortstop, second base, third base, outfield, right field, center field, and left field. The San Francisco Giants signed him on September 18, 1966, and the Expos signed him as a free agent on August 27, 1969. He debuted in the major leagues on April 6, 1973, for the Montreal Expos. He was traded to the Atlanta Braves on March 31, 1979, to the Texas Rangers on December 6, 1979, and to the Los Angeles Dodgers on September 13, 1980, and played his final game on August 26, 1981, for a total of nine seasons in the major leagues. Frías was a great defender and committed only 5 errors as second baseman and 10 errors as shortstop.

Rafael Batista

Rafael Sánchez Batista was born on October 20, 1947, in Consuelo. A first baseman, he debuted in the major leagues on June 17, 1973, for the Houston Astros and played his final game on April 27, 1975. He played in the major leagues for only two seasons, for a total of 22 games. In 1975 he had a .300 batting average.

1976

Joaquín Andújar

Joaquín Andújar was born on December 21, 1952, in the La Barca section of San Pedro de Macorís. A right-handed pitcher, he was signed by the

Cincinnati Reds on November 14, 1969, and was traded to the Astros on October 24, 1975. He debuted in the major leagues on April 8, 1976, for the Houston Astros. He was traded to the Cardinals on June 7, 1981, and pitched his best seasons with them. He won the National League Most Valuable Player Award in 1982, received a Gold Glove in 1984, won 20 games in 1984 and 21 games in 1985, and won the World Series in 1985. In December 1985 he was traded to the Oakland Athletics and then back to the Astros, for whom he pitched his final game on September 30, 1988. He played a total of thirteen seasons in the major leagues, with a 3.58 ERA. He had to retire early because of leg problems.

Santo Alcalá

Santo Anibal Alcalá was born on December 23, 1952, in Villa Providencia, San Pedro de Macorís. A right-handed pitcher, the Reds signed him prior to the 1970 season. He debuted in the major leagues on April 10, 1976, for the Cincinnati Reds. His career was cut short by an injured pitching arm. During his two years in the majors he struck out 140 batters and had an ERA of 4.76. He pitched his final game on September 25, 1977, for the Montreal Expos.

Juan Ramón Bernhardt

Juan Ramón Coradin Bernhardt was born on August 31, 1953, in San Pedro de Macorís. He debuted in the major leagues on July 10, 1976, for the New York Yankees and played his final game on April 8, 1979. He primarily played as a designated hitter and third baseman.

Alfredo Griffin

Alfredo Claudino Baptist Griffin was born on October 6, 1957, in Consuelo. The Indians signed him on August 22, 1973. He played shortstop, second base, and third base, and was also a designated hitter. He debuted in the major leagues on September 4, 1976, for the Cleveland Indians. In 1978, while playing for the Cleveland Indians, he had a .500 batting average. On December 5, 1978, he was traded to the Toronto Blue Jays to play shortstop. He was named Rookie of the Year in 1979. On December 8, 1984, he was traded to the Oakland Athletics. In 1985 he received a Gold Glove for his fielding skills. On December 11, 1987, he was traded to the Los Angeles Dodgers. On March 19, 1992, he started playing with the Blue Jays as a free agent. On October 3, 1993, he played his final game for a total of eighteen seasons in the major leagues, in which he hit 245 doubles and 78 triples, had 527 RBIs, and stole 192 bases.

Ignacio "Al" Javier

Ignacio Alfredo Wilkes Javier was born on February 4, 1954, in Consuelo. He played outfield, left field, and right field. The Astros signed him in 1971. He debuted in the major leagues on September 9, 1976, for the Houston Astros and played his final game on October 1, 1976, an 8-game single-season major-league career.

1978

Arturo DeFreitas

Arturo Marcelino Simon DeFreitas was born on April 26, 1953, in San Pedro de Macorís. He played first base and right field. The Reds signed him on May 27, 1970. He debuted in the major leagues on September 7, 1978, for the Cincinnati Reds, and played two seasons for the team. His final game was on June 27, 1979.

Alberto Lois

Alberto Lois Pie was born on May 6, 1956, in Consuelo. He played outfield, left field, and center field. The Pittsburgh Pirates signed him in 1974. He debuted in the major leagues on September 8, 1978, for the Pirates and played his final game on September 29, 1979. His career, only fourteen games in two seasons, was ended by debilitating injuries from a car crash.

Pedro Guerrero

Pedro Guerrero was born on June 29, 1956, in Santa Fe. A first baseman, he was signed by the Cleveland Indians on January 15, 1973; they traded him to the Dodgers the following year. He debuted in the major leagues on September 22, 1978, for the Los Angeles Dodgers. He was awarded the title of Most Valuable Player in 1981. His Dodger year of 1982 was his best: he had 32 home runs, 100 RBIs, and a .304 batting average. He played for the Dodgers for eleven of the sixteen seasons of his career. He played for five seasons with the St. Louis Cardinals. He was then traded to the Cardinals on August 16, 1988, and signed as a free agent with them on January 7, 1992, playing his final game on October 4, 1992. He had career totals of 267 doubles, 215 home runs, and 898 RBIs, and an overall .300 batting average.

1980

Rafael "Rafelin" Ramírez

Rafael Emilio Peguero Ramírez was born on February 18, 1958, in Angelina. He was signed to the Atlanta Braves by Pedro González in September 1976. Primarily a shortstop, he debuted in the major leagues on August 4, 1980, for the Atlanta Braves. He played a total of thirteen seasons in the major leagues: eight seasons with the Braves and five with the Houston Astros. He played his final game on October 3, 1992. He hit 224 doubles, stole 112 bases, and had 484 RBIs.

1981

George Bell

George Antonio Bell was born on October 21, 1959, in Santa Fe. The Philadelphia Phillies signed him on March 7, 1978. He played outfield, left field, right field, third base, and second base, and was a designated hitter. He debuted in the major leagues on April 9, 1981, for the Toronto

Blue Jays, and played his final game on October 2, 1993, for the Chicago White Sox. He played nine seasons with the Blue Jays, one with the Chicago Cubs, and two with the White Sox. During those twelve seasons he had a batting average of .278, hit 265 home runs and 308 doubles, and had 1,002 RBIs. In 1987, while on the Blue Jays, he became the first Dominican to be named Most Valuable Player in the league. He was also the first player in the major leagues to hit three home runs on an opening day.

Rufino Linares

Rufino de la Cruz Linares was born on February 28, 1951, in Quisqueya. He played mostly outfield and left field. He debuted in the major leagues on April 10, 1981, for the Atlanta Braves and played his final game on October 6, 1985, for the California Angels. He played a total of four seasons in the major leagues: three with the Braves and one with the Angels. He died on May 16, 1998.

1982

Julio Franco

Julio César Franco was born on August 23, 1958, in Consuelo. He debuted in the major leagues on April 23, 1982, for the Philadelphia Phillies, who signed him as a free agent on April 23, 1978.

Julio Franco had one of the longest careers in major-league history, spanning twenty-five years from April 1982 until September 2007, when he retired at age forty-nine. He maintained an impressive career batting average of .298, getting a hit one out of every three times at bat for twenty-five years. There were many years in which he had a batting average of .300 or above: 1986 (.306), 1987 (.319), 1988 (.303), 1989 (.316), 1991 (.341), and 1994 (.319). His total of 2,586 hits was the highest of any Dominican major-league player.

Franco mostly played shortstop and second base, but he also played first base, third base, left field, outfield, and right field, and he was also a designated hitter. He was traded to the Cleveland Indians on December 9, 1982, and then traded to the Texas Rangers on December 6, 1988. The Chicago White Sox signed him as a free agent on December 15, 1993, and the Indians signed him as a free agent on December 7, 1995. The Milwaukee Brewers signed him as a free agent on August 13, 1997, and the Tampa Bay Devil Rays on February 19, 1999. On August 31, 2001, the Atlanta Braves purchased him from the Mexico City Tigers. The Braves signed him as a free agent on January 8, 2003, on January 12, 2004, and on December 9, 2004. The New York Mets signed him as a free agent on December 12, 2005, and then the Braves signed him as a free agent on July 18, 2007. He finished out his 2007 season playing for the Braves. In 1990 he was named Most Valuable Player.

Franco was the oldest regular-position (everyday) player in major-league history. From 2004 until his retirement he was the oldest player in baseball and made age records on a regular basis: the oldest player ever to hit a home run, the oldest player to hit a grand slam, the oldest player ever to hit two home runs in the same game, and the oldest to steal two bases in the same game.

Alejandro Sánchez

Alejandro Pimental Sánchez was born on February 14, 1959, in San Pedro de Macorís. The Phillies signed him in 1978. He played outfield, right field, left field, and center field, and was a designated hitter. He debuted in the major leagues on September 6, 1982, for the Philadelphia Phillies and played his final game on May 16, 1987, playing a total of six seasons in the majors. He played for the Phillies from 1982 to 1983. He was traded to the San Francisco Giants on March 24, 1984, to the Detroit Tigers on April 5, 1985, and to the Minnesota Twins on January 16, 1986. He became a free agent on October 15, 1986, and then played for the Oakland Athletics in 1987.

1983

Juan Samuel

Juan Milton Samuel was born on December 9, 1960, in Barrio Restauración. The Phillies signed him on April 29, 1980. He played second base, center field, first base, right field, left field, and third base, and was a designated hitter, but he played mostly second base, with a total of 1,190 games at that position. He debuted in the major leagues on August 24, 1983, for the Philadelphia Phillies and played his final game on September 26, 1998, for the Toronto Blue Jays. He was traded to the New York Mets on June 18, 1989, to the Los Angeles Dodgers on December 20, 1989, and to the Kansas City Royals on September 8, 1995. He was signed as a free agent by the Royals on August 6, 1992, by the Cincinnati Reds on December 11, 1992, by the Detroit Tigers on February 14, 1994, and by the Blue Jays, the team with which he finished out his major-league career, on January 16, 1996. In his first four seasons, he was the first player in history to reach double-digit home runs, stolen bases, doubles, and triples. He played a total of sixteen seasons in the major leagues, collecting 161 home runs, 287 doubles, 102 triples, and 703 RBIs, and stealing 396 bases. He was the National League's Most Valuable Player in 1984 and 1987. He holds the major-league record for most at-bats by a right-handed hitter in a season. He also tied the major-league record for consecutive strikeouts—four—which is shared by Hack Wilson and Vince DiMaggio.

Tony Fernández

Octavio Antonio Castro Fernández was born on June 30, 1962, in Barrio Restauración. The Blue Jays signed him on April 24, 1979. He debuted in the major leagues on September 2, 1983, for the Toronto Blue Jays. In 1990 he was traded to the Padres, then traded to the Mets in 1992, to the Reds as a free agent in March 1994, to the Yankees in December 1994, to the Indians in 1996, back to the Blue Jays in 1997, and to the Brewers in February 2001; he played his final game for the Brewers, on October 7, 2001. He played shortstop as well as a smaller number of games as a second baseman, third baseman, and designated hitter. For four consecutive seasons, from 1986 to 1989, he received a Gold Glove and was the American League's Most Valuable Player. In his seventeen seasons in the major leagues, he hit 414 doubles and 92 triples, had 844 RBIs, and stole 246 bases.

1984

Ramón Romero

Ramón de los Santos Romero was born on January 8, 1959, in Barrio Restauración. A left-handed pitcher, he was signed by the Cleveland Indians on October 1, 1976. He debuted on September 18, 1984, with the Cleveland Indians, and played his final game on September 21, 1985, with the Indians. He had a career 6.28 ERA.

1985

Mariano Duncan

Mariano Nalasco Duncan was born on March 13, 1963, in Angelina. He played mostly second base but also shortstop, outfield, left field, third base, first base, and right field, and was a designated hitter. The Dodgers signed him on January 7, 1982, and he debuted in the major leagues on April 9, 1985, for the Dodgers. He stole 38 bases his rookie year. He was traded to the Cincinnati Reds. The Philadelphia Phillies signed him as a free agent on April 14, 1995. The New York Yankees signed him as a free agent on December 11, 1995, and they then traded him to the Blue Jays on July 29, 1997. He played his final game on September 17, 1997, for the Blue Jays, for a total of twelve seasons in the major leagues. His batting average was .306 in 1990 and .340 in 1996. He had 233 doubles, 491 RBIs, and 174 stolen bases. After his playing career ended, Duncan became a coach for the L.A. Dodgers.

Manny Lee

Manuel Lora Lee was born on June 17, 1965, in Villa Magdalena. The Mets signed him on May 10, 1982, and he debuted in the major leagues on April 10, 1985, for the Toronto Blue Jays. At ages nineteen and twenty (in 1985 and 1986) he was the youngest player in the American League. During his eleven-season major-league career, he played shortstop in 522 games, second base in 358 games, third base in 32 games, and right field in 1 game, and was a designated hitter in 25 games. He played his final game on April 26, 1995, for the St. Louis Cardinals.

1986

Juan Castillo

Juan Bryas Castillo was born on January 25, 1962, in Placer Bonito. He was signed by the Milwaukee Brewers on October 11, 1979, and debuted in the major leagues on April 12, 1986, for the Brewers. He played second base, shortstop, third base, and left field, and also was a designated hitter, but was primarily a second baseman, playing a total of 135 games at second base. Castillo played his final game on April 17, 1989. He played for the Brewers for his entire four-season major-league career.

Balvino Galvez

Balvino Jerez Galvez was born on March 31, 1964, in Batey Monte Cristi. He was a right-handed pitcher signed by the Dodgers on September 10, 1981. He debuted in the major leagues on May 7, 1986, for the Dodgers and pitched his final game on October 5, 1986, playing only one season and pitching only 10 games in the major leagues, with an ERA of 3.92. Despite his good year, he was sent down to the minors, then had a stormy but illustrious career in Japanese baseball. In 2001 Galvez was about to go back to the majors to play for the Pirates when he got into an argument with the pitching coach in spring training, walked off the field, and went back to the Dominican Republic without talking to anyone. He was immediately released, and his career ended.

1988

Ravelo Manzanillo

Ravelo Manzanillo was born on October 17, 1963, in Placer Bonito. He was a left-handed pitcher. He debuted in the major leagues on September 25, 1988, for the Chicago White Sox and played for them until 1994, when the Pirates signed him as a free agent. He spent his final two seasons, 1994 and 1995, playing for the Pirates. Manzanillo played his final game on May 9, 1995, for the Pittsburgh Pirates. His career ERA was 4.43.

1989

Sammy Sosa

Samuel Peralta Sosa was born on November 12, 1968, in Consuelo. The Texas Rangers signed him on July 30, 1985, and he debuted in the major leagues on June 16, 1989, for the Texas Rangers. He was traded to the Chicago White Sox, then to the Cubs on March 30, 1992, and to the Baltimore Orioles on February 2, 2005. The Rangers signed him as a free agent on January 30, 2007, and he retired at the end of the season, although he still held out hopes for a comeback.

Sosa played mostly outfield and also was a designated hitter. In 1993 he scored more than 30 home runs and stole more than 30 bases, breaking the 30–30 record. In 1998 he was awarded the titles of National League Most Valuable Player and Major League Player of the Year. In 1998 he and Mark McGwire competed for the National League home-run title. Although Sosa's sixty-second home run in September was hit after McGwire's, enabling McGwire to win the contest—and Sosa's 66 home runs that season fell short of McGwire's 70—Sosa went on to be the only batter in history to hit 60 or more home runs for three consecutive seasons. On June 20, 2007, in his last season, Sosa became one of only five players to hit 600 home runs.

José Canó

Joselito Soriano Canó was born on March 7, 1962, in Boca del Soco. A right-handed pitcher, he was signed by the New York Yankees on March 10, 1980; the Yankees released him on August 6, 1980. The Atlanta Braves signed him as a free agent on December 1, 1981, and released him on June 4, 1982, and again in 1983 and 1985. The Astros signed him as a free agent on April 15, 1987, and he debuted in the major leagues on August 28, 1989, for the Houston Astros, playing his final game on September 30, 1989. In his only major-league season, Canó pitched in six games, starting twice, with a 1–1 win-loss record and an ERA of 5.09.

Juan "Tito" Bell

Juan Mathey Bell was born on March 29, 1964, in Los Cuatro Caminos, San Pedro de Macorís: he was the brother of George Bell. The Los Angeles Dodgers signed him as a free agent on September 1, 1984, but then traded him to the Baltimore Orioles on December 4, 1988. He debuted in the major leagues on September 6, 1989, for the Baltimore Orioles. On August 11, 1992, he was traded to the Philadelphia Phillies. After playing for the Phillies, he spent his final two seasons playing for the Montreal Expos and the Boston Red Sox. His major-league career consisted of seven seasons. Bell played his final game on August 25, 1995, for the Boston Red Sox. He played mostly second base, but also shortstop, outfield, third base, right field, center field, and left field, and was a designated hitter.

1990

José Offerman

José Antonio Dono Offerman was born on November 8, 1968, in Barrio Blanco, San Pedro de Macorís. A switch-hitter and right-handed thrower, he was signed by the Dodgers on July 24, 1986. He debuted in the major leagues on August 19, 1990, for the Dodgers. He has played shortstop, second base, first base, outfield, left field, right field, and center field, and is a designated hitter. He was traded to the Kansas City Royals on December 17, 1995. The Boston Red Sox signed him as a free agent on November 16, 1988. A conditional deal sent him to the Seattle Mariners on August 8, 2002. The Montreal Expos signed him as a free agent on February 26, 2003, and released him on April 1, 2003. The Minnesota Twins signed him as a free agent on February 6, 2004. The Philadelphia Phillies signed him as a free agent on January 19, 2005, and released him on May 20, 2005. The New York Mets signed him as a free agent on June 8, 2005. In 1996, he had a .303 batting average, and in 1998 he had a .315 batting average.

Victor Rosario

Victor Manuel Rivera Rosario was born on August 26, 1966, in Callejón Ortiz in San Pedro. The Boston Red Sox signed him on December 5, 1983, but traded him to the Atlanta Braves, the team on which he debuted in the major leagues on September 6, 1990. He played shortstop and second base for the Braves for one season and played his final game on October 3 of that same year.

Andrés Santana

Andrés Confesor Belonis Santana was born on February 5, 1968, in Quisqueya. The San Francisco Giants signed him as a free agent in 1985. A shortstop, he debuted in the major leagues on September 16, 1990, for the Giants and played the final game of his one-season career on October 3, 1990.

1991

Tony Eusebio

Raul Antonio Bare Eusebio was born on April 27, 1967, in Los Llanos, San Pedro de Macorís. The Astros signed him on May 30, 1995. He played all nine seasons of his career with the Astros as a backup catcher. He debuted in the major leagues on August 8, 1991, for the Astros and played his final game on October 7, 2001. He had 241 RBIs. Although his batting average for his career was only .275, his postseason batting average from 1997 to 2001 was .375. In 2000 he had a record 24-game hitting streak, although, because he was not a regular player, it took him 51 days to accomplish this.

Esteban Beltré

Esteban Valera Beltré was born on December 26, 1967, in Quisqueya. The Montreal Expos signed him on May 9, 1984, and he debuted in the major leagues on September 3, 1991, for the Chicago White Sox. He played shortstop, second base, and third base, and was a designated hitter. He played his final game on June 5, 1996, for the Boston Red Sox.

Luis Mercedes

Luis Roberto Santana Mercedes was born on February 15, 1968, in Miramar. The Orioles signed him on February 16, 1987, but then traded him to the Giants on April 29, 1993. He played right field, left field, and center field, and was a designated hitter. He debuted in the major leagues on September 8, 1991, for the Baltimore Orioles and played his final game on September 23, 1993. He played a total of three seasons in the major leagues, his first two on the Orioles and his last one on both the Baltimore Orioles and the San Francisco Giants.

Josias Manzanillo

Josias Adams Manzanillo was born on October 16, 1967, in Placer Bonito, the brother of Ravelo Manzanillo. A right-handed pitcher, he was signed by the Red Sox on January 10, 1983, and debuted in the major leagues for the Red Sox on October 5, 1991. The Kansas City Royals signed him as a free agent on April 3, 1992, the Milwaukee Brewers signed him as a free agent on November 20, 1992, the Seattle Mariners signed him as a free agent on December 21, 1996, the Houston Astros signed him as a free agent on July

27, 1997, the Tampa Bay Devil Rays signed him as a free agent on December 18, 1997, the New York Mets signed him as a free agent on July 3, 1998, the Pittsburgh Pirates signed him as a free agent on February 9, 2000, the Cincinnati Reds signed him as a free agent on January 22, 2003, and finally the Florida Marlins signed him as a free agent on May 6, 2004. He ended his career playing for the Florida Marlins and played his final game on September 22, 2004. In his eleven-year career he had a 4.71 ERA, pitching 300 strikeouts.

1992

Juan Guerrero

Juan Antonio Guerrero was born on February 1, 1967, near the Porvenir sugar mill. He primarily played shortstop but also played third base, left field, and second base. He debuted in the major leagues on April 9, 1992, for the Houston Astros, playing with them until the final game of his one-season major-league career, on October 3, 1992.

Ben Rivera

Bienvenido Santana Rivera was born on January 11, 1968, in San Pedro de Macorís. A right-handed pitcher, he was signed by the Braves in 1986. He debuted in the major leagues for the Braves on April 9, 1992. On May 28, 1992, he was traded to the Philadelphia Phillies, ending his three-season career with the Phillies on July 31, 1994. He had a career ERA of 4.52.

Manny Alexander

Manny de Jesús Alexander was born on March 20, 1971, in Restauración. He played mostly shortstop but also second base, third base, outfield, left field, right field, and first base, and also was a designated hitter. The Baltimore Orioles signed him on February 4, 1988, and he debuted in the major leagues for the Orioles on September 18, 1992, at age twenty-one, the youngest player in the American League in 1992. He was traded to the New York Mets on March 22, 1997, given to the Chicago Cubs as part of a deal on August 14, 1997, and traded to the Boston Red Sox on December 12, 1999. The Seattle Mariners signed him as a free agent on February 18, 2001, and the New York Yankees signed him as a free agent on February 4, 2002. The Milwaukee Brewers purchased him on August 10, 2002, and the Texas Rangers signed him as a free agent on November 15, 2004. He was then traded to the San Diego Padres on August 31, 2005. In 2007 he was released by the Padres during spring training.

1993

Domingo Jean

Domingo Luisa Jean was born on January 9, 1969, in Consuelo. A right-handed pitcher, he was signed by the Chicago White Sox on May 8, 1989, and traded to the New York Yankees on January 10, 1992. He debuted in the major leagues on August 8, 1993, for the Yankees and played his final game on October 3, 1993. He played only one season in the major leagues, with a 4.46 ERA.

Salomón Torres

Salomón Ramírez Torres was born on March 11, 1972, in Barrio Blanco. A right-handed pitcher, he was signed by the San Francisco Giants on September 15, 1999, and debuted in the major leagues for the Giants on August 29, 1993. He was traded to the Seattle Mariners on May 21, 1995. The Pittsburgh Pirates signed him as a free agent on December 30, 2001, and then traded him to the Milwaukee Brewers on December 7, 2007. In his career as of 2008, he had struck out 540 batters and had an ERA of 4.31.

Norberto Martin

Norberto Edonal McDonald Martin was born on December 10, 1966, in Villa Velasquez, San Pedro de Macorís. The White Sox signed him on March 27, 1984. He debuted in the major leagues on September 20, 1993, for the Chicago White Sox. He played mostly second base. He played his final game on May 4, 1999, for the Toronto Blue Jays. He had a .357 batting average in his first season (1993), a .350 batting average in 1996, and a .300 batting average in 1997. His major-league career average was only .278, largely because of low batting averages in his final two years.

1994

Héctor Carrasco

Héctor Pacheco Pipo Carrasco was born on October 22, 1969, in Barrio México. A right-handed pitcher, he was signed by the New York Mets on March 20, 1988. The Houston Astros signed him as a free agent on January 21, 1992. He was traded to the Florida Marlins on November 17, 1992, given to the Cincinnati Reds on September 10, 1993, and debuted in the major leagues on April 4, 1994, for the Cincinnati Reds, then traded to the Kansas City Royals on July 15, 1997, drafted by the Arizona Diamondbacks on November 18, 1997, selected by the Minnesota Twins on April 3, 1998, and then traded to the Boston Red Sox on September 9, 2000. The Toronto Blue Jays signed him as a free agent on January 9, 2001, the Minnesota Twins signed him as a free agent on March 30, 2001, the Texas Rangers signed him as a free agent on January 23, 2002, the Baltimore Orioles signed him as a free agent on March 1, 2003, the Washington Nationals signed him as a free agent on February 3, 2005, the Los Angeles Angels of Anaheim signed him as a free agent on December 2, 2005, the Nationals signed him as a free agent on July 18, 2007, the Pittsburgh Pirates signed him as a free agent on January 24, 2008, and the Chicago Cubs signed him as a free agent on May 6, 2008. At the end of his twelfth season, in 2008, he had a 3.99 ERA and had hit 69 home runs.

José Oliva

José Galvez Oliva was born on March 3, 1971, in San Pedro de Macorís. He played third base and first base and was signed by the Texas Rangers on November 12, 1987. He debuted in the major leagues on July 1, 1994, for the Atlanta Braves and then was traded to the St. Louis Cardinals on August 25, 1995. He played his final game on October 1, 1995, for the Cardinals, concluding a brief two-season major-league career. He died on December 22, 1997, in Santo Domingo from injuries from a car crash.

Armando Benítez

Armando Germán Benítez was born on November 3, 1972, in Ramón Santana, San Pedro de Macorís. A right-handed pitcher, he was signed by the Baltimore Orioles on April 1, 1990. He debuted in the major leagues on July 28, 1994, for the Orioles. On December 1, 1998, he was traded to the New York Mets; he was traded to the New York Yankees on July 16, 2003, and traded to the Seattle Mariners on August 6, 2003. On January 6, 2004, he started playing for the Florida Marlins as a free agent, and on December 2, 2004, he started playing with the San Francisco Giants as a free agent. On May 31, 2007, he was traded to the Florida Marlins. On March 11, 2008, he started playing for the Toronto Blue Jays as a free agent. A hard-throwing closer whose fastball has been clocked at faster than 100 miles per hour and whose sly splitter is difficult to find, as of 2008 he had an ERA of 3.12. In 2004 he led the National League in saves, with a total of 47. He would have been recognized as one of the best closers in the game were it not for a tendency to lose accuracy in big games at critical moments.

1995

Rudy Pemberton

Rudy Hector Perez Pemberton was born on December 17, 1969, in Placer Bonito. An outfielder, he was signed on June 7, 1987, by the Detroit Tigers. He debuted in the major leagues on April 26, 1995, for the Tigers. He played in the majors for three seasons, two for the Tigers and one for the Boston Red Sox. He played his final game on June 2, 1997, for the Boston Red Sox. In the 1996 season he had an amazing .512 batting average; his career average for the three seasons was .336. His .512 average is the highest in history for a player with more than thirty at-bats.

1996

Miguel Mejía

Miguel Mejía was born on March 25, 1975, in Quisqueya. The Baltimore Orioles signed him on January 22, 1992. He was drafted by the Kansas City Royals, then was traded to the St. Louis Cardinals on December 4, 1995. He debuted in the major leagues on April 4, 1996, for the Cardinals and played his final game for them, on September 29, 1996. At age twenty-one he was the youngest player in the National League. In his only season in the majors, he played 21 games in all three outfield positions.

Manny Martínez

Manuel de Jesús Martínez was born on October 3, 1970, in Barrio México. He played all three outfield positions and was signed by the Oakland Athletics on March 10, 1988. He debuted in the major leagues for the Seattle Mariners on June 14, 1996, played a total of three seasons in the majors for the Chicago Cubs and the Pittsburgh Pirates, and played his final game on October 3, 1999, for the Montreal Expos.

Luis Castillo

Luis Antonio Donato Castillo was born on September 12, 1975, in Barrio Restauración. A second baseman, he was signed by the Florida Marlins on August 19, 1992, and debuted in the major leagues on August 8, 1996, for the Marlins and then was signed by the Marlins as a free agent on December 7, 2003. He was traded to the Minnesota Twins in 2005 and then to the New York Mets in 2007. The Mets then signed him as a free agent that same year. As of 2008, he has played thirteen seasons in the major leagues and has hit 178 doubles, made 386 RBIs, and stolen 342 bases. His batting average exceeded .300 multiple times: it was .302 in

1999, .334 in 2000, .305 in 2002, .314 in 2003, and .301 in 2005 and 2007. He received Gold Gloves in 2003, 2004, and 2005, and was the National League's Most Valuable Player in 2003.

1997

Julio Santana

Julio Franklin Santana was born on January 20, 1973, in Consuelo. A nephew of Rico Carty, this right-handed pitcher was signed by the Texas Rangers on February 18, 1990, and debuted in the major leagues for the Rangers on April 6, 1997. He started playing for the Tampa Bay Devil Rays in 1998 and was then traded to the Boston Red Sox in 1999. The Red Sox signed him as a free agent on February 2, 2000, the Montreal Expos signed him as a free agent on June 18, 2000, and the San Francisco Giants signed him as a free agent on November 10, 2000. The New York Mets drafted him on December 11, 2000, but then the San Francisco Giants took him back on March 30, 2001. The Detroit Tigers signed him as a free agent on November 16, 2001, and again on January 27, 2003. The Philadelphia Phillies signed him as a free agent on March 29, 2003, and the Mikwaukee Brewers signed him as a free agent on December 23, 2004. The Phillies then signed him again on November 30, 2005, but released him on October 11, 2006. As of the end of 2008, he had a career ERA of 5.30, with 308 strikeouts.

Fernando Tatis

Fernando Tatis, Jr., was born on January 1, 1975, in Miramar. He has played third base, left field, right field, first base, outfield, shortstop, and second base, and has been a designated hitter. The Texas Rangers signed him on August 25, 1992, and he debuted in the major leagues for the Rangers on July 26, 1997. He was then traded to the St. Louis Cardinals on July 31, 1998. On December 14, 2000, he was traded to the Montreal Expos and played with them through 2003, when he was injured, retiring for one season. Then the Tampa Bay Devil Rays signed him as a free agent on January 6, 2004. The Baltimore Orioles signed him as a free agent on November 25, 2005. The Los Angeles Dodgers signed him as a free agent on February 9, 2007. The Mets signed him as a free agent on March 23, 2007, and again on January 7, 2008. Not only is Tatis one of the few players ever to hit two grand slams in the same game, he is the only player in baseball history to hit two grand slams in the same inning. As of the end of the 2008 season, he had hit 149 doubles and 103 home runs, and had 394 RBIs.

1998

Marino Santana

Marino Santana was born on May 10, 1972, in Consuelo. A right-handed pitcher, he was signed by the Seattle Mariners on April 28, 1990, and the Detroit Tigers signed him as a free agent on November 26, 1996. He debuted in the major leagues for the Tigers on September 4, 1998. He played a total of two seasons in the major leagues, playing for the Tigers for the 1998 season and for the Red Sox for the 1999 season. His final game was on July 23, 1999, for the Red Sox. His career ERA was 7.94.

Angel Peña

Angel Peña was born on February 16, 1975, in Miramar. He was a catcher. The Los Angeles Dodgers signed him in 1992. He debuted in the major leagues on September 8, 1998, for the Dodgers and played his final game on June 1, 2001, for a total of three seasons in the majors, all for the Dodgers.

José Jiménez

José Jiménez was born on July 7, 1973, in San Pedro de Macorís. A right-handed pitcher, he was signed by the St. Louis Cardinals on October 21, 1991. He debuted in the major leagues on September 9, 1998, for the

Cardinals and was traded to the Colorado Rockies on November 16, 1999. The Cleveland Indians signed him as a free agent on January 8, 2004, and he played his final game on July 5, 2004, for the Indians. His career ERA was 4.92.

1999

Guillermo Mota

Guillermo Reynoso Mota was born on July 25, 1973, in Barrio México. A right-handed pitcher, the New York Mets signed him on September 7, 1990. He debuted in the major leagues on May 2, 1999, for the Montreal Expos, who had taken him from the Mets on December 9, 1996, in a minor-league draft. He was traded to the Los Angeles Dodgers on March 23, 2002, traded to the Florida Marlins on July 30, 2004, traded to the Boston Red Sox on November 24, 2005, and traded to the Cleveland Indians on January 27, 2006. He was returned to the Mets on August 20, 2006, in a deal, then traded to the Milwaukee Brewers on November 20, 2007. As of the end of the 2008 season he had a career ERA of 3.93 and had hit 67 home runs.

Alfonso Soriano

Alfonso Pacheco Soriano was born on January 7, 1976, in Quisqueya. He debuted in the major leagues on September 14, 1999, for the New York Yankees and played with them until 2004. He started as a second baseman and then became an outfielder. While playing for the Yankees in 2002 he had a .300 batting average. He was then traded to the Texas Rangers on February 16, 2004; he played for them from 2004 to 2006. On December 8, 2005, he was traded to the Washington Nationals and played for them in the 2006 season. On November 20, 2006, he started playing for the Chicago Cubs. He broke the world record of 40–40 by stealing more than 40 bases and hitting more than 40 doubles, and he is the first major-league player to reach 40–40–40, or 40 stolen bases,

40 home runs, and 40 doubles. Consistently a productive hitter, by the end of the 2008 season he had hit 309 doubles and 270 home runs, and had 705 RBIs. He had also stolen 248 bases.

2000

Lorenzo Barceló

Lorenzo Barceló was born on August 10, 1977, in Miramar. He was a right-handed pitcher signed by the Chicago White Sox, for whom he played his entire three-season major-league career. He debuted on July 22, 2000, and played his final game on April 19, 2002. His career ERA was 4.50.

Carlos Casimiro

Carlos Casimiro was born on November 8, 1976, in San Pedro de Macorís. The Baltimore Orioles signed him on April 15, 1994. He debuted in the major leagues on July 31, 2000, playing for the Orioles as a designated hitter, and played his final game on August 1, 2000. Used only as a designated hitter, Casimiro was released by the Orioles on November 1, 2000.

Lesli Brea

Lesli Brea was born on October 12, 1973, in Barrio Villa Providencia. He was a right-handed pitcher signed by the Seattle Mariners on January 20, 1996, but he debuted in the major leagues on August 13, 2000, for the Baltimore Orioles. He played two seasons for the Orioles and his final game, on June 16, 2001, was for them as well. His brief career saw the extremely poor ERA of 12.27.

Elvis Peña

Elvis Peña was born on August 15, 1974, in San Pedro de Macorís. He played shortstop and second base and was signed by the Colorado Rockies on June 22, 1993. He debuted in the major leagues on September 2, 2000, for the Rockies and played his final game on October 7, 2001, for the Milwaukee Brewers. In 2000 he had a .333 batting average.

Luis Saturria

Luis Saturria was born on July 21, 1976, in San Pedro de Macorís. An outfielder, he debuted in the major leagues on September 11, 2000, for the St. Louis Cardinals and played his final game on October 5, 2001, also for the Cardinals.

2001

Victor Santos

Victor Irving Santos was born on October 2, 1976, in Barrio Restauración. A right-handed pitcher, he was signed by the Tigers on June 11, 1995. He debuted in the major leagues on April 9, 2001, for the Detroit Tigers. He did not give up one earned run in his first 27.1 innings—an ERA of 0.00. On March 25, 2002, the Tigers traded him to the Colorado Rockies. The Texas Rangers signed him as a free agent on November 17, 2002, the Milwaukee Brewers signed him as a free agent on December 2 2003, and the Kansas City Royals signed him as a free agent on November 18, 2005. In 2006 he started playing for the Pittsburgh Pirates. The Cincinnati Reds signed him as a free agent on January 8, 2007, and then sold him to the Baltimore Orioles on September 7. The San Francisco Giants signed him as a free agent on January 11, 2008. In 2002 he had a .500 batting average. At the end of the 2008 season he had a career ERA of 5.21.

Jesús Colome

Jesús de la Cruz Colome was born on December 23, 1977, in Barrio Azul. A right-handed pitcher, he was signed by the Oakland Athletics on September 29, 1996. He was traded to the Tampa Bay Devil Rays on July

28, 2000. He debuted in the major leagues on June 21, 2001, for the Devil Rays. The New York Yankees signed him as a free agent on April 15, 2006, and the Washington Nationals signed him as a free agent on November 8, 2006. At the end of the 2008 season he had a major-league career ERA of 4.50.

Pedro Santana

Pedro Santana was born on September 21, 1976, in Barrio México. A second baseman, his entire major-league baseball career was one game on July 16, 2001, for the Detroit Tigers against the Cincinnati Reds.

2002

Eddie Rogers

Edward Antonio Rogers was born on August 29, 1978, in Los Llanos, San Pedro de Macorís. The Orioles signed him on November 7, 1997. He debuted in the major leagues on September 5, 2002, for the Orioles, playing three seasons for them, then signing with the Red Sox in 2006 and the Washington Nationals in 2007. He played shortstop, second base, outfield, third base, left field, and right field, and was a designated hitter.

2003

José Valverde

José Rafael Valverde was born on July 24, 1979, in San Pedro de Macorís. A right-handed pitcher, the Arizona Diamondbacks signed him on February 6, 1997, and he debuted in the major leagues for the Diamondbacks on June 1, 2003. He was a closer and in 2007 his record of 47 saves was the highest of any major-league pitcher. Then, on December 14, 2007, the Diamondbacks traded him to the Houston Astros. He became the National League's Most Valuable Player in 2007 and 2008. At the end of the 2008 season he had a major-league career ERA of 3.31.

2004

Daniel Cabrera

Daniel Alberto Cruz Cabrera was born on May 28, 1981, in San Pedro de Macorís. He was a six-foot-seven-inch right-handed fastball pitcher. The Baltimore Orioles signed him on March 15, 1999, and Cabrera debuted in the major leagues for the Orioles on May 13, 2004, and threw six shutout innings. For a few months he seemed almost unhittable, but then he began losing control of his pitches. In 2006, still devastating when in control, he led the major leagues in both walks and wild pitches, was sent down to the minors, but was later recalled. On August 19, 2006, he almost pitched a no-hitter against the Yankees until the ninth inning, when fellow Macorisano Robinson Canó spoiled it with a hit for the Yankees. In August 2007 he blew a three-run lead against the Texas Rangers and lost 30 to 3. His career ERA is 5.05. The Orioles did not pick up his contract in 2009, and he signed with the Washington Nationals.

Eddy Rodríguez

Eddy Rodríguez was born on August 8, 1981, in Ramón Santana, San Pedro de Macorís. He is a right-handed pitcher signed by the Orioles on March 11, 1999. He debuted in the major leagues on May 31, 2004, for the Baltimore Orioles and played for the Orioles for 2004 and 2006. He signed with the Florida Marlins on October 30, 2006.

Jerry Gil

Jerry Bienvenido Manzanillo Gil was born on October 14, 1982, in Placer Bonito. The Arizona Diamondbacks signed him as a shortstop on November 15, 1999. He debuted in the major leagues on August 22, 2004, for the Diamondbacks and played only that one season for them. In 2007 he played one season for the Cincinnati Reds.

2005

Robinson Canó

Robinson José Canó, the son of José, was born on October 22, 1982, in Villa Magdalena, San Pedro de Macorís. The New York Yankees signed him as a second baseman on January 5, 2001. He debuted in the major leagues for the Yankees on May 3, 2005, and as of 2009 has continued playing for them. As of the end of the 2008 season, he had hit 151 doubles and 309 RBIs and maintained a .303 batting average.

2006

Sendy Rleal

Sendy Aquino Rleal was born on June 21, 1980, in San Pedro de Macorís. A right-handed pitcher, the Baltimore Orioles signed him on June 30, 1999. He debuted in the major leagues on April 5, 2006, for the Orioles. This was his only major league season, which he finished with a 4.44 ERA. The Orioles released him on September 5, 2007.

Agustín Montero

Agustín Alcántara Montero was born on August 26, 1977, in San Pedro de Macorís. A right-handed pitcher, he was signed by the Oakland Athletics as a free agent on January 20, 1995. He debuted in the major leagues on May 12, 2006, for the Chicago White Sox. In 2007 he went back down to the minor leagues. His major-league ERA was 5.14.

Juan Morillo

Juan Bautista Morillo was born on November 5, 1983, in San Pedro de Macorís. A right-handed pitcher, he debuted in the major leagues on September 24, 2006, for the Colorado Rockies, who signed him as a free agent on April 26, 2001. As of the close of the 2008 season, he had an 11.42 ERA, mainly because of a slider he has trouble controlling. He throws his fastball up to 100 miles per hour.

2008

José Arredondo

José Juan Arredondo was born on March 30, 1984, in San Pedro de Macorís. A right-handed relief pitcher, he signed with the Los Angeles Angels of Anaheim on June 25, 2002. He debuted for the Angels in the major leagues on May 14, 2008, against the Chicago White Sox and gave up a home run to the first batter he faced, Nick Swisher. Nevertheless he finished the season with a promising 1.62 ERA.

A Dominican Chronology

The Country, Sugar, and Baseball

600   Tainos drive off the Ciboney and become the dominant population on the island, calling it Quisqueya, meaning "mother of the earth."

1492   Christopher Columbus arrives.

1493   La Isabela, the first permanent European settlement in the Americas, is founded by Columbus on the north coast of the island.

1496   Santo Domingo is founded.

1506   First Dominican sugar harvest is brought in.

1586   Sir Francis Drake attacks and nearly destroys Santo Domingo.

1605   In an attempt to stop smuggling, the Spanish force settlers to abandon the west of the island. French move in.

1697   Spain cedes the western third of the island to the French, who make it a prosperous sugar colony built on African slavery.

1791   Uprising takes place by the 480,000 slaves in the French colony.

1795   While putting down the rebellion in their colony, French troops take over the Spanish side.

1801   Toussaint-L'ouverture, a former slave, declares an independent nation of Haiti. Napoleon sends his troops.

1804   Napoleon is defeated. Jean-Jacques Dessalines becomes the leader of the first independent black republic and gives it the Arawak name Haiti.

1808 French troops are overthrown by colonists and the eastern side is returned to Spain.

1821 Spanish colonists declare the independent state of Haiti Español and ask to join Simón Bolívar's Gran Colombia.

1822 Haiti Español invaded and occupied by Haitian forces.

1844 Dominicans declare their independence and drive out the Haitian military.

1845 **A Manhattan book dealer, Alexander Cartwright, writes first definitive rule book for baseball.**

1861 Country again comes under Spanish rule.

1863 Civil war breaks out between pro-Spanish and pro-independence movements.

1864 During civil war, last documented record of pure Tainos is written by Dominican soldiers who were being attacked by them.

1865 Dominican Republic becomes an independent nation again.

1866 **According to popular legend, first baseball game in Cuba takes place in Matanzas.**

1871 Annexation of the Dominican Republic is rejected by the U.S. Senate.

1879 Juan Antonio Amechazurra, a Cuban, opens the first *ingenio*, Ingenio Angelina, a steam-powered sugar mill.

1880 San Pedro de Macorís granted permission to become an international port.

1881 Another Cuban, Santiago W. Mellor, founds Ingenio Porvenir.

1882 At the height of a sugar boom, Ulises Heureux becomes the first Dominican dictator. He plunges country so deeply into debt that it has never recovered.

1882 Ingenio Cristóbal Colón and Ingenio Consuelo start up.

1891 **Cubans form two competing baseball clubs in Santo Domingo.**

1893 Sugar companies in San Pedro start recruiting workers from Saint

Thomas, Saint John, Saint Kitts, Nevis, Anguilla, Antigua, and Saint Martin.

1898 **After this season, blacks are completely banned from both major-league and minor-league baseball.**

1899 Heureux is assassinated.

1906 **Licey team is founded in Santo Domingo.**

1911 **Licey defeats San Pedro.**

1916 United States Marines invade and occupy.

1920 **Kenesaw Mountain Landis, known for racist views as judge, is appointed the first U.S. commissioner of baseball.**

1922 Cuba, Puerto Rico, and Dominican Republic produce thirty-eight percent of the world's cane sugar and twenty-seven percent of total world sugar.

1924 U.S. Marines leave.

1930 Rafael Leonidas Trujillo comes to power.

1936 Santo Domingo is renamed Ciudad Trujillo.

1936 **San Pedro's Estrellas win the championship from Ciudad Trujillo.**

1937 **Ciudad Trujillo beats Estrellas and bankrupts Dominican baseball in the process.**

1937 Trujillo massacres between 20,000 and 30,000 Haitians in the Dominican Republic.

1945 **Brooklyn Dodgers sign Jackie Robinson, first black major-league player since 1898. Eleven weeks later, second black player, Larry Doby, is signed by the Cleveland Indians.**

1948 **Cuban Minnie Miñoso breaks color line for Latinos by playing for Cleveland Indians.**

1951 **Dominican League is reorganized as professional baseball again.**

1954 **Estrellas win championship.**

1956 **Ozzie Virgil becomes first Dominican major leaguer.**

1956 Jesús de Galíndez is kidnapped by Trujillo agents in New York, tortured, and murdered.

1959 Mirabal sisters are murdered.

1959 **Stadium is built in San Pedro for the Estrellas; later named Tetelo Vargas Stadium.**

1961 Trujillo is assassinated.

1962 United States embargoes Cuba.

1962 **Amado Samuel, shortstop, is first Macorisano to play in major leagues.**

1963 Juan Bosch is elected president but after nine months is overthrown by military.

1965 A pro-Bosch rebellion leads to civil war. U.S. invades.

1966 U.S. military leaves after engineering an election that brings former Trujillo puppet president Joaquín Balaguer to power.

1968 **The Estrellas win championship.**

1978 After twelve years of Balaguer, opposition leader Silvestre Antonio Guzmán is elected president.

1982 Jorge Blanco from Guzmán's party is elected.

1986 Balaguer returns to power.

1994 Although this is Balaguer's third corrupt election victory in a row, international outcry is so great, he agrees to hold another election in two years.

1996 Leonel Fernández, from Juan Bosch's party, is elected. Unlike Bosch, he emphasizes infrastructure for international business rather than social programs and claims to be building "Singapore of the Caribbean."

2000 Fernández is barred by law from running a second term. Opposition candidate Hipólito Mejía comes to power on popular platform of social programs.

2004 Mejía uses legislative majority to end term limit. His opponent Fernández is elected.

2008 Fernández is reelected.

ACKNOWLEDGMENTS

Me gustaría agradecer a Manuel Corporán, mi hermano Manolo, por toda la ayuda, la buena conversación, la perspicacia y las risas y para dejarme conocer su familia valiente y afectuosa. I thank Major League Baseball for their cooperation, and particularly Ronaldo Peralta for answering all of my questions for years with the utmost courtesy, speed, and professionalism. Thanks to José Canó for his openness and help, even though we still haven't gone fishing, and to Arturo D'Oleo.

My deep-felt thanks to my friend of many years now, Bernard Diederich, whom I first met on Hispañola—no longer remember which side first—and who writes of this world with rare insight and grace. And to Elizabeth Macklin for her help in translating Deligne: I could translate the lean twentieth-century lines of Mir but could never have done Deligne without her poet's touch.

I owe a debt to Tim Wiles and Freddy Berowski, who pleasantly and efficiently helped me in the library of the Baseball Hall of Fame in Cooperstown, New York.

Thanks to Geoffrey Kloske for doing it all and so well, to Rebecca Saletan for her great advice, and to the whole Riverhead family for being such great partners. A special thanks, as always, to my dear friend Charlotte Sheedy for representing me. And thanks to Susan Birnbaum for all her help.

Thank you, Marian Mass, my beautiful Marian, for a hundred things, but especially for having stopped rooting for the Yankees.

BIBLIOGRAPHY

DOMINICAN HISTORY

Atkins, G. Pope, and Larman C. Wilson. *The Dominican Republic and the United States: From Imperialism to Transnationalism.* Athens: University of Georgia Press, 1998.

Balaguer, Joaquín. *Historia de la Literatura Dominicana.* Rafael Calzada, Argentina: Gráfica Guadalupe, 1972.

———. *La Isla al Revís: Haiti y el Destino Dominicano.* Santo Domingo: Fundación José Antonio Caro, 1983.

———. *Memorias de un Cortesano de la "Era de Trujillo."* Santo Domingo: Fundación Corripio, 1988.

Black, Jan Knippers. *The Dominican Republic: Politics and Development in an Unsovereign State.* London: Allen & Unwin, 1986.

Bosch, Juan. *Composición Social Dominicana: Historía e Interpretacion.* Santo Domingo: Alfa y Omega, 1981.

Brown, Isabel Zakrzewski. *Culture and Customs of the Dominican Republic.* Westport, CT: Greenwood Press, 1999.

Crassweller, Robert D. *Trujillo: The Life and Times of a Caribbean Dictator.* New York: Macmillan, 1966.

Deligne, Gastón F. *Obra Completa* vol. 1: *Soledad y Poemas Dispersos.* Santo Domingo: Fundación Corripio, 1996.

Diederich, Bernard. *Una Cámara Testigo de la Historia: El Recorrido Dominicano de un Cronista Extranjero, 1951–1966*. Santo Domingo: Fundación Cultural Dominicana, 2003.

———. *Trujillo: The Death of the Goat*. Boston, MA: Little Brown, 1978.

———, and Al Burt. *Papa Doc and the Tonton Macoutes: The Truth About Haiti Today*. New York: McGraw-Hill, 1969.

Fuller, Captain Stephen M., and Cosmas, Graham A. *Marines in the Dominican Republic, 1916–1924*. Washington, D.C.: U.S. Marine Corps, 1974.

Galíndez, Jesús de. *La Era de Trujillo: Un Estudio Casuístico de Dictadura Hispanoamericana*. Buenos Aires: Editorial Americana, 1976.

Leopoldo Richiez, Manuel. *Historia de la Provincia y Especialmente de la Ciudad de San Pedro de Macorís*. Santo Domingo: Sociedad Dominicana de Bibliófilos, 2002.

Moya Pons, Frank. *El Pasado Dominicano*. Santo Domingo: Fundación J. A. Caro Alvarez, 1986.

Nelson, William Javier. *Almost a Territory: America's Attempt to Annex the Dominican Republic*. Newark: University of Delaware Press, 1990.

Pacini Hernandez, Deborah. *Bachata: A Social History of a Dominican Popular Music*. Philadelphia: Temple University Press, 1995.

Peguero de Aza, Maximiliano. *Quinientos Años de Historia de los Pueblos del Este (Origen y Evolución)*. Santo Damingo: Soto Castillo, 2004.

Rood, Carlton Alexander. *A Dominican Chronicle*. Santo Domingo: Fundación Corripio, 1986.

Sellers, Julie A. *Merengue and Dominican Identity: Music as National Unifier*. Jefferson, N.C.: McFarland, 2004.

Valldeperes, Manuel. "La Temporalidad Histórico-Espiritual en el Poeta Gastón Fernando Deligne," in *Revista Interamericana de Bibliografia* 14, no. 2 (1964), pp. 151–58.

SUGAR HISTORY

Ayala, César J. *American Sugar Kingdom: The Plantation Economy of the Spanish Caribbean, 1898–1934*. Chapel Hill: University of North Carolina Press, 1999.

Martínez, Samuel. *Peripheral Migrants: Haitians and Dominican Republic Sugar Plantations*. Knoxville: University of Tennessee Press, 1995.

Murphy, Martin F. *Dominican Sugar Plantations: Production and Foreign Labor Integra-tion*. New York: Praeger, 1991.

Plant, Roger. *Sugar and Modern Slavery: A Tale of Two Countries*. London: Zed Books, 1987.

BASEBALL HISTORY

Alou, Felipe, with Herm Weiskopf. *My Life and Baseball*. Waco, TX: Word Books, 1967.

Bell, George, and Bob Elliott. *Hardball*. Toronto: Key Porter, 1990.

Bjarkman, Peter C. *Baseball with a Latin Beat*. Jefferson, NC: McFarland, 1994.

Bretón, Marcos, and José Luis Villegas. *Away Games: The Life and Times of a Latin Ball Player*. New York: Simon & Schuster, 1999.

Collado, Lipe. *Yo, Rico Carty*. Santo Domingo: Collado, 2002.

Fernández Reguero, Victor. *Tetelo (Su Vida)*. San Pedro de Macorís (no publisher noted, no date).

González Echevarría, Roberto. *The Pride of Havana: A History of Cuban Baseball*. New York: Oxford University Press, 1999.

Hample, Zack. *Watching Baseball Smarter: A Professional Fan's Guide for Beginners, Semi-Experts, and Deeply Serious Geeks*. New York: Vintage Books, 2007.

Jamail, Milton H. *Full Count: Inside Cuban Baseball*. Carbondale: Southern Illinois University Press, 2000.

Joyce, Gare. *The Only Ticket off the Island: Baseball in the Dominican Republic*. Toronto: McClelland & Stewart, 1991.

Klein, Alan M. *Growing the Game: The Globalization of Major League Baseball*. New Haven, CT: Yale University Press, 2006.

———. *Sugarball: The American Game, the Dominican Dream*. New Haven, CT: Yale University Press, 1991.

Koppett, Leonard. *The Thinking Fan's Guide to Baseball*. Wilmington, DE: Sport Media Publishing, 2004.

Krich, John. *El Béisbol: Travels Through the Pan-American Pastime*. New York: Atlantic Monthly Press, 1989.

Levine, Peter. *A. G. Spalding and the Rise of Baseball: The Promise of American Sport*. New York: Oxford University Press, 1985.

Monk, Cody. *The Dominican Dream Come True: Alfonso Soriano*. Champaign, IL: Sports Publishing, 2003.

Paige, Leroy (Satchel), as told to David Lipman. *Maybe I'll Pitch Forever*. Lincoln: University of Nebraska Press, 1993.

Pérez Guante, Carlos. *Macorisanos al Bate: Macorisanos at Bat*. Santo Domingo: Graphic Colonial, 2007.

Ruck, Rob. *The Tropic of Baseball: Baseball in the Dominican Republic*. Westport, CT: Meckler, 1991.

Sosa, Sammy, with Marcos Bretón. *Sosa: An Autobiography*. New York: Warner Books, 2000.

Veeck, Bill, with Ed Linn. *Veeck as in Wreck: The Autobiography of Bill Veeck*. Chicago: University of Chicago Press, 1962.

Wendel, Tim. *The New Face of Baseball*. New York: Rayo, 2004.

WEB SITES

www.baseball-almanac.com

www.baseballhalloffame.org

www.baseball-reference.com

INDEX

Aaron, Hank, 91
Abreu, Abner, 181–82
Abreu, Enrique, 180, 182
Abreu, Esdra, 182–84
Abreu, Gabriel, 184
Abreu, Senovia, 180, 182
academies
    academy system, 151- 53, 159, 160, 161
    Atlanta Braves, 156–59
    Baseball Towers facilities, 156–57
    California Angels, 159–61
    José Canó Baseball Academy, 175
    Chicago Cubs, 155, 161–62
    forerunner of, 97
    Hiroshima Carp Baseball Academy,
        162–63
    multiteam facilities, 155–56
Acevedo, Quiqui, 104, 105, 110
Acosta, José, 68
Acta, Manny, 141
Adair, Robert K., 199
African-Americans
    declining numbers in major leagues,
        207–9
    early major leaguers, 70
    first all-black outfield, 70
    first tryouts for, 69
    Garvey movement, 52

    harassment of, 84, 93–94
    Negro League, 59, 60, 62–63, 64, 68–69
    segregation of, 67–70
Águilas Cibaeñas
    in Dominican League, 64, 186, 188
    founding of, 58
    in 2008 playoff, 185, 191
Aguirre, Gary, 158
Alcalá, Santo, 227
Alcantara, Ervin, 140
Alexander, Manny, 6–7, 159, 179, 201,
        239–40
Aloma, Ignacio and Ubaldo, 51
Alomar, Roberto and Sandy, 204
Alou, Felipe, 75, 88
Alou, Matty, 76, 91
Amechazurra, Juan Antonio, 36
America. See United States
Amorós, Sandy, 73
Anacaona, 18
Andújar, Cristófar, 143
Andújar, Joaquín
    abandonment of San Pedro, 216–17
    erratic behavior and drug use, 195–96
    major-league career, 226–27
    testimony in Rosa sex scandal, 204
    wealth and status symbols, 7, 132
Angelina mill, 2, 36, 41

Angels, California, 101, 159–61, 189, 191
Anson, Cap, 67–68
Aramboles, Ricardo, 204
Arizona Diamondbacks, 178, 203
Arredondo, José, 252
Astin Field, 142
Astros, Houston, 80, 140, 143, 171–72, 178
Athletics, Kansas City, 82
Athletics, Oakland, 148, 178
Atlanta Braves
    academy in San Pedro, 153, 156–59
    Betemit, Wilson, 204
    Canó, José, 171
    González, Pedro, 85, 111
    Olivo, Chi-Chi, 76
    Paulino, Dario, 153
    Rogers, Danilo, 141
    Rymer, Carlos, 104
Avila, Rafael, 96–97
Aybar, José E., 61–62
Azucareros del Este, 171, 172, 186

bachata music, 20, 131
Báez, Buenaventura, 23
Báez, Mauricio, 26
Balaguer, Joaquín, 29–31, 43, 44, 72, 92
Baltimore Orioles, 6, 148, 159, 179, 188
Barceló, Lorenzo, 130, 247
Barceló family, 220
baseball fundamentals
    batting averages, 60
    curveballs, 55–56
    fastballs and changeups, 161–62
    home runs and stolen bases, 133
    rules and equipment, 48, 53–54
    shortstops, 97–98
    switch-hitters, 100
Batey Experimental, 8–9
Batista, Apollinaire, 149–50
Batista, Rafael, 226
Bell, James "Cool Papa," 62
Bell, George
    in America, 108
    on Andújar's honesty, 196
    on ballplayers' lack of education, 221
    childhood, 105–7
    Hard Ball, 194
    investment in academies, 156
    major-league career, 229–30
    mansion, 132
    in retirement years, 216–18

self-confidence, 111
tantrums and confrontations, 193–95
university training, 104–5
Bell, Juan "Tito," 236
Bellán, Esteban, 73
Beltré, Adrián, 203
Beltré, Esteban, 238
Benítez, Armando, 242
Bernhardt, Juan Ramón, 227
Berry, Ken, 159
Betancourt, Rómulo, 27
Betemit, Wilson, 204
Bithorn, Hiram, 68
Bjarkman, Peter, 49
Blakely, Gordon, 163
Blue Jays, Toronto, 96, 101, 164, 193
Bolívar, Simón, 22
Bonds, Barry, 198
Borbón, Pedro, 91
Bosch, Juan, 29–31, 43
Boston Red Sox
    Alexander, Manny, 201
    as all-white team, 70
    curse of the Bambino, 186
    signing-bonus payment, 148–49
    Tartabull, José, 159
    Williams, Ted, 91
Braves, Atlanta
    academy in San Pedro, 153, 156–59
    Betemit, Wilson, 204
    Canó, José, 171
    González, Pedro, 85, 111
    Olivo, Chi-Chi, 76
    Paulino, Dario, 153
    Rogers, Danilo, 141
    Rymer, Carlos, 104
Braves, Milwaukee, 77, 81–82, 87–88
Brea, Lesli, 247
Brooklyn Dodgers, 69, 73
Brown, Willard, 70
Browns, St. Louis, 70

Cabassa, Carlos, 109
Cabrera, Daniel, 148, 188, 189, 250
California Angels, 101, 159–61, 189, 191
Calvo, Jacinto "Jack," 68
Cambria, Fred, 208
Candalario, Rogelio, 80, 159, 183
Canó, Charlie, 169
Canó, José
    Baseball Academy, 175

Club Las Caobas, 175
on Estrellas' losing streak, 189
family and childhood, 168–69
hitting advice, 174
major-league career, 169–70, 171–72, 236
on San Pedro ballplayers, 222
Canó, Joselito, 174
Canó, Robinson, 172–73, 177, 188–89, 251
Cardinals, St. Louis, 7, 76, 93
Carrasco, Héctor, 241
Carrasquel, Alex, 68
Cartwright, Alexander, 48
Carty, Rico, 85–92, 94, 188, 218, 224–25
Cashman, Brian, 203
Casimiro, Carlos, 247
Castillo, Bonny, 154–55, 187, 188, 189
Castillo, Juan, 125, 234
Castillo, Luis, 243–44
Cedeño, Sergio, 197, 214
CEMEX, 116, 183
César Iglesias factory, 119
Céspedes, Carlos Manuel de, 36
Chandler, Happy, 69
Chapman, Ben, 93
charitable foundations, 141, 215, 218
Chicago Cubs, 155, 161–62, 199–200
Chicago White Sox, 73, 159, 202
Cincinnati Reds, 78, 91
Circuito de los Ingenios, 99–100
Claxton, Jimmy, 68
Clemens, Roger, 200, 213
Clemente, Roberto, 91
Cleveland Indians
    Abreu, Abner, 181
    Doby, Larry, 70
    González, Pedro, 84–85
    Griffin, Alfredo, 100–101
    Miñoso, Minnie, 73
    Otero, Reggie, 97, 100
    Veeck, Bill, 70
Cobb, Ty, 196
Colome, Alexander, 143
Colome, Jesús, 248–49
Colón, Bartolo, 191
color line, 67–70
"Concierto de Esperanza para la Mano Izquierda" (Mir), 113
Congress of Racial Equality (CORE), 215–16
Consuelo team

Carty, Rico, 86–87, 92
equipment, 103–4
Franco, Julio, 103
gifted players from, 53, 97, 99
Griffin, Alfredo, 97, 99
Consuelo village
    cane harvest, 7–8
    Carty family in, 85–86
    houses, 213
    production of baseball players, 99
    sugar mill, 2
    in twenty-first century, 121–23
Contón, Alfredo "Chico," 53
Córdova, Cuqui, 63
CORE (Congress of Racial Equality), 215–16
Corporán, Alcadio, and family, 177–78
Corporán, Manuel, 179–80
cricket, 52, 105–6
Cristóbal Colón mill, 2, 37, 220
Cruz, Victor, 101
Cuba
    ballplayers from, 73, 209
    baseball in, 17, 48–50
    sugar industry, 36
    U.S. trade embargo against, 17, 81, 209
Cubs, Chicago, 155, 161–62, 199–200
Cummings, Candy, 56
Cunningham, Bill, 79
curses, 186–87
curveballs, 55–56
Cy Young Award, 77–78, 191

dances, 18–19, 28–29, 52, 127–28
Dark, Al, 78
DeFreitas, Arturo, 228
"Del Trapiche" (Deligne), 13
Deligne, Gastón Fernando, 13, 43, 44, 52
Detroit Tigers, 74–75, 84–85
Diamondbacks, Arizona, 178, 203
Diederich, Bernard, 27
Dihigo, Martín, 74
DiMaggio, Joe, 196–97
Doby, Larry, 70
Dodgers, Brooklyn, 69, 73
Dodgers, Los Angeles
    Avila, Rafael, 96
    Beltré, Adrián, 203
    Canó, Charlie, 169
    Galvez, Balvino, 195
    Griffin, Alfredo, 101

Dodgers, Los Angeles (*cont.*)
  Guerrero, Pedro, 111
  Roseboro, Johnny, 79
Dominican baseball players
  in Dominican military, 77
  first major leaguers, 74–80
  lack of education, 86, 104, 145–46,
    181, 221
  in major and minor leagues, 207
  stereotypes, 79, 82, 101–2, 193–94,
    195
Dominican League
  budget inequality, 187
  draft system, 188
  foreign players, 62
  professional status, 59, 64
  salaries, 140–41, 189
  teams in, 58
Dominican Republic
  ambiguous identity, 15–20
  anti-Haitianism, 19, 41, 123
  Balaguer and Bosch presidencies,
    29–31
  chronology, 253–56
  curses, 186–87
  European invasions and annexations
    of, 20–24
  immigration to United States from,
    123, 152
  major-league scouts in, 96
  poetic description of, 15
  racial tensions, 19, 40–42, 71–72
  regionalism, 33–34, 41
  Santo Domingo, 21–22, 46, 137, 210
  steroid availability, 205–6
  sugar industry, 38–40, 42–43, 45
  Tainos, 33–35
  Trujillo dictatorship, 25–29
  upper class, 219–20
  U.S. invasion and occupation of, 24–25,
    27, 31, 39, 57
  women, 18
  See also San Pedro de Macorís
Dominican Summer League, 146, 147,
  151–52
Dominican Winter Baseball League, 56
Doubleday, Abner, 47–48
Dragones de Ciudad Trujillo, 62–63
Dressen, Charles, 84
Drysdale, Don, 77
Duncan, Mariano, 233

Eastern Stars. *See* Estrellas Orientales
Echavaría, Tony
  on crime, 17, 134
  on investment by major-league players,
    218, 220–21
  on San Pedro economy, 116, 136
Escogido Lions, 58, 61, 91, 185, 186, 187
Espaillat, Ulises Francisco, 20
Estadio Tetelo Vargas, 2–3, 64–65, 190, 221
Esteban Bastardo, Raquel, 167–68
Estrellas Orientales
  fans, 190–91
  founding of, 2
  losing streak, 185–89, 191
  professional status, 58
  stadium, 2–3, 64–65
  top players in, 61, 64, 85
  in 2008 playoff, 185, 191
Eusebio, Tony, 237–38
Expos, Montreal, 75

Fernández, Leonel, 2, 72, 134
Fernández, Ramón "Sanbobi," 117–18, 119
Fernández, Tony, 96, 97, 102–3, 219, 232–33
Fernández de Oviedo, Gonzalo, 34
Fiallo, Federico, 62
five-tool players, 153
Flood, Curt, 93–94
Florida Marlins, 188, 204
foods
  chicken, 83, 88, 108, 157
  congrejos al ajillo, 119
  crabs in coconut, 167–68
  Dominican diet, 88, 129, 135, 157, 160
  English steamed fish, 176
  fungi, 52, 129
  ham and eggs, 83, 88–89
  mofongo, 141
  pescado y domplin, 130, 178
  restaurant orders, 83, 88–89, 110
Foster, Rube, 68
Franco, Felicia, 211–12
Franco, Julio
  in America, 108–9
  childhood home, 109
  on Consuelo team, 99, 103, 107
  determination, 111
  major-league career, 82, 97, 108, 212–13,
    230–31
  mother's house, 211–12
  in retirement years, 213–14

Franco, Vicente, 211
Frías, Pepe, 97, 226
Furcal, Rafael, 111

Galíndez, Jesús de, 26, 27
Galvez, Balvino, 195, 234
García, Antonio "El Chico," 103
García, Julio, 161–62, 186
García, Silvio, 69
Garvey, Marcus, 52
Gehrig, Lou, 196–97
Giants, New York
    Alou, Felipe, 76
    Latham, Arlie, 212
    Martínez, Horacio, 76
    Pompez, Alejandro, 74
    Thompson, Hank, 70
    Virgil, Ozzie, 17, 74, 75
Giants, San Francisco, 77, 79, 156, 204
Gibson, Bob, 77
Gibson, Josh, 60, 62
Gil, Jerry, 250
Glanville, Doug, 219
Goldberg, Arthur, 93–94
Gómez, Petronila Angélica, 44
González, Juan, 204
González, Pedro
    as Atlanta Braves scout, 85, 96, 107, 111
    background, 82–83
    as Consuelo manager, 99
    major-league career, 83–85, 84, 224
    racism endured by, 84, 194
    temper, 84–85
González Echevarría, Roberto, 49–50
Gooden, Dwight, 155
Grant, Ulysses S., 24
Greenberg, Hank, 196–97
Greene, Graham, 28
Griffin, Alfredo
    on Andújar's behavior, 196
    background, 98–99
    charity golf tournament, 218
    as Estrellas manager, 185–86, 187, 188, 189, 191
    investment in San Pedro, 131, 220
    major-league career, 97, 100–101, 227–28
    mansion, 213
    temperament, 101–2
Gross, Kevin, 206
"Guavaberry" (song; Guerra), 222

Guerra, Felito, 57
Guerra, Juan Luis, 222
Guerrero, Epifanio "Epy," 96, 97, 102, 145, 164
Guerrero, Felito James "Ñato," 176–77
Guerrero, Juan, 239
Guerrero, Julio, 189
Guerrero, Mario, 96
Guerrero, Pedro, 111, 229
Guillén, Ozzie, 204
Guillot, Ernesto and Nemesio, 49
Guzmán, Santiago, 226

Haiti
    and abolition of slavery in Dominican Republic, 22, 38
    blackening of Dominican Republic, 22, 41
    Creole language, 26, 42
    Dominican Republic compared with, 16
    invasion and occupation of Dominican Republic, 19, 22–24, 128
    migrant workers in Dominican Republic from, 42
    as threat to Dominican Republic, 71–72
Hall, Toby, 199
Hall of Fame
    Anson, Cap, 68
    induction process, 79, 196
    Marichal, Juan, 75, 79–80, 196
Hard Ball (Bell), 194
Hart, Clemente, 99
Hazín family, 220
Hemingway, Ernest, 78–79, 115, 117
Henderson, Donald Warner, 127, 130
Hernández, Enrique, 56, 57–58
Hernández, Rudy, 76
Hiroshima Carp Baseball Academy, 162–63
Houston Astros, 80, 140, 143, 171–72, 178
Howe, Art, 186

Indians, Cleveland
    Abreu, Abner, 181
    Doby, Larry, 70
    González, Pedro, 84–85
    Griffin, Alfredo, 100–101
    Miñoso, Minnie, 73
    Otero, Reggie, 97, 100
    Veeck, Bill, 70
ingenios, 36–37
Inoa, Michael, 148

Irvin, Monte, 70
Isla al Revés, La (Balaguer), 72

Jackson, "Shoeless" Joe, 200
Jacobo, Astin, Sr., 143
Jacobo, Astin, Jr., 142, 143, 150–51, 202–3
Japanese training system, 162–63
Javier, Ignacio "Al," 228
Javier, Julián, 76
Jean, Domingo, 240
Jiménez, Elvio, 83, 225
Jiménez, José, 245–46
Jiménez, Manny, 82, 83, 223–24
Johnson, Lyndon, 31
Johnson, Randy, 148
José, Gladys María, 129
José Canó Baseball Academy, 175
Joseph, Rick, 225

Kahn, Roger, 200
Kake, Yasushi, 162
Kansas City Athletics, 82
Kansas City Royals, 143
Kennedy, John F., 27, 30
Knapp, Harry Shepard, 45
Knickerbockers, New York, 48
Koufax, Sandy, 77–78, 79, 201

La Romana Azucareros, 171, 172, 186
Landis, Kenesaw Mountain, 68–69
Las Pajas mill, 2, 37
Latham, Arlie, 212
Lee, Manny, 233–34
Licey Tigers
    in Dominican League, 58, 186, 188
    foreign players, 57
    founding of, 56–57
    major-league pitching staff, 6
    in 2008 playoff, 185
    wealth, 187–88
Linares, Rufino, 230
Lions, Escogido, 58, 61, 91, 185, 186, 187
Lois, Alberto, 228
Los Angeles Dodgers
    Avila, Rafael, 96
    Beltré, Adrián, 203
    Canó, Charlie, 169
    Galvez, Balvino, 195
    Griffin, Alfredo, 101
    Guerrero, Pedro, 111
    Roseboro, Johnny, 79

Lugo, Julio, 210
Lugo Martínez, Ludín, 44
Luque, Adolfo, 73, 78–79

Macorixes, 35
Major League Baseball
    budget disparities among teams, 188
    dead-ball eras, 90
    as Dominican industry, 220
    draft system, 95
    first Dominicans, 73–75
    first Latinos, 73
    first Macorisanos, 81–2
    foreigners in, 95–96, 206–10
    minimum signing age, 145–46
    numbers of teams and players, 95, 209
    off-season play, 188
    racism, 67–70, 84, 93
    record comparisons, 200–201
    reserve-clause rule, 93
    rule changes, 53–54
    salaries and bonuses, 94–95, 145,
        147–49, 154
    scouting in Dominican Republic, 96–97
    selection of prospects, 153–54
    steroid abuse, 196, 197–99, 200, 204–6
    See also academies; scandals
Manny Acta Foundation, 141
Manzanillo, Josias, 125, 238–39
Manzanillo, Ravelo, 235
Marichal, Juan, 75, 76–80, 196, 204
Mariners, Seattle, 143
Maris, Roger, 64, 197
Marlins, Florida, 188, 204
marriage scandal, 201
Martí, José, 49
Martin, Norberto, 240–41
Martínez, Elio, 5, 8–9, 11
Martínez, Herman, 149, 182
Martínez, José, 158, 161
Martínez, Manny, 243
Martínez, Pedro, 80, 183, 219
Mateo, Victor, 202
Mays, Willie, 70, 77
McGwire, Mark, 197, 198, 201, 214,
    215, 235
McNally, Dave, 94
Medina, Alberto, 147
Mejía, Hipólito, 134
Mejía, Miguel, 243
Mellor, Santiago W., 37

Mena, Rafael, 203
Mercedes, José, 6–7, 89, 185, 187–88, 189
Mercedes, Luis, 130, 238
merengue, 19–20, 28–29
Messersmith, Andy, 94
Mets, New York, 82, 150, 155, 212
Milwaukee Braves, 77, 81–82, 87–88
Minaya, Omar, 111
Miñoso, Minnie, 73, 74
Mir, Pedro, 15, 43–44, 113
Mirabal sisters, 18, 27
Montero, Agustín, 251
Montreal Expos, 75
Morales, Dionicio, 7–9
Morales, José Ignacio, 125
Moreno, Jose, 107–8
Morillo, Juan, 251
Mota, Guillermo, 246
Moya Pons, Frank, 23
music, 16, 19–20, 98, 128–29, 131

Nationals, Washington, 141
Negro League, 59, 60, 62, 64, 67–69, 74
New York Giants
    Alou, Felipe, 76
    Latham, Arlie, 212
    Martínez, Horacio, 76
    Pompez, Alejandro, 74
    Thompson, Hank, 70
    Virgil, Ozzie, 17, 74, 75
New York Mets, 82, 150, 155, 212
New York Yankees
    Alexander, Manny, 201
    Blakely, Gordon, 163
    Boston Red Sox curse on, 186–87
    Canó, José, 169–70
    Canó, Robinson, 173, 189
    first Dominican pitcher to defeat, 143
    González, Pedro, 83–84
    Jiménez, Elvio and Manny, 83
    Maris, Roger, 64
    Rodriguez, Alex, 188
    Soriano, Alfonso, 133, 163, 203
Nina Santana, Federico, 61, 62
Noboa, Junior, 156
Norman, Nelson, 99
Nuevo Club, 55, 57–58

Oakland Athletics, 148, 178
Oakland Oaks, 68
Offerman, José, 236–37

Old Man and the Sea, The (Hemingway), 79,
    115, 117
Oliva, José, 241–42
Olivo, Chi-Chi, 76
Olivo, Diomedes, 76
Orioles, Baltimore, 6, 148, 159, 179, 188
Ortiz, David, 186
Otero, Reggie, 97, 100
Our Man in Havana (Greene), 28
Ozama Club, 55

Paige, Satchel, 62, 63, 69
Pan American baseball team, 87
Paredes, Andre, 167
Paulino, Dario, 153, 157
Peguero, Héctor, 110
Pemberton, Rudy, 242–43
Peña, Ángel, 130, 245
Peña, Elvis, 247–48
Peña Gómez, José Francisco, 72
Pérez, Julio Eladio, 27
Pérez, Lulu, 55–56
Pérez, Rafael, 203
Pérez Tolentino, Ramón, 141
Philadelphia Phillies, 93, 104–5, 110
Physics of Baseball, The (Adair), 199
Pittsburgh Pirates, 76, 142, 189, 195
Pompez, Alejandro, 74
Ponce de León, Juan, 35
Porvenir mill, 1, 2, 37, 120–21
Puerto Rico
    music and culture, 19, 20
    sense of identity, 14–15
    slavery, 37, 38
    sugar industry, 37–38, 42–43
    U.S. occupation of, 46, 57
Punta de Pescadores, 35, 115

Quisqueya mill, 2, 37

racism and racial tensions
    in Dominican Republic, 19, 40–42,
        71–72
    harassment of Dominicans in U.S., 84,
        89–90, 194
    in Major League Baseball, 67–70, 84, 93
Ramírez, Carlos, 89–90
Ramírez, Rafael "Rafelin," 97, 99, 111, 229
Rangers, Texas
    Abreu, Esdra, 184
    academy in San Pedro, 156–57

Rangers, Texas (*cont.*)
  Franco, Julio, 212
  Minaya, Omar, 111
  Sosa, Sammy, 111
  Tatis, Fernando, 179
  2007 victory over Baltimore Orioles, 148
Ravelo, Yan Carlos, 204
Ray, Kenny, 191
Rays, Tampa Bay, 143–44, 155, 181, 183, 199
RBI (Revitalizing Baseball in Inner Cities), 183, 208–9
recipes
  congrejos al ajillo, 119
  crabs in coconut, 167–68
  domplin con pescado, 178
  English steamed fish, 176
  fungi, 52, 129
  mofongo, 141
Reds, Cincinnati, 78, 91
Red Sox, Boston
  Alexander, Manny, 201
  as all-white team, 70
  curse of the Bambino, 186
  signing-bonus payment, 148–49
  Tartabull, José, 159
  Williams, Ted, 91
Reed, Alberto, 98
Reilly, Rick, 198, 205
Revitalizing Baseball in Inner Cities (RBI), 183, 208–9
Reyes, José, 76, 155
Rickey, Branch, 69
Rincón Cocolo restaurant, 129
Ripken, Cal, Jr., 98, 159
Risco Bermúdez, René del, 44
Rivera, Ben, 239
Rleal, Sendy, 251
Robby Mar restaurant, 118–19
Robinson, Jackie, 69–70
Robles, Rafael, 225
Rodríguez, Aaron, 147, 160
Rodriguez, Alex, 98, 188, 205
Rodríguez, Eddy, 250
Rodríguez, Iván, 204
Rodríguez Montaño, Benancio, 139
Rodríguez Perozo, Evangelina, 44
Rogers, Danilo, 141
Rogers, Eddie, 249
Romero, Charlie, 160, 163–64, 174, 181
Romero, Ramón, 233

Rosa, Luis, 204
Rosario, Adriano, 203
Rosario, Victor, 237
Rose, Pete, 200
Roseboro, Johnny, 79
Royals, Kansas City, 143
Ruth, Babe, 196
Rymer, Carlos, 104

Sabourín, Emilio, 50
Samuel, Amado, 81, 223
Samuel, Juan, 105, 107–8, 232
San Francisco Giants, 77, 79, 156, 204
San Pedro de Macorís
  affluence, 43–45, 130, 132, 140
  baseball connections, 141
  baseball equipment, 82–83, 86, 103–4, 130
  baseball games and fields, 142
  baseball origins, 9–10, 51–54, 99–100
  black migrant workers, 40–41
  cricket, 52–53, 105–6
  crime, 17, 134
  fishing and crabbing business, 115–19, 166–68
  hurricane devastation, 197, 214
  immigrant culture, 42, 127–30
  manufacturing zone, 135–36
  origin of town, 35–36
  poets, 43–44
  poverty, 134–35, 137
  production of major-league players, 11, 17, 99, 106, 130, 210, 222
  shortstops from, 97
  sugar industry, 1–5, 36–39, 43, 51–53, 120–25
  tourism, 123–25, 130–31, 136
  university, 135
  women's rights, 44
  See also Dominican Republic
Sánchez, Alejandro, 231
Sandino, Augusto César, 58
Sandoval, Art, 215
Santa Fe mill, 2, 123
Santa Fe team, 81, 82, 104–7
Santana, Andrés, 237
Santana, Danny, 142, 143–45, 153, 183–84
Santana, Ervin, 189
Santana, Julio, 92, 244
Santana, Marino, 245
Santana, Pedro, 249

Santana, Rafael, 99
Santo Domingo teams, 55–58, 60–61, 185
Santos, Ángel Valera de los, 137
Santos, Francisco de los, 150
Santos, Isabel de los, 177–78
Santos, Victor, 248
Saraceno, Jon, 199
Saturria, Luis, 248
scandals
  age falsification, 203–4
  corked bats, 199–200
  Dominican marriages, 201
  sex scandal, 204
  signing-bonus scams, 201–3
  steroid abuse, 196, 197–99, 200, 204–6
  violence, 79, 84–85, 194, 195
  World Series fixing, 196, 200
Seattle Mariners, 143
Senators, Washington, 76
Serra, José, 155, 161
Shamsky, Art, 78
Sheffield, Gary, 207
Sherry, Larry, 84–85
signing bonuses
  average, 145, 147–48
  buscones, 149–50, 161
  increase in, 94–95, 148–49, 154
  scams, 201–3
  significance of, 181, 183
Smith, Red, 94
Soriano, Alfonso, 133, 163, 203, 219,
  246–47
Sosa, Rosa Julia, 216
Sosa, Sammy
  abandonment of San Pedro, 197,
    214–15, 216
  arrogance, 216
  charitable foundation, 197, 215
  childhood, 109–10
  corked-bat scandal, 199–200
  major-league career, 110, 132–33, 214,
    235
  shopping center, 132–33, 215, 220
  steroid scandal, 197–98, 200, 204–5,
    216
Soulouque, Faustin-Élie, 23
South Porto Rico Sugar Company, 38
Spahn, Warren, 77
St. Louis Browns, 70
St. Louis Cardinals, 7, 76, 93
Stengel, Casey, 79

steroid abuse, 196, 197–99, 200, 204–6
Sumner, Charles, 24

Tainos, 33–35
Tampa Bay Rays, 143–44, 155, 181, 183, 199
Tartabull, José, 159
Tatis, Fernando, 130, 178–79, 189, 196,
  244–45
Tetelo Vargas Stadium, 2–3, 64–65, 190,
  221
Texas Rangers
  Abreu, Esdra, 184
  academy in San Pedro, 156–57
  Franco, Julio, 212
  Minaya, Omar, 111
  Sosa, Sammy, 111
  Tatis, Fernando, 179
  2007 victory over Baltimore Orioles, 148
Thompson, Hank, 70
Tiant, Luis, Sr., 60
Tigers, Licey, 74–75, 84–85
Toledo, Eddy, 144, 153, 154, 155
Toribio, Domingo, 202
Toronto Blue Jays, 96, 101, 164, 193
Torres, Salomón, 125, 156, 240
Trautman, George, 87
Trujillo, Rafael Leónidas
  control of baseball, 60–62
  control of sugar mills, 60, 64
  dictatorship, 25–29
  extravagance, 30
  racial quotas, 72
  reconstruction of Santo Domingo, 46
Trujillo, Ramfis, 64–65, 77, 83
"Trujillo en la Frontera" (Pérez), 27

United States
  Cuban baseball and, 48–50
  Cuban trade embargo, 17, 81, 209
  declining interest in baseball, 208–9
  deportation of Dominicans, 116–17
  Dominican immigration to, 123, 152
  invasion and occupation of Dominican
    Republic, 24–25, 27, 31, 39, 57
  manufacturing in San Pedro, 135–36
  origin of baseball in, 47–48
  resentment of foreigners in baseball,
    206–7
  spread of baseball throughout
    Caribbean, 57
  sugar consumption, 38

Valverde, José, 249
Vargas, Juan Esteban "Tetelo," 59, 64,
    197
  Tetelo Vargas Stadium, 2–3, 64–65,
    190, 221
Vásquez, Rafael, 142–43, 154
Veeck, Bill, 70, 84
Vicini Cabral family, 220
Virgil, Ozzie, 17, 73–75

Walker, Moses Fleetwood, 67
Washington Nationals, 141
Washington Senators, 76
White Sox, Chicago, 73, 159, 202
Whitman, Walt, 206
Wilder, David, 202
Williams, Ken, 133
Williams, Spin, 195
Williams, Ted, 91
World Series
  Andújar's pitching (1982), 7
  Andújar's violent outbreak (1985),
    195
  Berra's double play (1955), 73
  billy-goat curse (1945), 186

Doby, first black to hit home run (1948),
    70
  fixing scandal (1919), 196, 200
  Florida Marlins victories, 188
  Pedro González in (1964), 85
  Alfredo Griffin in, 101, 191
  Robinson's final season (1956), 70
  Tampa Bay Rays in (2008), 183

Yankees, New York
  Alexander, Manny, 201
  Blakely, Gordon, 163
  Boston Red Sox curse on, 186–87
  Canó, José, 169–70
  Canó, Robinson, 173, 189
  first Dominican pitcher to defeat, 143
  González, Pedro, 83–84
  Jiménez, Elvio and Manny, 83
  Maris, Roger, 64
  Rodriguez, Alex, 188
  Soriano, Alfonso, 133, 163, 203
Yastrzemski, Carl, 91
Yawkey, Tom, 70
Young, Cy, 196
  Award, 77–78, 191

MARK KURLANSKY is the *New York Times*–bestselling author of many books, including *The Food of a Younger Land; Cod: A Biography of the Fish That Changed the World; Salt: A World History;* and *The Last Fish Tale: The Fate of the Atlantic and Survival in Gloucester, America's Oldest Fishing Port and Most Original Town.* He reported from the Caribbean for the *Chicago Tribune* for seven years and wrote both *A Continent of Islands: Searching for the Caribbean Destiny* and *The White Man in the Tree and Other Stories* about the area. A finalist for the *Los Angeles Times* Book Prize for science writing and a winner of the Dayton Literary Peace Prize, he lives in New York City.